INTELLIGENCE, RACE, AND GENETICS

INTELLIGENCE, RACE, AND GENETICS

Conversations with Arthur R. Jensen

FRANK MIELE

Westview
PRESS

A Member of the Perseus Books Group

Copyright © 2002 by Westview Press, A Member of the Perseus Books Group

Westview Press books are available at special discounts for bulk purchases in the United States by corporations, institutions, and other organizations. For more information, please contact the Special Markets Department at the Perseus Books Group, 11 Cambridge Center, Cambridge MA 02142, or call (617) 252-5298.

Published in 2002 in the United States of America by Westview Press, 5500 Central Avenue, Boulder, Colorado 80301-2877, and in the United Kingdom by Westview Press, 12 Hid's Copse Road, Cumnor Hill, Oxford OX2 9JJ

Find us on the World Wide Web at www.westviewpress.com

A Cataloging-in-Publication data record for this book is available from the Library of Congress.

ISBN 0-8133-4008-X

The paper used in this publication meets the requirements of the American National Standard for Permanence of Paper for Printed Library Materials Z39.48–1984.

10   9   8   7   6   5   4   3   2   1—05 04 03 02

To my late father, Edward J. Miele,
and my mother, Cecilia Miele,
who gave me both my genes and my environment;
and to my brother, Edward F. Miele,
who shares them with me.

CONTENTS

PREFACE

"Compensatory education has been tried and it apparently has failed." With that opening sentence of a 123-page-long article solicited by the prestigious *Harvard Educational Review*, Professor Arthur R. Jensen, of the University of California, Berkeley, went from being a highly respected but little-known educational psychologist to one of the most controversial figures in science.

Written in 1969 during the tumultuous days of the rioting in the Black inner cities and White voter disenchantment with Lyndon Johnson's Great Society programs, Jensen's *HER* article set off a firestorm of controversy. The title, "How Much Can We Boost IQ and Scholastic Achievement?" and Jensen's conclusion, "Not much," made him a headliner in *Time, Newsweek, Life, U.S. News & World Report,* and *The New York Times Magazine,* on the one hand, and the target of student protests, sit-ins, resolutions of condemnation, and even acts of vandalism and death threats on the other. The word "Jensenism"—shorthand for Jensen's theory that an individual's IQ is largely due to heredity, including racial heritage—found its way into some dictionaries.

In this book, I skeptically cross-examine Arthur R. Jensen on Jensenism—how and why he believes the scientific evidence is even stronger today that:

- IQ is real, biological, and highly genetic, and not just some statistic or the result of educational, social, economic, or cultural factors;

- race is a biological reality, not a social construct; and, most controversially of all,
- the cause of the 15-point average IQ difference between Blacks and Whites in the United States is partly genetic.

The late Stephen Jay Gould's *Mismeasure of Man*, Howard Gardner's numerous books on "multiple intelligences," and Joseph Graves's *The Emperor's New Clothes* argue that Jensenism and the controversial best-seller *The Bell Curve* (which draws heavily on Jensen's work) are marginal science at best, pseudoscience at worst. Here, Jensen replies to these and other critics. He also answers the questions I think you yourself would like to ask him. He tells you why he believes the scientific basis of Jensenism is as solid as the Rock of Gibraltar, why the experts in the relevant disciplines of behavior genetics and psychometrics agree with him and not his critics, and why the public has been so misinformed.

This book also introduces you to Arthur Jensen, the man behind the "ism," so that you can understand why he took up such a controversial research program and why he has pursued it so relentlessly. Finally, it takes you on the intellectual odyssey of the behavioral sciences over the past third of a century, detailing the sea changes that have taken place since Jensen and Jensenism first hit the front pages in 1969.

Frank Miele
Sunnyvale, California

ACKNOWLEDGMENTS

I could not have written this book without the help and encouragement that so many people have given me over the years. I would like to give particular thanks to publisher and editor-in-chief Michael Shermer and the staff of *Skeptic*, to all those who have given so generously of their time in allowing me to interview them for the magazine, and to my editor Karl Yambert and the staff at Westview. Additionally, the photos in the book were provided by courtesy of Arthur Jensen and the cover photo by courtesy of Lois V. Jensen, his sister, and I thank them for their permission to use the photos.

F. M.

INTRODUCTION

Jensenism and Skepticism

Jensenism, n: the theory that an individual's IQ is largely due to heredity, including racial heritage; after Arthur R. Jensen (born
  1923), U.S. educational psychologist, who first propounded
  this hypothesis in 1965.

and

Skepticism, n: the search for provisional, not metaphysical, truth through
  the continuous and vigorous application of the methods of
  science, that is, formulating hypotheses and gathering data
  against which to test them.

Jensenism and skepticism—what's the connection? What does a controversial
theory linking intelligence, race, and genetics have to do with a growing movement that promotes better understanding of the scientific method
and greater use of critical thinking by the general public?

On the one hand, one skeptic icon, the late Stephen Jay Gould, who was
then America's best-known science writer, a distinguished though controversial scientist in his own right, and a past president of the American
Association for the Advancement of Science, once claimed to have
debunked Jensenism as resting on "a rotten edifice." On the other, *Intelligence,*
the most prestigious journal in the field of IQ research, devoted an entire
issue to honoring Jensen and his work, which its editor, Douglas Detterman,
titled "A King Among Men: Arthur Jensen."

If these wildly varying assessments of Arthur R. Jensen and his theories of race, genetics, and human intelligence don't invite a skeptical examination and some critical thinking, what does? As senior editor of *Skeptic*, I've
interviewed some of the world's leading scholars on differing sides of the
race-IQ issue and related controversies in biological and behavioral sciences.
Who better to interview than the namesake of the most controversial "ism"
of them all—the relation between race, intelligence, and genetics?

I realized that a fair treatment of Jensen and Jensenism would require a
book, not just an article. Jensen accepted, but could he commit the time?
That year, 1999, he was based in London, England, working at the Galton
Library on biographies of Charles Spearman and Hans Eysenck commissioned by the American Psychological Association (APA) and delivering the
annual Galton Lecture as well as invited lectures at universities and research
institutes in the United Kingdom, Denmark, Germany, Austria, Italy, and
Spain. It wasn't possible for me to spend the year in Europe attending the
lectures while we did the interviews. Even long-distance phone calls presented a difficulty because of the eight-to-nine-hour time difference, and
they would be a budget buster. So we decided to conduct the conversations
via E-mail. I wrote a series of questions on a particular topic, and Jensen
replied. We had our printed transcript proofed, but the only other modifi-
cations are those requested by the publisher, Westview Press, to remove rep-
etition, to clarify some of the more technical passages, or to update information and references to the scientific literature where appropriate.

Many reject Jensenism without examining the evidence because they
fear what might follow if it gained widespread public acceptance. I want
you to be able to decide for yourself whether Jensenism represents one
man's search for provisional, not metaphysical, truth through the continuous and vigorous application of the methods of science, that is, by formulating hypotheses and gathering data against which to test them, or a
dangerous diversion back down a blind alley of old and disproven ideas,
deceptively dressed up in modern scientific jargon.

The Prelude introduces you to "the man behind the 'ism.'" It includes
a biographical and professional sketch of "Jensen before Jensenism."

Chapter I, "Jensenism: A New Word in the Dictionary," provides a
perspective on "Jensenism" and explains how a well-respected and previ-

ously noncontroversial educational psychologist gave rise to a controversial word in the dictionary. We discuss how in the late 1960s Jensen's research interest turned from the serial position effect (how and why it's easier to remember the first and last items in a list than those in the middle) to the importance of general intelligence, as opposed to specific task learning, in education and in life; and then to the important role of heredity in intelligence, a subject that previously had been almost completely neglected.

Jensen recounts his discussions while in Washington, D.C., with Daniel Patrick Moynihan, who was then Nixon's presidential assistant for urban affairs, and with George H. W. Bush, who was then a Republican congressman from Texas. Jensen's own disdain, not for individuals but for things political as opposed to scientific, is apparent.

In Chapter 2, "What Is Intelligence? The g Factor and Its Rivals," Jensen defends the theory of general intelligence (the g factor) against the criticism that the g factor is merely a statistical artifact. When I present the best-known rival theories of intelligence, Jensen explains why he believes that the difference between the g factor theory and Robert Sternberg's Triarchic Theory of Analytical, Practical, and Creative Intelligence is a semantic one, while he sees Howard Gardner's Theory of Multiple Intelligences as a form of psychological biography, but not true science. The chapter concludes with Jensen explaining how state-of-the-art technologies such as PET scans provide even more support for his conclusions than just IQ tests.

In Chapter 3, "Nature, Nurture, or Both? Can Heritability Cut Psychology's Gordian Knot?" we discuss the meaning of heritability—the statistic used in quantitative genetics to resolve the nature-nurture question—what it can tell us and what it can't. Jensen's critics often accuse him of misinterpreting heritability. Still others deny that the heritability statistic (as opposed to the concept of heredity) has any meaning in human research, where controlled experiments are ethically unacceptable. As evidence for the genetic basis of intelligence, Jensen describes how closely the observed correlations between various degrees of kinship (identical twins, ordinary siblings, parents and their natural children, parents with their adopted children) fit with the correlations predicted by the genetic theory, but go against those predicted from a purely cultural theory. In particular, he draws a comparison between the high correlation of 0.87 (1.00 being perfect correlation) between the IQs of identical twins separated early in life and reared apart (who share 100 percent of their genes, but 0 percent of their environment), and the much lower correlation of 0.32 between the IQs of unrelated children reared together (who share 0 percent of their genes, but 100 percent of their environment). The chapter also includes a discussion of the Burt Affair—the controversy surrounding the accusation that Sir Cyril Burt had "faked" his twin studies, whose results Jensen had quoted in his *HER* article—and of Jensen's involvement in it.

Chapter 4, "What Is Race? Biological Reality or Cultural Construction?" examines the biggest taboo of all—the subject of race. I ask Jensen how he, an educational psychologist, can reject the official statement of the American Anthropological Association that race is a mere cultural construction and has no biological validity. Jensen counters that the most state-of-the art population genetic studies and statistical procedures identify "population clusters" that correspond quite closely to the racial classifications of traditional anthropology and even of "the man on the street," although the term "race" is avoided.

Jensen then presents three lines of argument to support what he calls the Default Hypothesis—that both genetic and environmental factors play about the same part in causing the average difference in IQ between Blacks and Whites as they do in causing differences in IQ within either race. First, he claims that the attempts to explain the Black-White IQ difference in terms of social, economic, or cultural factors alone have been tested and they have failed. When I cite ten of the best-known theories, Jensen explains why he believes they have been disproven. He draws particular attention to the results of trans-racial adoption studies, which show that Black children adopted by White middle-class parents end up with IQs at about the Black average, while mixed-race adopted children have intermediate IQs, and White adopted children have IQs around the White average.

Jensen's second argument, drawn from evolutionary biology, is that whenever two groups differ in physical characteristics, they will differ in behavior as well. He cites a famous study that demonstrated that Black, White, and Chinese American babies, all in the same hospital and tested in the first days after birth, differed in movement and activity. Next, Jensen claims that both the correlation between brain size and intelligence within either race, and the average difference in brain size and in intelligence between Blacks and Whites, are well established in the scientific literature.

Jensen's final argument that genes play a role in the Black-White IQ difference is based on what he calls Spearman's hypothesis. Charles Spearman, the famous British psychologist who first used the term g (general mental ability), also remarked that the more a given test measures the g factor, the greater the average Black-White difference on that test. Jensen explains that his research has confirmed Spearman's hypothesis for a number of different mental tests, given in different countries, by different examiners. Further, he has shown that g is related to a number of biological measures such as brain-wave patterns, glucose metabolism in the brain, and well-known genetic phenomena such as inbreeding depression (that is, the reduction in height, physical development, and IQ in children born of close-relative marriages).

Chapter 5, "From Jensenism to The Bell Curve Wars: Science, Pseudoscience, and Politics," draws Jensen out on subjects he has until now touched on only sparingly, if at all—the questions of race, science, and politics in American history, why he believes the race-genetics-IQ question has been so systematically misrepresented in the mass media and in many textbooks, his analysis of the most vocal opposition individuals and groups, and the role of the Pioneer Fund (which has supported much of his own work) in race-IQ research. I ask why, if he is correct, Jensenism is so often treated as pseudoscience, and organizations such as the American Psychological Association (APA), the Behavior Genetics Association (BGA), and the Educational Testing Service (ETS) have either disagreed with Jensenism (at least on the issue of race, genetics, and IQ) or remained silent. Jensen cites a survey of the members of the Behavior Genetics Association and the Test and Measurement Division of the APA (Division 5), as well as a statement in the *Wall Street Journal* signed by 50 experts in the behavioral sciences, as evidence that among experts in the relevant disciplines, Jensenism is considered mainstream science, not pseudoscience. (See Appendix B for the *Wall Street Journal* statement.)

The final chapter, Chapter 6, "Science and Policy: What's to Be Done?" invites Jensen onto truly new ground. He presents his view of the proper role of scientific fact in setting public policy, including Affirmative Action in the public and private sectors, especially in the military, government bureaucracy, and the educational system. Jensen also speculates on what the future holds in terms of policies such as welfare and eugenics.

Appendix A lists Jensen's large and ever-growing bibliography. In addition to the references at the end of each chapter, readers looking for more information can refer to Jensen's bibliography for relevant articles.

Appendix B reproduces the statement that appeared in the *Wall Street Journal* by 50 behavioral scientists on 25 points the signatories (including Jensen) considered "scientifically well-established."

Throughout this book my aim has been neither to praise Jensen and Jensenism nor to bury them. Rather, my goals are:

- First, to ask the questions you would ask if you were interviewing Jensen for a print or TV newsmagazine. Each chapter opens with an introduction that provides the background knowledge necessary to understand the topics covered in that chapter, much like the material talk show hosts get to "prep" them for interviews.
- Next, since most of Jensen's prolific output has been in technical books and journals, to allow Jensen to respond directly and conversationally to the objections of his best-known and severest critics in the academic world.
- Finally, whether you conclude that Jensenism is scientifically rock solid, rotten, or somewhere in between, I want you to meet Arthur R. Jensen, the man behind the "ism."

Further Reading

The reference to debunking Jensenism and its "rotten core" is: Gould, S. J. (1996). *The mismeasure of man* (Revised and expanded edition). New York: Norton. The special journal issue in which 13 experts, including some critics, honored Jensen and his work is: Detterman, D. K. (Ed.), 1998. A king among men: Arthur Jensen. *Intelligence*, 26 (3), 175–318. The major books and articles cited here are listed with the corresponding chapters.

PRELUDE

The Man Behind the "Ism"

For all the controversy that has raged around Jensenism, the general public knows relatively little about Jensen himself. Why? First, almost all of his more than 400 publications have appeared in technical journals or books. What's more, he's a born introvert. If you sat next to him on an airplane, you'd probably assume he was an auditor or bank examiner rather than a professor at the University of California at Berkeley. If you met him during his long tenure on the Berkeley campus, you'd be much more likely to think he taught business or law than psychology.

So who is Arthur R. Jensen? Did anything in his past—nature or nurture—play prologue to Jensenism? The play on the words "nature" and "nurture" comes from Shakespeare's *The Tempest*, but the enigma of heredity versus environment goes back to the ancient Greek philosophers. When they encountered non-Greeks they wondered whether heredity or environment (especially climate) could account for the differences in appearance and behavior. Similar observations were made by the ancient civilizations in Egypt, China, and India. In the age of science, first anthropology, then psychology, then sociology has each tried to resolve in its own way the riddle of human differences. How qualified is Arthur Jensen to speak on so enduring, so difficult, and so emotionally loaded a topic as the connection between intelligence, race, and genetics?

The authoritative *Corsini Encyclopedia of Psychology* describes him as:

One of the most visible educational and differential psychologists in the past half-century. Jensen is professor emeritus of educational psychology in the Graduate School of Education, University of California, Berkeley. During the forty years of his tenure at Berkeley, he was a prolific researcher in the psychology of human learning, individual differences in cognitive abilities, psychometrics, behavioral genetics, and mental chronometry, and his activity has continued since his official retirement in 1994. His work, published in seven books and some 400 articles in scientific and professional journals, has placed him among the most frequently cited figures in contemporary psychology, and his name has become one of the "isms" of our language.

JENSEN BEFORE JENSENISM

Arthur R. Jensen was born in 1923 in San Diego, California, where his father owned a lumber and building-supplies business. His paternal grandparents, the Jensens, were immigrants from Copenhagen, Denmark. On his mother's side, Jensen's grandfather was German. His maternal grandmother came from a Polish Jewish family. Both families disapproved of the marriage across religious lines, and the couple left Berlin and put down new roots in the San Diego area. Fluent in Polish, his grandmother was selected to greet the world-famous pianist Ignacy (Jan) Paderewski when he came to San Diego. Early on, Jensen noted how the dour demeanor of his Danish relatives contrasted with the fun-loving atmosphere of his mother's side of the family.

As a boy, Jensen attended San Diego public schools. He was a loner who read voraciously and said little—except when he had a subject to speak on. Then he would hold forth at the dinner table, enthusiastically recounting all he had read, until his only sibling, a younger sister, would plead, "Do we have to listen to another one of his lectures?" Young Jensen had little interest in team sports; he preferred hiking through the woods or swimming. His hobbies, which he pursued with diligence, were herpetology and classical music. He collected snakes, which he would trade to the reptile keeper of the San Diego Zoo to feed the zoo's king cobra, in exchange for white rats, which Jensen in turn fed his snakes.

Jensen's first goal in life was to become a clarinetist in a symphony orchestra, or better yet, a conductor. His playing was good enough to earn an audition with Leopold Stokowski's American Youth Symphony, and Jensen performed as second clarinet with the San Diego Symphony for a year when he was only seventeen. He soon realized, however, that no matter how much or how hard he practiced, he lacked the "special something" required to make it to the peak of the musical world. So Jensen switched career paths, entered the University of California at Berkeley, and majored in psychology.

Jensen's interests in herpetology and classical music provide clues to the eventual rise of Jensenism. He clearly had an interest in biology. Catching and keeping snakes and lizards required carefully observing their behavior. At 15 he performed experiments to determine whether it was temperature or light that caused the lizards to go underground. (He found it was temperature.)

Jensen remains passionate about music, though he hasn't performed in years. He has a massive collection of recordings and he and his wife are season ticket holders for the San Francisco Opera. When lecturing in Europe he makes it a point to attend symphony and opera performances. Jensen's decision to abandon a musical career provides a key insight into his view not only of himself but of the world. Clearly, he had the ability to make a living from music. But the fire that burns inside Arthur Jensen, though invisible from the outside, is to perform at the very highest level he can. As he states in Chapter 1, he has always been interested in people who have "made it." It is not a desire for the trappings or rewards of success that drives Jensen but the conviction that he's doing what he does best. As he once told me, "The two smartest things I ever did were to decide to become a professor because it's the only thing I can really do at a level I'm truly satisfied with and to marry Barb because she does so much that allows me to focus on my work and brings so many things into my life I wouldn't have without her."

Perhaps because of his personal experience with music, Jensen has been keenly aware of his own and others people's limitations, and he is therefore skeptical of pie-in-the-sky claims that "If you can dream it, you can be it!" Instead, he has always practiced and preached a methodical approach of setting stepwise goals and reevaluating the next step to take as each successive rung is reached or not.

AN INTELLECTUAL ODYSSEY

But why psychology? As we follow the career of Arthur Jensen and the story of Jensenism, we will also trace the intellectual odyssey of psychology in our time. From its beginning, psychology has varied wildly in what, how, and why it studies. One tradition—exemplified by B. F. Skinner's behaviorism—searches for universal laws that describe the behavior of all organisms. Differences between individuals, species, or groups are treated as random error, much as a chemist allows for the measurement errors that come from using imperfectly calibrated scales. A second tradition, based more on the biological sciences, sees observed differences as psychology's wheat, not its chaff. That tradition tries to explain human differences in terms of the best mix of hereditary, biological, and cultural causes. Whether the focus is on universal laws or individual and group differences, however, both these traditions are "reductionist" approaches because they reduce the dizzying multiplicity of behavior to either universal laws or a small number of factors.

In contrast, depth psychology and dynamic psychology are more humanistic and holistic. They try to solve each individual's "problems" by understanding the totality of his or her existence. Sigmund Freud's psychoanalysis is the classic example. Those who follow the model of the hard sciences reject such methods as being literary or mystical, not scientific. But to many, the methods of hard science are too cold and detached. They argue that an obsessive drive for scientific purity produces a sterile psychology, indifferent to individual suffering and irrelevant to the problems of society.

These then are psychology's Scylla and Charybdis—a summons for methodological purity that steers research further and further toward impersonal generalization versus a cry for commiseration that leads into the mists of mythology, not science. Jensen was drawn to psychology because he believes that it can produce answers to important problems for individuals and society. He became disenchanted with pure experimental psychology because he saw it sharpening its focus by excessively narrowing it. He wasn't interested in spending his career determining the precise difference in reaction time in two experimental situations for its own sake. However, when he wanted to know what differences in a purely objective measure such as reaction time could reveal about individual and group differences in IQ, he revived and reestablished the field of mental chronometry, even designing some of the measuring instruments himself.

When Jensen turned to clinical psychology, he again became disenchanted—this time because his own studies proved that tests based on the assumptions of depth psychology simply were not valid predictors of anything except how that person answered that test. The situation is much like trying to measure people's musical or athletic ability by asking them to name their favorite artists or players. The test is reliable. Most people will have the same personal picks from one day to the next. But this tells us nothing about their own ability.

After graduating from Berkeley in 1945, Jensen returned home and worked at his father's business, then as a technician in a pharmaceutical laboratory, as a social worker, and as a high school biology teacher and orchestra conductor while getting a master's degree in psychology from San Diego State University. Then in 1952 Jensen went to Teachers College, Columbia University, to study educational and clinical psychology. There he worked as a laboratory technician in Columbia's Zoology Department and as a research assistant to his major professor and mentor, Percival Symonds, an exponent of dynamic psychology and projective tests. Together, they co-authored *From Adolescent to Adult* (1961), based on their research. Jensen's doctoral dissertation, "Aggression in Fantasy and Overt Behavior" (1956), cast doubt on the scientific ability of one such test, the Thematic Apperception Test, to predict individual differences of aggression, either in degree or type.

During a year's clinical internship at the University of Maryland's Psychiatric Institute in Baltimore (1955–1956), Jensen became further disillusioned with dynamic psychology. At the same time, he was drawn to quantitative and experimental research on personality by Hans J. Eysenck at the University of London's Institute of Psychiatry. A postdoctoral fel-

Jensen's first appearance on TV (Channel 2, Oakland) after he first wrote on the role of genetics and IQ in school achievement while a fellow at the Center for Advanced Study in the Behavioral Sciences, Stanford University. (Spring 1967)

lowship from the National Institute of Mental Health (NIMH) allowed Jensen to spend 1956–1958 working in Eysenck's lab. There he thrived, his passion for research that emphasized both scientific rigor and real-life relevance being shared not only by Eysenck but also by others in the London School of psychology. The intellectual origins of Jensenism lie in the scientific worldview and methods of the London School, which was established by Sir Francis Galton and Charles Spearman, the founders of psychometrics, differential psychology, and behavioral genetics.

Inspired by his work at Eysenck's lab, Jensen returned to the States and was appointed assistant professor of educational psychology in the University of California at Berkeley in 1958. In 1966 he became full professor and then research psychologist in the Institute of Human Learning there. Jensen spent his first sabbatical year (1964–1965) in Eysenck's lab. In 1966–1967 he was an invited fellow at the Center for Advanced Study in the Behavioral Sciences at Stanford.

It was only in the late 1960s, after he had established a solid reputation based on a decade of careful, noncontroversial research and over 30 publications on human learning, that Jensen expanded his focus to include individual differences in scholastic performance among culturally disadvantaged minority groups such as Mexican Americans and Blacks. He began by assuming that any observed group differences were the result of socioeconomic and cultural factors. Increasingly, however, Jensen realized that the prevailing opinion among educational psychologists at that time just didn't tell the whole story. His reading and research interests turned more and more to biology and genetics.

Then in 1969 the *Harvard Educational Review,* one of the most prestigious journals in the field, asked Jensen to contribute an article to be entitled "How Much Can We Boost IQ and School Achievement?" The outline *HER* gave Jensen requested that he include a clear statement of his position on social class and racial differences in intelligence. Jensen discussed race and IQ briefly, saying only that while cultural factors were clearly involved in causing the 15-point difference in average IQ between Black and White Americans, genes couldn't be ruled out. As for the article's central question, "How Much Can We Boost IQ and Scholastic Achievement?" Jensen's conclusion, based on his review of the evidence, could be summed up in two words: Not much.

Jensen's *HER* article came at a time when "Black power" was clashing with the "White backlash" against Lyndon Johnson's Great Society programs. Against that backdrop, Jensen rocketed from relative anonymity as a respected but low-profile expert on human learning to blazing notoriety in the pages of *Time, Newsweek, Life, U.S. News & World Report,* and *The New York Times Magazine.* He soon became a target of student protests, sit-ins, resolutions of condemnation, acts of vandalism, and death threats. The word "Jensenism" entered the Random House and Webster's unabridged dictionaries.

During his academic career at UC Berkeley, including the 30-plus years after he became "controversial," Jensen received every promotion possible—even to "super-grades" beyond the rank of full professor, which required recommendation by a panel of distinguished international experts not on the Berkeley faculty. Indeed, the closer one gets to expert opinion in the relevant disciplines of psychometrics (mental testing) and behavior genetics, the greater the support for Jensen and his work; and each year, that support increases. Of his more than 400 publications, none has been in fringe journals, and the overwhelming majority have been in the most prestigious peer-reviewed journals in the relevant fields—journals such as *Intelligence, Behavior Genetics, Personality and Individual Differences, The Psychological Bulletin,* and *Behavioral and Brain Sciences*—and in such authoritative works as *The Encyclopedia of Psychology* and *The Encyclopedia of Intelligence,* where articles are by the editor's invitation. In 1970 Jensen was a founding member of the Behavior Genetics Association. He has served as a consulting editor to both *Intelligence* and *Behavior Genetics,* and published articles in their first issues. Jensen is often asked to serve as a peer reviewer by these and by many other academic journals because their chief editors recognize the fairness and thoroughness with which he treats every article sent to him, regardless of whether or not it agrees with his own position.

In 1998 *Intelligence* published a special issue entitled "A King Among Men: Arthur Jensen." It included Jensen's own account of his career, his massive and ever growing bibliography, and commentaries on his life and works by some of his most important admirers and thoughtful, if grudging, critics.

Many reject Jensenism not because a careful study of the evidence has convinced them that it is scientifically wrong, but because they fear that racism might find scientific support if Jensenism gained general acceptance. That is, they reject Jensenism on moral rather than scientific grounds, often while attributing political rather than scientific motives to Jensen himself. However, Arthur Jensen is the least political person I know and also the most straightforward. What you see with Arthur Jensen is what you get. He is consumed by a Gandhian dedication to following principle in making decisions, but is willing to reevaluate his decisions based on new information.

Perhaps that dedication to principle above pragmatism in part explains why through all the turmoil and vituperation he has endured, Jensen really doesn't hold any grudge against his opponents. Some, he believes, simply hold religiously to a different view of the world, where stubborn facts have to be subordinated to what they believe is the good of society. Others, he thinks, just don't possess the quantitative or analytical skills or background to comprehend the issues objectively. About the worst thing I've ever heard him call such individuals, indeed the harshest word I've heard him use, is "mush-heads." But Jensen is most put off by those who say they agree with his conclusions completely but do not understand how he arrived at them. "I'd rather sit across the table from either of the first two groups than the third, someone who likes what he thinks I'm saying just because it seems to agree with his own prejudices," he once told me. Jensen has pursued the role heredity plays in the Black-White difference in average IQ not because he is obsessed with race but because he is dedicated to understanding what he believes is society's most important possession—intelligence. To dodge the race question would be to ignore an important piece in the puzzle—an act of intellectual cowardice.

Our conversations on intelligence, race, and genetics now begin with my asking Jensen how a once noncontroversial name gave rise to the most controversial "ism" in contemporary behavioral science.

Further Reading

The juxtaposition of "nature" and "nurture" comes from Shakespeare's *The Tempest* (Act IV, Scene I), where Prospero refers to Caliban as "a devil, a born devil on whose nature nurture can never stick." Sir Francis Galton, the father of the study of human differences in mental ability, picked up what he termed the Bard's "alliterative antithesis." (See Galton, F. [1874, 1970]. *English men of science: Their nature and nurture.* London: Frank Cass [1970 reprint]; and Galton, F. [1875]. The history of twins, as a criterion of the relative powers of nature and nurture. *Fraser's Magazine, 12,* 566–576.) In the chapters that follow, you will see how much Jensen and others in the London School of psychology have followed in Galton's footsteps.

The source of the brief Jensen biography is: Craighead, W. E., and Nemeroff, C. B. (2001). *The Corsini encyclopedia of psychology.* New York: Wiley. The special journal issue in which 13 experts, including some critics, honored Jensen and his work is: Detterman, D. K. (Ed.), 1998. A king among men: Arthur Jensen. *Intelligence, 26* (3), 175–318.

For Jensen's own account of his 1969 *Harvard Educational Review* article, the origin of "Jensenism" and the reaction to it, see the 67-page preface to: Jensen, A. R. (1972). *Genetics and education.* New York: Harper and Row. The other biographical information comes from my many conversations with Jensen.

1

JENSENISM

A New Word
in the Dictionary

In this chapter I ask Jensen to explain how in 1969 his name became inextricably linked with the controversial issue of intelligence, race, and genetics. At that time, America was as deeply divided over race relations as it was by the Vietnam War. Numerous studies financed by the federal government and leading foundations all documented that the average IQ of Black Americans (85) was 15 points below that of Whites (100). At first, Jensen agreed with other educators and psychologists—and just about every other social scientist—that environmental factors such as limited opportunities, lower average income, and the legacy of slavery, Jim Crow, and segregation, were the cause. Academic research aimed at finding the best method to alleviate the 15-point Black-White IQ gap came to focus more and more on early intervention to circumvent environmental obstacles to cognitive development. Head Start remains the best known of the resultant programs for early cognitive stimulation of the disadvantaged.

Outside of academia, however, many White Americans—and not just those in the South—had become disenchanted with the Great Society programs. Aided by a political backlash among Whites opposing such programs, Richard Nixon was elected president on a law-and-order platform in 1968.

In 1969, the respected *Harvard Educational Review* (*HER*) commissioned Jensen to write an evaluation of educational intervention programs. The resulting 123-page article, "How Much Can We Boost IQ and Scholastic Achievement?" remains one of the most cited works (either vilified or praised, depending on the reviewer's point of view) in the social science literature.

Based on his review of the evidence, Jensen reached three conclusions that were diametrically opposite to the prevailing view:

- Compensatory education had been tried, and it had failed to raise significantly either the IQ or the school performance of disadvantaged children.
- Genetic differences were more important than cultural or socioeconomic differences in explaining individual differences in IQ within the White population (the only group for which there were adequate data at that time).
- Most explosively—it was therefore only reasonable to ask whether genetic differences played some role in the 15-point Black-White average-IQ difference.

The *HER* article became a major media event. Its three main points, dubbed "Jensenism," entered our vocabulary. Jensen became the target of student protests, sit-ins, acts of violence, and even death threats. Academic criticism came in the form of resolutions from scholars and professional organizations condemning Jensenism. In May 1969, in a three-hour symposium held for security's sake in a closed studio on the Berkeley campus (but broadcast to an outside audience), Jensen defended Jensenism before a panel of questioners who were among the most distinguished figures in their respective disciplines. They were geneticists Joshua Lederberg (1958 Nobel laureate in Physiology or Medicine) and William J. Libby; mental testing expert Lee J. Cronbach; Arthur Stinchombe of the UC Berkeley Sociology Department; and Aaron Cicourel of UC Santa Barbara, an authority in the field of psycholinguistics. The distinguished geneticist Curt Stern acted as moderator. Obviously, the symposium failed to resolve the issue, but it showed that Jensen could go toe-to-toe with eminent critics and give at least as good as he got.

Jensen also gives us his firsthand observations and impressions of important people in science, music, and politics. Through Jensen's eyes we meet Columbia University professors Henry E. Garrett and Otto Klineberg, who opposed each other vigorously in an earlier debate on race and IQ; anthropologist Margaret Mead, who would later lead a protest against Jensen's election as a fellow of the Psychology Section of the American Association for the Advancement of Science (AAAS) after his *HER* article appeared; Sir Cyril Burt, who years later, after his death, would be accused of faking his famous study of identical twins reared apart, which Jensen cited in the *HER* article (see Chapter 3 for a discussion of the Burt Affair and Jensen's involvement in it); George H. W. Bush, then a Texas congressman; Daniel Patrick Moynihan, whose report to President Nixon on the Black family produced a race controversy of its own; and conductor Arturo Toscanini, whose concerts and rehearsals Jensen attended regularly while a graduate student at Columbia. Jensen reserves his greatest praise for his mentor, the late British psychologist Hans J. Eysenck, for having shaped fundamentally his attitudes about psychology and science.

Miele: Back in 1969 you were an educational psychologist in the Graduate School of Education and a research psychologist in the Institute of Human Learning at the University of California in Berkeley. Your work was well respected and you had no history of enjoying or even seeking controversy. If anything, the opposite was the case—you were best known for researching things like the serial position effect in learning.

Then your article "How Much Can We Boost IQ and Scholastic Achievement?" appeared in the Winter 1969 issue of the *Harvard Educational Review*. Most *HER* articles are read by professionals and graduate students in educational psychology and attract little outside notice. But yours produced a national controversy that was covered in the major news magazines as well as on TV and radio. It generated heated discussion in professional journals, resolutions condemning you and the article, student protests, sit-ins, acts of violence, and even death threats. Eventually, the word "Jensenism" even entered the dictionary.

What did you say in that lengthy, 123-page *HER* article that hadn't been said before? After all, you'd given a talk with the same title two years earlier.

Jensen: Three things about the *HER* article combined synergistically to set off all the commotion. Each of them was quite contrary to the prevailing zeitgeist.

First, I examined the available research and concluded that compensatory educational programs had failed to show any strong or lasting effect in raising IQ or scholastic achievement. Second, I reviewed the existing evidence showing that genetic factors played a large part in individual differences in IQ. And third, I said the totality of evidence was most consistent with the *hypothesis* that genetic as well as environmental factors are involved in the average difference between Blacks and Whites in IQ and scholastic achievement. Although it was less than 5 percent of the whole article, this small part—hypothesizing a genetic component in the racial IQ difference—produced the most vehement vituperation.

The 15-point difference in average IQ between Blacks and Whites in the United States had been well established by the psychological research. But never before (including in the talk you just mentioned) had I suggested the *plausible hypothesis* that both environment and genes were involved. This hypothesis was plausible because research had not found any compelling explanation for all of the 15-point difference, and because genetic factors as well as environmental factors were responsible for individual differences in IQ within either racial group.

Miele: But claims about racial differences in brain size in fact go all the way back to Paul Broca, discoverer of one of the important speech centers in the brain. And there was Robert Bennett Bean's study of Black-White differences in brain size, which was cited by Henry Garrett and others, such as W. C. George in his pamphlet *The Biology of the Race Problem*, issued by the Governor of Alabama (George Wallace's predecessor, John Patterson). The mainstream trend in anthropology and psychology was to debunk those studies. Were you aware of all this?

Jensen: I'm chagrined to say that at the time I wrote my *HER* paper I wasn't. A year or two later someone sent me a copy of George's pamphlet. As he was a professor of anatomy, I thought it might be worth reading. At that time I was on a committee chaired by the late Professor Harry Harlow, the famous researcher on primate behavior. Harlow was quite knowledgeable about brain research, physiological psychology, and the like. I gave him a copy of George's essay and asked for his opinion. Harlow believed that genetics played a part in racial differences and that there are racial differences in brain size. But he was unimpressed by George's evidence. He thought it was antiquated and questionable and said he would put very little stock in it. So I ignored it.

The study by Bean doesn't ring a bell. I can't recall having come across it in my fairly extensive review of studies on brain correlates of intelligence. But if it's a reputable piece of research, I should have it in my files. The fact that it was cited in an essay issued by the Governor of Alabama back around the time of federally enforced school desegregation in the South should lead one to examine it carefully to see if it actually has any scientific merit.

After the publicity surrounding my *HER* article, I did receive a number of letters from so-called citizens' groups in various Southern states, asking if I would write letters to their local newspapers in support of racial segregation in public schools. I replied that I was, and always have been, absolutely opposed to racial segregation of any kind. One of these people wrote back calling me "just another Berkeley pinko!" He at least gave me the satisfaction of knowing that I had angered him.

Miele: Well, Sir Cyril Burt had already made the case for genetic factors in IQ and scholastic ability in a number of papers, including his famous 1957 Bingham Award Lecture sponsored by the American Psychological Association titled "The Inheritance of Mental

Ability." So did a 1963 review article by Nikki Erlenmeyer-Kimling and Lissy Jarvik in *Science*.

Jensen: I had heard of Burt as one of the preeminent figures in psychology since I was an undergraduate student in Berkeley. And so I attended his Bingham Award Lecture during the second year of my postdoctorate at London University, though I had no special interest in the topic at that time. I went simply because I wanted to see Britain's most famous psychologist in person. He was then 75 years old, and I thought I might never get another chance to see the great man. Little did I imagine then that about 13 years later I would get to know him quite well personally and eventually become involved in the Burt Affair. [See Chapter 3 for a discussion of the Burt Affair and Jensen's involvement in it.]

Miele: Did he live up to your expectations?

Jensen: His Bingham Lecture was the best lecture I had ever attended. Burt spoke entirely without a script and had the kind of eloquence, showmanship, and authority that really held his audience spellbound. A brilliant and impressive man.

Miele: The third and most controversial part of your *HER* article, the genetic role in racial differences in IQ, had been made by Audrey Shuey in the two editions of her lengthy 1966 book, *The Testing of Negro Intelligence*, which you cite in the *HER* article. And Henry Garrett, a past president of the American Psychological Association, had been carrying on a running debate with Otto Klineberg and others on the subject (though you do not cite those).

So was it really your novel combination of the themes that garnered all the headlines? Or was it the fact that you came to the race-IQ debate with clean hands, so to speak, because you were a respected researcher in compensatory education who had never supported—and who, indeed, opposed—attempts to overturn the *Brown v. Board* school desegregation decision?

Jensen: What you've said is true, but I'd like to qualify it a bit.

By 1969, Shuey's book and Garrett's writings, if not Klineberg's, were far in the background. Shuey got her Ph.D. under Garrett at Columbia University. They both wrote as if the fact that hundreds of studies consistently found a mean Black-White difference of about 15 IQ points constituted sufficient evidence that the difference was largely, if not entirely, genetic. Of course it is not sufficient evidence. Neither Shuey nor Garrett attempted to examine the issue in a way that could lead to any conclusion. That requires investigating a whole network of relationships and different lines of empirical evidence. A hundred or a thousand times as many IQ test comparisons as the three hundred or so that were compiled by Shuey could not have brought us any closer to understanding the causes of the Black-White IQ difference.

Miele: Then why did you cite Shuey's work, if not Garrett's?

Jensen: Because when I viewed the purely psychometric evidence presented by Shuey in relation to the fact that genetic and environmental factors play a part in individual variation in intelligence within either race, along with a number of other facts, I thought it was scientifically necessary to investigate the possibility of genetic as well as environmental factors in explaining the Black-White average-IQ difference.

Miele: Since you were all at Columbia University, did you ever meet Garrett, Shuey, or Klineberg? If so, what were your impressions of them?

Jensen: I met both Garrett and Klineberg when I was a grad student there. I even audited Klineberg's course on social psychology, not because I was interested at that time in any of these topics we're now discussing, but simply because he was one of the famous names in psychology. For the same reason, I audited an anthropology course given by Margaret Mead, and I became acquainted with the venerable dean of experimental psychology, Robert S. Woodworth, whose classic textbook I had used as an undergraduate psychology student at Berkeley. I was always interested in what people who had "made it" were like in person.

Miele: And Garrett?

Jensen: Yes. I wanted to take a course in factor analysis given by Professor Helen M. Walker. She was a noted statistician and one of the two or three best professors I ever had. Unfortunately she was on sabbatical that year. Since Garrett offered a less specialized course, I went to him to find out just what it covered. He asked about my previous courses in statistics and suggested I audit just the couple of lectures on factor analysis. They were very introductory and covered less than I had already picked up from the chapter on factor analysis in J. Paul Guilford's famous textbook *Psychometric Methods.*

I found Garrett a rather lackadaisical and perfunctory lecturer, and I was glad that I hadn't enrolled for his full course. He seemed friendly, but was quite impersonal and matter-of-fact. Nothing about him left me with any clear personal impression. In this respect, he was a rather typical professor.

Klineberg was a very precise and professorial fellow, short and compact, with very close-cropped gray hair. He was a good lecturer, though not very animated; he usually sat at a desk while lecturing but he nearly always had considerable enthusiasm for his subject. Personally, he was quite formal but very cordial and courtly, much as I later found to be more common among the older European professors. Sir Cyril Burt, for example, had a similar personal style.

Miele: While we're strolling down memory lane, what were your impressions of Mead and Woodworth?

Jensen: Margaret Mead was truly an unforgettable character. I never met her personally, but audited her lectures at Columbia. She always came across as a woman of great energy, with boundless enthusiasm for whatever she was talking about. Her lectures were immensely colorful and entertaining. And it was clear that she thoroughly enjoyed her showmanship. I still vividly remember some of her anecdotes and descriptions, such as her telling, complete with hilarious arm-waving gestures—about the swinging pendulous breasts of the older Samoan women. It brought the house down. She was usually quite "earthy," and never high-flown. As an entertaining lecturer, few college professors could compete with her.

I found many of her statements involving psychological matters highly provocative because they so completely contradicted what I had learned from other professors at Columbia. For example, she thought schizophrenia was a cultural condition, defined as a disease only in modern Western cultures. I mentioned this to Joseph Zubin, who, in his course on abnormal psychology, taught that schizophrenia is a genetic brain disorder. He was most annoyed that Margaret Mead was teaching "such blatant nonsense" to so many students. My major professor, Percival Symonds, was greatly amused when I told him I was auditing Mead's course. He said something like, "I hope you're not taking it seriously, because when it comes to psychology she doesn't know what she's talking about."

Robert Woodworth was an impressive man and a most interesting lecturer. He personally knew every big name in the history of American and European psychology, from William James on. This wealth of personal, anecdotal knowledge, combined with his fantastic scholarly erudition, made his course on history and systems of psychology a memorable experience. It was also an inspiration to see someone in his late 80s who was so physically fit and mentally sharp.

The first time I met Woodworth personally, I took along one of his books for him to autograph, which he did. I asked him some questions about E. L. Thorndike, co-author of his famous study on the "transfer of training." I wanted to get Woodworth's personal impressions of Thorndike the man. But he rather dismissed my question, saying he would be discussing Thorndike in his course.

Then to my surprise, Woodworth proceeded to more or less interview me, saying, "Well, you already know about me. I'd like to know something about you." He asked me about the other courses I was taking, which professors I had—he knew them all and commented knowingly about each one. Then he asked me a most interesting question to which I wasn't prepared to give a very good answer: "What do you want to be doing ten years from now? That's the way to think about what you're doing now." I frequently recall Woodworth's good influence on me.

Miele: You said, "I was always interested in what people who had 'made it' were like in person." Who were the most impressive people you've met? What did they have in common?

Jensen: I have already mentioned my major professor, Percival Symonds. I learned something about good work habits from him. He was also the first person who ever took the trouble to offer quite detailed criticisms of things I wrote. He emphasized that if I was ever to become what he called "a real professor," it was essential that I "research and publish." Symonds himself was a prolific and clear writer, and he knew all the ropes for getting published. Though he never tried to indoctrinate me in his own beliefs, he did want me to develop the habit of writing. I liked this and profited greatly from his mentoring.

By far the most important person in my career, of course, was Hans Eysenck. I spent two years with him as a postdoc and another year on my first sabbatical leave from Berkeley. From his writings, I had great expectations of Eysenck when I went to England to work in his department, and they were more than fulfilled. Eysenck was a kind of genius, or at least a person of very unusual talents, and the only person of that unusual caliber that I have come across in the field of psychology. I have known a number of very capable and truly outstanding persons in psychology, and persons whose scientific contributions are on a par with, or may even exceed, Eysenck's, but none who were what I would think of as some kind of phenomenon.

I got perhaps as much as 90 percent of my attitudes about psychology and science from Eysenck. The three years I spent in his department have been a lasting source of inspiration. I dread to think where my own career might have gone had I never made the Eysenck connection. I think Eysenck was a great man and have written in detail about my impressions of him.

Miele: What about people outside of psychology?

Jensen: I've never really gotten to know any politicians personally. Once after testifying in Congress I met former president George H. W. Bush—at that time a congressman from Texas—and chatted with him for a few minutes. He knew something about my 1969 *HER* article but seemed more interested in my personal background—where I was born, where I grew up, where I went to college, things like that. He acted rather amazed by my answers, especially the fact that up to that time I had never set foot in the Deep South. When he said, "Isn't that interesting, you've never been in the South?" I assumed he was testing my credentials for my discussing the nature of the Black-White difference in IQ. But that topic never came up in our brief conversation.

The one really great politician that I observed at close hand was Jawaharlal Nehru, the then prime minister of India. I had read Nehru's autobiography *Toward Freedom* and his *The Discovery of India*, both beautifully written books, so I enjoyed the opportunity of seeing him in person. So many people were in line to shake hands with him that I got out of the line and went up to where I could observe him up close for longer than if I had remained in line and waited my turn to shake hands. He was shorter than I had imagined (five feet, six and a half inches, to be exact), but he was surprisingly handsome. Even at age 65, Nehru had a dynamic and charismatic quality, fitting for a prime minister.

Miele: And Gandhi? Briefly.

Jensen: I'll try to be brief. Mahatma Gandhi has been my number one hero since I was 14 years old. I never saw him in person, of course, but up until perhaps 20 years ago I thought I had read everything written about him in English, certainly more than I have ever read on any other person or subject. Then, in 1980, when I visited the Gandhi Library at the Punjab University in Chandigarh, India, I discovered that I had read only a fraction of the nearly 500 books and several thousand articles then written about Gandhi, not to mention the handsome 90-volume set of his own writings published by the Indian government.

Miele: Why Gandhi? He wasn't a scientist.

Jensen: The greatest thing about Gandhi was his truly great and moving life. When a newspaper reporter asked him, "What is your message?" Gandhi replied, "My life is my message." And an absolutely extraordinary life it was! One of those rare individuals who, as they say, is larger than life. He was also one of the few people I know of who lived nearly his whole adult life by principle, entirely by principle. And they were difficult principles to live up to. Even to have made the attempt and to have succeeded to the extent that Gandhi did is, I think, awesome. As *Life* magazine wrote, one has to go back in history to the Buddha and Jesus for comparisons. Gandhi's greatness far overshadowed his personal idiosyncrasies and eccentricities.

One wonders how many people could possibly follow Gandhi's example. Yet, properly studied, his well-documented life can be a continual source of example and inspiration. He is the one who first comes to mind whenever I feel puzzled as to the right course of action.

Miele: And in your other love, the world of music?

Jensen: The one who impressed me the most was the great maestro Arturo Toscanini. During my three years in New York I rarely missed one of the concerts he conducted with the NBC Symphony. I even attended his rehearsals. Toscanini, too, was a charismatic figure, emitting electricity, and performing magic with his orchestra. His rehearsals were rather terrifying, even when several rows back from the stage and not directly in the line of fire as were the musicians in the orchestra. Sparks flew. They had to become inured to his sudden explosions of temper. There must have been some very good musicians who could not play under him.

I last saw Toscanini in rehearsal when he was 87. What seemed so interesting was the phenomenal passion and the extreme care he had for the quality of the performance. I have never seen such a high degree of concentration and effort brought to any task by anyone else. At times his tremendous concentration and mental energy struck me as abnormal and a bit frightening—like the sun being brought to a white-hot focus by a great magnifying glass. It's clear why all other conductors, famous and obscure alike, were in awe of him. On the podium he was an elemental force of nature.

Miele: And what qualities did all these exceptional people have in common?

Jensen: Three things: An exceptional level of ability or talent, unstinting energy, and an intensely concentrated, sustained interest in what they were doing.

Miele: Couldn't your interest in "people who had made it" reflect a certain underlying elitism on the one hand and almost clinical coldness towards those who haven't on the other? Could that have affected your whole approach to the question of IQ, genetics, and race?

Jensen: A colleague who knew me quite well once accused me of having an unusual interest in people who were in some way exceptional. I can't deny that; but what I will deny is the implied corollary of what you call elitism, some "clinical coldness," towards people who aren't known for any conspicuous achievement.

I do believe that the factors that cause some individuals to be exceptional are largely genetic. Of course, they also need opportunities and environments that favor the expression or development of their exceptional traits. I believe that people of really exceptional achievement are examples of *emergenesis*—a term in behavioral genetics. It means that exceptional achievement depends upon a particular, rare combination of genetic traits that act multiplicatively, not additively. If any one of the traits is lacking, the exceptional achievement will not occur.

According to Sir Francis Galton, the three traits that are essential for outstanding achievement are a high level of ability, drive or zeal, and persistence of effort. Real genius also requires creativity.

Miele: Let's get back to Jensenism. In the 67-page preface to your 1972 book, *Genetics and Education,* and in other places, you describe how this controversy just "burst around you" and how you've acted as a scholar just going where the evidence took you. Some critics say you deliberately courted controversy as a path toward advancement. In that preface you describe how you gave your manuscript to a reporter for *U.S. News & World Report,* a conservative news magazine, especially at that time, which had in 1965 run a controversial article along similar lines by William Shockley, "Is the Quality of the U.S. Population Declining?"

So weren't you looking for a chance to get into the fray in those tumultuous times?

Jensen: Not at all, but I don't think it would be in the least reprehensible if that were the case. I did think that the issues dealt with in my *HER* article were very important. And I suppose I must accept my late colleague Lee Cronbach's claim that I had a certain "missionary zeal," and I wanted to get my message out. All true. But I wasn't seeking the commotion that ensued, nor did I do anything to promote it. It was unfortunate, but as I view it all in retrospect, I think it was necessary if discussion of the issues was to be brought into the open.

Miele: Then how did your manuscript get into the hands of the reporter from *U.S. News & World Report?*

Jensen with a graduate assistant at the University of California, Berkeley, about the time of the publication of his HER *article in 1969, which led to the term* Jensenism *becoming part of our vocabulary.*

Jensen: It was a curious happenstance. The reporter was on the Berkeley campus to cover the student unrest going on at that time. He came to my office to get my opinion. I don't know why he picked me, because I wasn't very interested in the matter. I had been away in Europe during the height of the so-called Free Speech Movement that seemed to dominate the Berkeley campus at that time.

I told the reporter I was involved with something I thought far more important and was about to have an article on it come out in the *Harvard Educational Review.* He seemed interested so I told him the gist of the article. He asked for a copy of my 200-page typescript, which I gave to him. He followed up with the editors of the *HER.* They sent him copies of the seven commentaries on my article they had solicited and said they intended to hold a press conference about it. Within a week or so, the article was published and the controversy was reported in *U.S. News & World Report,* the *New York Times, Time, Life,*

Newsweek, and other places. Some accounts were superficial or inaccurate. Only *U.S. News & World Report* and *Fortune,* both of which have interviewed me from time to time over the years, have consistently taken pains to check everything with me for factual and technical accuracy before going to press.

Miele: But why did you jump into the race-IQ issue at that time?

Jensen: Because educational psychologists were trying to discover and to ameliorate the conditions that caused the large average shortfall in Blacks' scholastic performance. They were investigating a host of supposed environmental causes and hypothesizing others. In the 1960s it was quite taboo to mention genetic factors in connection with IQ differences, except perhaps only to completely dismiss them even as a possibility. But I could find no scientific basis for dismissing the *plausibility* of a genetic hypothesis, which of course always allows for environmental influences as well. So I thought it was important to put it on the table along with all the social-cultural-psychological hypotheses being investigated. Moreover, there was already sufficient evidence to disconfirm some of these hypotheses.

I still feel confident that I was right in what I did in 1969. And if you read my *HER* article carefully, you'll see that I stated a hypothesis. I made no claims that weren't at least as justified scientifically as any of the purely environmental hypotheses that were so popular at that time.

Miele: So that's all there is to the origin of Jensenism? There's no "rest of the story"?

Jensen: If you are looking for some deeper or hidden motive on my part, I'm afraid I can't be of much help. If anything, my attitudes are based on a rather lifelong antipathy to believing anything without evidence. As a kid I was more or less kicked out of Sunday school because of my argumentativeness and resistance to accepting things on faith. Scientific ways of thinking about things, however, have always appealed to me, and I feel no need to believe much of anything. Belief is really irrelevant to science. Its truth status doesn't consist of belief and doesn't depend on belief.

Any certitude I enjoy in my life is based on what could be called aesthetic experiences, particularly music, and also nature. The things I know and like at this direct sensory and subjective level are good and right, for me, without need of any evidence or argument beyond the experience itself. But I don't confuse them with the understanding of objective reality, which, in my opinion, should lie entirely within the purview of science.

Miele: Even in science, things don't happen in a vacuum. Let's recall what America was like back in 1969. Richard Nixon had just been elected president in a close election, helped by Governor George Wallace of Alabama, whose candidacy had been supported by a White backlash against programs of racial equalization. Nixon himself benefited directly from a demand for law and order and a feeling among the White majority that Lyndon Johnson's Great Society had been a failure or even counterproductive.

Did you have any involvement or even interest in the Civil Rights Movement, school desegregation, or the hope that intervention programs like Head Start could boost the academic achievement and IQ of disadvantaged children that motivated so many of your colleagues in the social sciences at that time? Hadn't you been the beneficiary of Great Society research grants?

Jensen: In fact, I voted for Johnson in the 1964 presidential election. I felt strongly enough about it that I voted by absentee ballot because I was in London on a sabbatical leave working as a Guggenheim Fellow in Eysenck's department.

I believed in the Great Society proposals, particularly with respect to education and Head Start. When I returned to California I gave talks at schools, PTA meetings, and conferences and conventions explaining why these things were important and should be promoted. I have always been opposed to racial segregation and discrimination. They go against everything in my personal philosophy, which includes maximizing individual liberties and regarding every individual in terms of his or her own characteristics rather than the person's racial or ethnic background. How could I think otherwise when at that time I had been steeped in Gandhian philosophy for over 20 years?

And yes, I did apply for and receive research grants and contracts from government agencies such as the Office of Education, National Science Foundation, Office of Economic Opportunity, and National Institute of Mental Health for research on individual differences in learning abilities and its possible applications to the education of pupils who at that time were called the "culturally disadvantaged." I met many of the prominent leaders in this effort, and attended meetings in the nation's capital. At that time I was quite enthusiastic about its promise. I considered it a socially valuable enterprise for educational psychology research.

Miele: Well, one of those colleagues, Martin Deutsch, with whom you had edited a book on the culturally disadvantaged, claimed your *HER* article contained a tremendous number of errors and misstatements. His exact words were, "Perhaps so large a number of errors would not be remarkable were it not for the fact that Jensen's previous work contained so few, and more malignant, all errors referred to are in the same direction: maximizing differences between Blacks and Whites and maximizing the possibility that such differences are attributable to hereditary factors." Others accused you of doctoring figures taken from well-known articles just to bolster your case. Thirty years have passed since your *HER* article: Is there anything in it you were forced to correct or that you would like to correct now, or clarify in the light of additional information?

Jensen: I did edit a book with Martin Deutsch and Irwin Katz, in 1968. Later, Deutsch, a professor at New York University, had recklessly claimed in a lecture at Michigan State University that there were 53 errors in my *HER* article, "all of them unidimensional and all of them anti-Black." I was shocked by such an outlandish accusation, and I wrote to him asking for a list of these purported errors, so I could correct them in subsequent printings of the article, which, incidentally, is still being reprinted and sold by Harvard. Two or three requests from me failed to elicit a reply from Deutsch. I urged him to publish any and all errors he claimed to find, but nothing of the kind was ever published.

Considering how hard some people were trying to put down this article, I was amazed at how little they could actually find wrong with it! A geneticist friend did inform me of one quite obscure technical error that only a very sharp-eyed expert would have caught, but it would take longer to explain than it's worth in this context. The idea that I had "doctored" figures or did anything at all like that to make a point is scurrilous nonsense, the last resort of a frustrated critic.

Miele: The other criticism I've heard is that you had your finger in the political wind. When the Nixon administration came in you decided to provide them with the scientific ammunition they needed to justify slashing all of those Great Society programs. Any comment?

Jensen: Absolutely false! That way of thinking is completely foreign to me. I am almost embarrassed by my lack of interest in politics and I was even less interested in those days than I am now. The idea of providing any kind of "ammunition," scientific or otherwise, to help any political regime promote its political agenda is anathema in my philosophy. One always hopes, of course, that politicians will pay attention to scientific findings and take them into consideration in formulating public policy. But I absolutely condemn the idea of doing science for any political reasons.

I have only contempt for people who let their politics or religion influence their science. And I rather dread the approval of people who agree with me only for political reasons. People sometimes ask me how I have withstood the opposition and vilification and demonstrations over the years. That hasn't worried me half as much as the thought that there may be people out there who agree with some of my findings and views for entirely the wrong reasons—political reasons, prejudice, ignorance, whatever. It is never the bottom line that I consider important, but the route by which one reaches it. The only route of interest to me is that of science and reason. I have no use for political or religious thinking when it comes to trying to understand real phenomena.

Miele: For the record, then, who first coined the term "Jensenism"? Was it you? Science writer Lee Edson in his article in *The New York Times Magazine*? Your arch-critic Leon Kamin? Wasn't it in fact Daniel Patrick Moynihan, then adviser on domestic affairs to Richard Nixon, and later Democratic senior senator from New York (now retired)?

Jensen: It has been my understanding that this term first appeared in the *Wall Street Journal*, which was quoting Moynihan. He made a statement in an interview that went something like "The winds of Jensenism are blowing through the nation's capital with gale force." Other media then began using the term. It is also in Lee Edson's *New York Times* article, which was one of the few balanced and accurate reports at that time.

Miele: Moynihan had already gotten into some controversy over his remarks about the Black family and "benign neglect." And John Ehrlichman claims Nixon said some very "Jensenist" things about Head Start. If you weren't interested in the policies of the Nixon administration, it certainly sounds as if they were interested in your article. What was your involvement with Moynihan back when he was a Nixon advisor?

Jensen: One day when I was in Washington to attend a council meeting of the AERA [American Educational Research Association], I received a message from Moynihan's secretary asking if I could come to his office while I was in town. So I met him in the White House at about 4:00 that afternoon. He was a very open and cordial fellow, quite jolly and immediately likable. He offered me a drink from the bar in his office and asked if I minded if he invited his "assistant on Jensenism" to come over from the Old Executive Office Building across the street and sit in on our conversation. He buzzed his secretary to call this assistant, explaining to me that one of this young fellow's assignments was to read my stuff and keep him [Moynihan] informed about it. Moynihan in turn forwarded this information to President Nixon, who was keenly interested in Jensenism. We talked about many things during the hour or so that I was there, including Moynihan's then forthcoming trip to India as ambassador. I had noticed Erik Erikson's biography of Gandhi on his desk, and of course I couldn't resist getting into a conversation about that, since I was an aficionado of the Gandhi literature and had met Erikson, the famous psychoanalyst, at the very time he was writing his book on Gandhi.

Miele: And regarding race?

Jensen: We compared notes on our treatment, or mistreatment, for having stuck our necks out on certain aspects of the race issue, even though we had each written quite different things from entirely different perspectives.

Moynihan was also interested in hearing about my directing a large-scale study of the effects of complete desegregation of the Berkeley public schools by means of two-way busing. The research design was rather ingenious and promised some quite definitive answers, but he thought it unlikely that it could ever be carried out, because of political pressures. I had already completed what we called the baseline testing the year before, when the Berkeley schools were quite de facto segregated. Moynihan was politically much less naive than I, and it turned out he was right.

The testing that was intended to assess the first year's effects of integration had no sooner begun than I received a phone call from the assistant superintendent telling me that they had halted the testing program, and that my research assistants should not return to the schools. I asked him "Why?" and I still remember his exact words: "Because the Berkeley School District is a political unit, not a research institute." The dean of the School of Education in the University tried to save the situation by offering to assume directorship of the project I had designed, but the school authorities wouldn't buy it, and so my research project was ended. I learned that the public protests against the project at school board meetings were based largely on my *HER* article, which had gotten considerable coverage in the local newspapers.

Miele: And was that the end?

Jensen: No, Moynihan later wrote to me asking if I knew why a much higher percentage of Black women than Black men passed the Federal Civil Service exams. At the time I didn't know this was a fact, so I looked into it and found the same thing was true for college entrance exams and aptitude exams used for hiring in the private sector. I told Moynihan that I would do some research on this matter.

I wrote a fairly technical book chapter about my findings, titled "The Race × Sex × Ability Interaction." I sent a copy to Moynihan, but by then he was no longer in the White House and I've not since had any contact with him. Subsequent studies have not consistently found the mean sex difference in IQ, so I no longer put much confidence in the theory.

Miele: At some point, however, you must have changed your point of view. Did the scientific evidence lead you to a new political philosophy or did a change in political philosophy lead you to reexamine the science?

Jensen: Changed my point of view about what? I did at one time believe that an individual's family and social environment and socioeconomic status were by far the most influential factors in determining individual and especially group differences in intelligence and every other psychological trait. Certainly I hold a rather different position today, because the scientific evidence that I have studied shows overwhelmingly that my previous belief was wrong. The evidence shows that genetic factors and also environmental factors that have biological effects are much more potent influences on mental development than the effects of family environment. The best evidence for this is based on monozygotic twins who were separated in infancy and reared apart in different families, and on genetically unrelated children adopted into the same family. If anyone wants to read an excellent introduction to this evidence, I suggest David Rowe's book *The Limits of Family Influence.*

You keep harping on politics. Over the years, I have become increasingly disillusioned about politics and increasingly suspicious of it. What I see of partisan politics and government's interference in people's lives these days lends considerable appeal to the philosophy of libertarianism, although I am not a libertarian with a capital L.

Miele: Then let's return to science. Take the three points that made your *HER* article so controversial: (1) the failure of compensatory education, (2) the evidence for a genetic basis to IQ, and (3) the likelihood of some genetic component to the Black-White IQ difference. Would you say that's a fair and accurate definition of "Jensenism"?

Jensen: I think that is a fair statement so long as no one views it as some kind of dogma but simply conclusions I have reached for the time being based on my studies of these matters.

Miele: Suppose the *Harvard Educational Review* now asked you to come out with a new and revised edition. What have 30 years of research told you that you didn't know then?

Jensen: That's a big order! I have answered it at length in my latest book, *The g Factor,* but here are a few key points.

First, we have learned that the family environment per se has exceedingly little—practically zero—effect in creating individual differences in mental development by the time children reach early maturity. This is true at least throughout the range of the normal, humane home environments that are typical of the vast majority of Whites and of Blacks in the present-day United States.

Second, I am even less optimistic today than I was in 1969 about the ability of compensatory educational programs to markedly or permanently raise either the IQ or school achievement for the vast majority of children who score below the national average. I now believe that quite radical innovations in education are needed to deal with the very wide range of individual differences in potential for academic achievement, regardless of race. Our schools must become much more diversified in their curricula, the pacing of instruction, and their educational goals for pupils in every segment of the bell curve. I have expressed these ideas in more detail in a book edited by Robert J. Sternberg, the noted psychologist at Yale University.

Third, I now believe, more strongly than I did earlier, that most of the environmental causes of individual differences in IQ, particularly in the g factor, are biological, rather than social-psychological.

Miele: We'll examine those strong assertions on intelligence, genetics, and race in depth in the chapters that follow. For now, let me ask whether the three heretical Jensenist theses have now become accepted?

Jensen: The only hard evidence I know of comes from the survey made by Snyderman and Rothman in their 1988 book *The IQ Controversy,* in which over 600 psychologists responded to a long list of questions related to my 1969 *HER* article. The majority were in agreement with my own position on every one of the major points, including the race question. Three times as many said they believed that both genetic and environmental factors are involved in the average Black-White difference as said the difference is entirely environmental.

Miele: If you could write the final word on the career of Arthur Jensen and how he became one of the most controversial figures in contemporary science, what would it be?

Jensen: That's simple: At some future point in time neither I nor Jensenism will any longer be seen as controversial. If scientific research is allowed to advance without political interference, the three parts of Jensenism will have proved either mostly right or mostly wrong.

I have faith in science as an ongoing and self-correcting process, not in some final conclusion. If that process finally puts me and Jensenism down, so be it.

Miele: And if someone else writes that final word, and it's "Arthur Jensen returned discussion of a genetic component for racial differences in IQ to academic respectability"?

Jensen: I'd think the inevitable had finally happened. It should have always been the case. I believe progress toward this inevitability is rapidly accelerating.

Further Reading

For Jensen's own account of his 1969 *Harvard Educational Review* article, the origin of "Jensenism," and the reaction to it, see the 67-page preface to: Jensen, A. R. (1972). *Genetics and education.* New York: Harper and Row.

For more on Jensen's work, see the bibliography of his publications in Appendix A.

2

WHAT IS INTELLIGENCE?

The *g* Factor and Its Rivals

In this chapter we discuss the first of the three components of Jensenism: intelligence. Is it one thing, or many things? Is it even a thing? Have psychologists agreed on a definition? If not, what are different theories of intelligence?

Surprisingly, Jensen says that experts in psychology have not been able to agree upon a definition of intelligence. Because of this lack of scientific precision, he has abandoned using the word. Instead, Jensen's research and conclusions are about what he terms "general mental ability" or "the *g* factor" (the latter is also the title of his most recent book). The theory of general mental ability grows out of the work of the London School of psychology, started by Sir Francis Galton, Charles Darwin's cousin. Other famous names associated with the London School and the *g* factor are those of Charles Spearman (who coined the term *g* to designate "general mental ability"), Sir Cyril Burt (whose controversial study of twins and Jensen's involvement in the Burt Affair are discussed in the next chapter), and Jensen's mentor, Hans J. Eysenck. Today, the theory of general mental ability and the *g* factor are accepted by many, but by no means all, psychometricians (mental testing experts) in the United States and worldwide.

Evidence for the *g* factor comes primarily from the use of correlation, also introduced by Galton, and of factor analysis and other newer and more powerful statistical methods. To understand the theory of general mental ability *(g)*, it may be helpful to think first about general athletic ability (let's call it *a*). We might start with a hunch that individuals who excel in one sport (say, the 40-yard dash) are more likely to perform better than average in other athletic events as well. They don't have to be the best or even better than average in *every* athletic event. But those who do better in one event, we might predict, should be more likely to do better in most other events. Or, to put it the other way, those who do below average in some events should be more likely to do poorly in others as well. If so, we have evidence for a *general factor* of athletic ability (that is, a single dimension of overall athletic prowess that runs from "klutz" at the low end to "jock" at the high end). But is there some scientific way to test our hunch?

The theory of general mental ability (the *g* factor) is like our hunch about general athletic ability. It says that on average, those who do well on one mental test also tend to do well on other tests. The statistical methods we use to test the *g* factor (or our *a*-factor hunch) are correlation and factor analysis. To take the simplest case, if the order of scores (best to worst) is exactly the same for two tests (athletic or mental ability), their correlation coefficient is +1.00. If the order is exactly the opposite for the two sets of scores, the correlation is −1.00. If there is no relation between them at all, the correlation has a value of zero. Such ideal correlations are seldom, if ever, found in real life. But based on the number of people we tested, we can determine how probable it is that the correlation we get is simply the result of chance. When just about all of the test scores have positive correlations with each other, we have strong statistical evidence for a general factor—*g* (for general mental ability) or *a* (for general athletic ability).

Besides the general factor, we can analyze the correlations between different tests and sort them into a number of group factors. Each group factor consists of the tests (or sports events) that are the most like each other in terms of how individuals perform (that is, they have the highest correlations with each other, even though they have some positive correlation with the other tests). For example, beneath our general athletic factor *(a)*, we might also find group factors for running *(r)*, strength *(s)*, and coordination *(c)*. The running factor might be further broken down into a sprinting factor *(sp)* and an endurance factor *(e)*. Even though the scores on all the events are correlated, the correlation between sprinting and endurance is much higher than correlations between either sprinting or endurance and any of the other tests. Likewise, a number of strength tests (for example, bench press, curls, push-ups) might also have the highest correlations with each other.

Evidence that there is one general mental ability, the g factor, rather than many distinct and independent abilities, is found in the fact that almost all mental, or cognitive, tests are positively correlated. Starting with Spearman, psychometricians have repeatedly found such a correlation, even between tests that look very different—for example, tests involving spatial relations, vocabulary, filling in missing pictures, or reaction time. Remember, this doesn't mean that the person who gets the best score on one test has to get the best score on all the others. All that's required to establish the existence of a g factor is that, on average, those who do well on one test also do well on the others, while those who do poorly on one tend to do poorly on the others.

Not all scientists, nor even all psychometricians, accept the theory of general mental ability. One of the theory's best-known critics was the late best-selling science writer and past president of the American Association for the Advancement of Science Stephen Jay Gould, who argued that the evidence for g is little more than statistical hocus-pocus.

Psychometrician Robert Sternberg, editor of *The Encyclopedia of Intelligence*, does not deny the existence of Spearman's—and Jensen's—g factor. But he thinks it is too narrow and fails to capture all that we mean by the word "intelligence." Sternberg believes that looking at g alone short-changes both the individuals tested and their potential contributions to society.

In place of the London School's hierarchical theory of a single, all-powerful factor of general mental ability, with a small number of group factors subordinate to it, and finally a host of specific factors subordinate to the group factors, Sternberg has developed his Triarchic Theory of Intelligence. For a rough analogy to Sternberg's mental triarchy, consider the three branches of the U.S. government—the Executive, the Legislature, and the Judiciary. Each branch is separate and has its own function; no one is superior; and the country cannot be governed without all of them. The first branch of Sternberg's triarchy, Analytical Intelligence, is similar to g. It involves the ability to see and apply logical relations. The second, Practical Intelligence, measures street savvy or "tricks of the trade." An example of Practical Intelligence would be a law school graduate who barely managed to pass the bar exam (which does measure g) but went on to excel as a trial lawyer because of his skill in "working a judge" and "badgering" hostile witnesses, which he picked up hanging around courtrooms rather than burying his nose in law books. The final branch of the triarchy, Creative Intelligence, is the ability to come up with new and imaginative answers to questions instead of simply applying familiar rules to get the same old answers. The difference between Sternberg's Triarchic Theory and the g factor theory goes beyond mere classification. Sternberg believes that Analytical, Practical, and Creative Intelligence can all be increased through training and that a person who is not as high on one can make up for it with high levels of one or both of the others. And even individuals who are at the very top in Analytical Intelligence may fall far short of what's expected of them based on g alone, if they haven't cultivated the other two aspects.

One of the theories most popular with the general public is Howard Gardner's Multiple Intelligences. Gardner developed the theory by carefully examining what exceptional people actually *do* in life. In Gardner's view, we can learn more from studying the biographies of Einstein, Gandhi, and Picasso to find out how and what they thought, than from knowing which one of them had the highest (or the lowest) IQ. He bolsters this assertion with evidence from medical cases in which injuries to certain brain areas produced specific impairments—for example, speech loss—but left other mental functions untouched. The fact that savants, like Dustin Hoffman's character in the movie *Rain Man*, can perform calculations or other mental operations better than geniuses but fail ordinary IQ tests also supports the idea of multiple, independent forms of intelligence.

In Gardner's view, the g factor confuses intelligence with a specific type of scholastic performance. Gardner instead defined intelligence as the potential to process information in a particular cultural setting to solve problems and create things. In place of Jensen's g or Sternberg's Triarchy, Gardner proposed seven types of intelligences—Linguistic, Logical-

Mathematical, Spatial, Musical, Bodily-Kinesthetic, Intrapersonal, and Interpersonal. To these he later added Naturalistic Intelligence (the ability to recognize plants and animals and to make sense of the natural world), and possibly Spiritual and Existential intelligence as well.

A new rival to the *g* factor theory comes from evolutionary psychology. Sometimes called the "Swiss Army Knife Model of the Mind," this theory says that evolution would not produce a general-purpose cognitive processor like *g*, but several independent mental modules. Each module, like the blades on the Swiss knife, serves a specific purpose. Since evolution produced the modules for important functions like recognizing kin or detecting cheaters, they should be present in everyone, with few if any individual differences. John Tooby and Leda Cosmides of the University of California at Santa Barbara have devised a series of experiments that have supported this view.

In this chapter, I cross-examine Jensen on the critical issue of whether *g* is a valid scientific measure. If not, the question of whether IQ is the result of nature or nurture is irrelevant and immaterial, and discussion of race differences in IQ is inadmissible. I ask Jensen to produce the evidence that supports existence of the *g* factor against these rival theories. In responding, Jensen first explains the statistical reality of *g*. Then he says the *biological* reality of *g* is demonstrated by the fact that it has higher correlations than any other psychological measure with a host of physiological, anatomical, and genetic variables, including the overall size of the brain, its glucose metabolic rate while solving problems, and the speed and complexity of brain waves, as well as heritability estimates (which measure the effects of genes versus environment) and inbreeding depression (the harmful effect on the offspring of close relatives).

Miele: The concept of intelligence is central to Jensenism. But many say that intelligence is like the Supreme Court Justice's famous statement about pornography—everybody knows what it is, but nobody can define it. Has psychology been able to define intelligence?

Jensen: No. There are almost as many definitions of intelligence as there are psychologists who define it. In 1921, the *Journal of Educational*

Psychology asked 15 noted psychologists to define intelligence and received 15 different definitions with little similarity. In Sternberg and Detterman's 1986 book *What Is Intelligence?*, 25 experts in mental abilities offered their definitions and conceptions of intelligence. There was hardly more consensus than in 1921. It's a ridiculous situation, of course.

The problem is that the word "intelligence" is such an umbrella term. It covers many definitions, but has little if any scientific precision. Intelligence is not a physical thing like a brain or a liver. It is not even a scientific concept or a construct. Intelligence is a word like "nature." We know more or less what we mean by it, but if we try to define it scientifically, we end up either listing a lot of other psychological traits or just talking gibberish.

Miele: Then how can you, or anyone, talk about IQ, or mental ability, or any of the other terms we use as rough equivalents of intelligence?

Jensen: I have solved this problem, at least to my own satisfaction, by exorcising the word "intelligence" from the discussion of individual differences *within* a given species, including *Homo sapiens*. I use the word "intelligence" only for objectively observable behavioral differences *between* different species. These include sensory sensitivity, perception, stimulus discrimination, stimulus generalization, various types of conditioning and learning, habit reversal, learning set formation, transfer of learning, concept formation, short-term and long-term memory, inference, reasoning and problem solving at different levels of abstractness, and denotative language.

All species do not display all of these capacities. But all biologically normal members of a species possess the same ones. By "biologically normal" I mean those without severe impairments due to chromosomal or genetic disorders, trauma, or disease.

The scientific study of individual differences in behavioral capacities within humans (or any species) calls for a different approach. The variables we measure must be defined operationally and kept explicit at every step. We work from the bottom up. We start with the simplest, most concrete, and least theoretical definitions, and move up through a hierarchy, linking each new definition unequivocally to one at a lower level.

Miele: But how does that get us closer to knowing what IQ, or mental ability, really means?

Jensen: In studying individual differences in humans, we call the lowest level in the hierarchy an ability. We define an ability as any specific action that the organism can perform in response to a specific stimulus or situation that can be objectively observed and classified, ranked, or graded on some kind of scale. It is a mental ability only if little or none of the differences between individuals are due to differences in sensory acuity, physical strength, or agility.

Miele: Fine, but what does that have to do with the g factor?

Jensen: First, the different abilities correlate with one another. The correlation matrix (that is, the table of all the correlations) between the abilities is then factor analyzed. This mathematical technique distills the large number of abilities into a smaller number of underlying, independent elements, termed factors, that account for most of the differences between individuals. As an analogy, think of how every point on earth can be located precisely in terms of just three factors—longitude, latitude, and distance above or below sea level.

Research in psychometrics, the science of mental measurement, consistently shows that the largest of all of these factors is general mental ability or the g factor. Discovered in 1904 by the great British psychologist Charles Spearman, the g factor measures some quality or property of the brain. It dominates every other factor and plays some part in every mental ability we can measure. Again, it may be useful to think of how just one number—temperature—gives us a good idea of whether it's colder or warmer in one city than another or on one day than another, though other "factors" such as humidity and wind chill also affect how warm or cold we feel.

Miele: Can you sketch the history of the *g* factor theory? Why did it arise? And why did it then fall out of favor—at least in popular books on the subject?

Jensen: I've written about this long and complex story in detail. In the latter half of the nineteenth century, philosophers and psychologists generally thought the human mind was made up of distinct faculties such as reason, discernment, wit, intuition, cleverness, perceptiveness, imagination, recollection, aesthetic sense—virtually every word describing some mental quality in the dictionary. Galton suggested that individuals differ in some general ability that enters into every cognitive task a person does. He also tried to show that this general ability was hereditary. Spearman also doubted the existence of so many separate, independent faculties. He realized the only way to find out was to devise some way to measure each of them and then determine which ones were highly correlated with one another.

But these conjectures of Galton and Spearman could not be tested rigorously until Karl Pearson invented the correlation coefficient around 1896. Spearman then began measuring various abilities and achievements and found them all positively correlated. He inferred that there was something in common that was measured by all the tests and invented a simple form of factor analysis to show the degree to which each test reflected it. He labeled this general factor *g*—always an italicized, lowercase *g*. It has now found its way into some dictionaries (e.g., *Random House Unabridged* and *Webster's Unabridged*), where it is defined as general mental ability (not to be confused with the much older *g* of physics, which signifies the acceleration of gravity).

Spearman's *g* is as important to psychology as Newton's law of gravitation is to physics. Interestingly, theories of the nature of *g*— the *g* of psychology and the *g* of physics—are still controversial! Each *g* can be measured, but we don't know precisely what it consists of.

Gravitation has been explained in terms of action at a distance, particles called gravitons, gravity waves, and the curvature of space. None of these theories is universally accepted as the correct one. It's much the same for Spearman's *g*. It's best to think of *g* as some property or properties of the brain (what else?) that causes individual differences on all cognitive tasks to be positively correlated.

The *g* factor is not the result of some mathematical machinations. There is no longer any doubt of the physical reality of *g*. We know it is heritable and that it correlates with many anatomical and physiological features of the brain.

Miele: Well, Stephen Jay Gould and others have argued that *g* is just an artifact of factor analysis.

Jensen: That argument is popular but scientifically invalid. The existence of *g* is not dependent on factor analysis, only its measurement. Would you say that weight doesn't exist because it has to be measured with a scale of some kind? My book *The g Factor* gives a detailed explanation of factor analysis in nonmathematical terms. Let me assure you that there is nothing at all arcane or mysterious about factor analysis or the *g* factor.

First, objective measurements with tests of various abilities have to be obtained in a fairly large sample of individuals who differ in the measured abilities. Then we calculate the correlation coefficients among all of these tests. If the tests measure various abilities, we find that their intercorrelations are always positive—that is, individuals' level of performance on any given test, on average, predicts to some degree their level of performance on any other test, depending on the magnitude of the correlation between the two tests. Every pair of tests shows this positive correlation. This is simply an empirical fact. There's nothing anyone has ever been able to do that will change it. Even though many attempts have been made to devise tests of mental ability that have zero or negative correlations with each other, no one yet has succeeded. It appears that zero and nonpositive correlations among ability tests are the psychometric equivalent of perpetual motion in physics—you can imagine them but you can never demonstrate them in the real world.

Factor analysis is simply a mathematical method for dividing up the amount of variation, the total of the individual differences (technically termed the "variance") in the scores on all the tests into what we call factors. Some factors account for more variance than do others, and factors differ in generality, that is, the number of different tests in which the factor accounts for some of the variance. We can array and display these factors in a quantitative, triangular hierarchy based on their degree of generality. At the highest level of the hierarchy of generality—the apex of the triangle—is general mental ability, the g factor. It is followed by two or more second-order group factors (such as, say, logical reasoning, verbal-educational skills and knowledge, and visual perception). Under each secondary group factor are two or more primary group factors (such as inductive reasoning and deductive reasoning under logical reasoning; or arithmetic reasoning, which involves both logical reasoning and verbal-educational skills and knowledge). At the lowest level are the actual psychometric tests such as the Raven's Matrices (which is a test of inductive reasoning) and letter series (which is a test of deductive reasoning and inductive reasoning). (See Figure 2.1.)

Similarly, the measurement of gravitation depends upon using measuring instruments such as meter sticks and chronometers and subjecting the measurements to mathematical calculations, from which we obtain an estimate of the physicist's g, whose value at the earth's sea level happens to be 32 feet per second per second. The value differs at various locations on the earth and on different planets in our solar system.

In principle, there's no essential difference between the measurement of psychometric g and physical g. If you think there is an essential difference, I'd like to know what it is. Both are constructs that can be defined in terms of objective procedures applied to data obtained under standardized conditions that meet certain criteria of accuracy or reliability. Factor analysis isn't only used in psychometrics. For example, it's used in archaeology, paleontology, geology, architecture, anatomy,

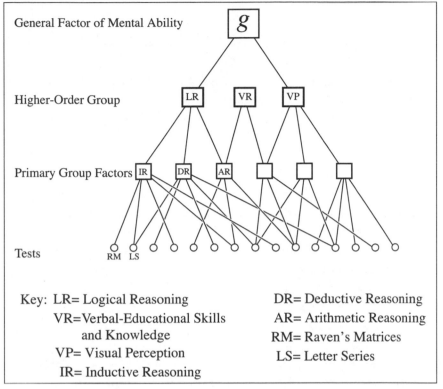

Figure 2.1: Factor Analysis of Mental Ability Tests Showing the General Factor of Mental Ability (Spearman's *g*), Higher-Order Group Factors, Primary Group Factors, and Tests.

The Raven's Matrices Test is almost a pure measure of Inductive Reasoning. The Letter Series Test is also a measure of Inductive Reasoning, though not so pure. The two tests correlate to produce a Primary Group Factor called Inductive Reasoning.

Letter Series also correlates with other tests (not called out in the figure) to form another Primary Group Factor called Deductive Reasoning.

The Primary Group Factors of Inductive Reasoning, Deductive Reasoning, and Arithmetic Reasoning correlate with each other to form the Higher-Order Group Factor called Logical Reasoning.

Logical Reasoning, in turn, correlates with two other Higher-Order Group Factors—Verbal-Educational Skills and Knowledge, and Visual Perception—to produce Spearman's *g*, the General Factor of Mental Ability.

g stands at the very top of the hierarchy of mental abilities. All of the mental ability tests, primary group factors, and higher-order group factors are *g*-loaded. That is, they correlate with *g* and to some degree measure it. The *g*-loadings can be thought of as analogous to the octane ratings of gasoline or the proof of alcoholic beverages. The higher a test's *g*-loading, the more purely it measures *g* and nothing else.

Sources: Adapted from A. R. Jensen, *Bias in Mental Testing* (New York: Free Press, 1980) and J. C. Carroll, *Human cognitive abilities: A survey of factor analytic studies* (Cambridge: Cambridge University Press, 1993).

zoological and botanical taxonomy, quantum mechanics, meteorology, medicine, sociology, political science, and economics as well.

Miele: The old cliché in law school is that a grand jury will indict a ham sandwich if a DA orders one. The old cliché I heard in graduate school was that what you get out of a factor analysis depends on what you put in and how you analyze it.

Jensen: That overworked canard is either meaningless or wrong. I have heard it only from persons who have never done a factor analysis and who know next to nothing about it. I'm not blaming you for bringing it up—I know it's your job to be provocative, and you're right, this point does provoke me a bit. I guess I've become rather tired of it. So what can I say?

You get factors from a factor analysis, and you didn't put those factors in to begin with. You begin just with scores on a variety of tests. The correlational structure of the tests that is revealed by factor analysis is not apparent in just looking at all the test scores or even by inspecting the matrix of correlations among the scores, although such inspection can give us a fair idea of whether the matrix probably contains a general factor—for example, all positive correlations and many of them large. Of course, it is obvious that no factors can emerge that are not latent in the various test scores, but you can say exactly the same thing about performing quantitative analysis in chemistry; in some complex substance you are analyzing, you can't find, say, calcium in some specific amount unless calcium is actually present in the substance. Similarly, in factor analysis, you can't identify a factor as spatial ability unless the collection of tests you have analyzed contains some tests that measure spatial ability. Nor can you tell by sheer inspection how much a particular test reflects, say, spatial ability; the same test might also reflect verbal ability, or we might find that there are several different types of spatial ability (as in fact there are), and the test will always reflect g as well. Or you might not even recognize from simple inspection that in addition to g and a numerical ability factor, a test of mental arithmetic also reflects a verbal component or a spatial component until the arithmetic test is included in a factor analysis with a number of other tests that reflect these components.

Miele: Can you provide a simple but real-life example of factor analysis?

Jensen: Years ago when I took a course on factor analysis one of our homework assignments was to analyze a set of 50 different body measurements—the diameters of the waist and the hips, the lengths of the total arm, upper arm, lower arm, and so on—obtained in a sample of 10,000 women by the British garment industry. In effect, factor analysis was used to "sort" the full set of 50 measurements into a smaller number of factors. To be technically precise, a factor is defined as a latent variable, or a hypothetical source of variance, that is common to two or more variables. Conceptually, you might want to think of a factor as a dimension that is made up of the measurements that "go together," that is, a subset composed of those measurements that correlate highly with each other and much less so with all the other measurements.

This was long before the advent of today's statistical software packages and personal computers that can do the job in a couple of minutes. Back then factor analyzing so many variables was a godawful calculating job. It took a full week of punching keys on an electrical desk calculator.

Miele: And the results of your Herculean labor?

Jensen: There was a very large general factor in all these body measurements—call it "general body size." That means that all 50 measurements correlated with each other to form a single factor (or dimension) of "general body size" on which each woman could be placed. In other words, on average, tall women tended to have longer arms, legs, fingers, and feet and also broader shoulders and hips and wider feet than shorter women. This makes sense because if it weren't true, women couldn't buy ready-made clothes based on one size but would have to get them tailor-made. The next largest factor was "latitude versus longitude." And this agrees with the fact that after their overall size, many garments are then "sized" or categorized by "width" (for example, narrow and wide, or A, B, C, D). Shoes are a good example. Then came a factor of "torso length versus leg length," which matches the fact that special sizes of slacks are available for women with relatively short and relatively long legs relative to their overall height. The next factor, as I recall, was "bust girth versus hip girth" (that is, generally bigger above or below the waist). So the original set of 50 body measurements could be mapped in terms of only those factors, just as any place on earth can be mapped in terms of longitude, latitude, and altitude. Adding one or two more factors to those four accounted for some 90 percent of the total variance in all 50 body measurements. As you can see from the examples, the results of such a factor analysis have real economic value to the garment industry.

When we do perform a similar factor analysis on a battery of psychometric tests there is always a large general factor, g (similar to the "general body size" factor described in the example I just gave), followed by various second-order group factors such as logical reasoning, verbal-educational skills and knowledge, visual perception, and so on (analogous to the other body-size factors in the example). (Refer back to Figure 2.1.)

Miele: Let's turn to the major rivals to g theory that are popular today: Sternberg's Triarchic Theory of Analytical, Practical, and Creative Intelligence; Gardner's Theory of Multiple Intelligences, which includes Linguistic, Logical-Mathematical, Spatial, Musical, Bodily-Kinesthetic, Interpersonal, and Intrapersonal forms of intelligence, to which he has recently added Naturalistic, Spiritual, and Existential forms of intelligence; and evolutionary psychology's Modular Theory of the Mind.

Isn't the difference between the g factor, Sternberg's Triarchy, and Gardner's Multiple Intelligences really a matter of terminology, not science? Don't they all tell part of the story?

Jensen: It's too simple just to say that these theoretical differences are merely a matter of terminology. If you performed a factor analysis of the traits in Sternberg's and Gardner's systems along with all the cognitive and personality variables we can now measure, most of them would fall into one of the group factors that are already known and quite well described in John B. Carroll's "three-strata model" of abilities, or the "big five" model of personality (Conscientiousness, Openness, Extraversion, Neuroticism, and Agreeableness). One or two new group factors might also emerge.

Miele: Well, I guess Sternberg's theory gets a lot of support from our everyday observations of "absent-minded professors" and "street-smart" characters with little or no education.

Jensen: Sternberg's triarchic model is an attempt to define the traits that contribute most to achievement and success of one kind or another in the intellectual domain. In a comprehensive factor analysis that included established reference tests of ability and personality, I would predict that most of the individual differences in Sternberg's triarchy (analytic ability, practical ability, and creativity) would be absorbed by g, while much of the rest of it would fall into the personality domain. There would also be a number of small group factors and specificity, too, mostly in his measures of "practical intelligence," which are highly specific to particular kinds of knowledge useful in certain job settings.

Except for g, the importance of all these various abilities and traits is problematic.

Miele: Why problematic? Why is g always the exception?

Jensen: Because the relative importance of each group ability factor or personality factor does depend on the context in which it operates. g is the exception because it enters into performance in virtually every context.

Miele: And Gardner's Theory of Multiple Intelligences?

Jensen: Until Gardner provides standardized measures for several of his multiple "intelligences," they can't be included in a factor analysis. That doesn't mean they don't exist or aren't important. But without some objective way of measuring the things Gardner calls "intelligences," his theory is more speculative literary psychology than psychometrics. There's nothing to stop anyone from claiming that Al Capone displayed the highest level of "Criminal Intelligence," or that Casanova was "blessed" with exceptional "Sexual Intelligence." And if you're going to use the word "intelligence" that loosely, you might as well say that Chess Grand Master Bobby Fischer is one of the world's great athletes. After all, chess players are called "wood pushers," and Fischer can "push wood" with the best of them.

Miele: But doesn't the fact that brain damage and certain genetic disorders produce very specific deficits in behavior (such as being unable to recognize faces but still recognize voices or geometric shapes) and the existence of savants like Dustin Hoffman's character in the movie *Rain Man* give Gardner's theory more hard neurological support than there is for the g factor?

Jensen: They do indeed support the "multiple abilities" aspect of Gardner's theory. No one denies that. But that does not contradict either the existence or the empirically demonstrated importance of the g factor.

There is one property of g that is seldom noted but is highly relevant to all other cognitive factors and talents and special abilities that are independent of g. I call it the threshold aspect of g. It means that these specific abilities or talents almost never result in notable life achievements unless the person who possesses them has a level of g above some threshold value. By definition, savants have very low IQ scores and a low level of g. But they display astonishing skills—say, numerical calculation, playing the piano by ear, memorizing pages from a telephone directory, or drawing objects from memory with nearly photographic accuracy. As remarkable as these savants certainly are, they never become mathematicians, scientists, professional musicians, or artists. That requires a fairly high level of g as well.

There are also people of quite normal general mental ability who possess some extraordinary savant-like ability. I tested Shakuntala Devi, probably the world's greatest mental calculating prodigy, in my reaction-time laboratory. Her IQ score was good, but not exceptional. But her calculating feats are amazing. We do know that functional efficiency in a particular domain can be markedly enhanced through extensive experience and practice.

The g threshold is important in most fields of endeavor. When the Institute of Personality Assessment and Research at Berkeley tested people recognized as successful in fields that call for special talents, all of them scored above average on IQ tests, with the vast majority scoring higher than 90 percent of the general population. The very highest levels of achievement, of course, require an absolutely extraordinary talent—actually, genius. But it is utterly silly to think that Newton, Beethoven, or Michelangelo possessed only a mediocre level of g. A level of g beyond the 90th percentile is probably necessary, though certainly not sufficient, for recognized achievement in science, the arts, or leadership in politics, the military, business, finance, or industry. But as Galton emphasized, that requires exceptional zeal and industry as well.

Miele: Research in the emerging disciplines of evolutionary psychology and cognitive neuroscience has also focused on the search for distinct modules in the brain, each with a specific function, rather than on the g factor and some general property of the brain. So do you accept or reject the existence of mental modules?

Jensen: Some people think that demonstrating the existence of modules in the mind proves that there are only separate abilities, each governed by a different module, and disproves the existence of g. This confuses individual differences and factors with the localized brain processes underlying the various kinds of abilities. Some modules such as quick-recognition memory of human faces or three-dimensional space perception can't possibly show up in a factor analysis of ability tests. These abilities are virtually universal in people who do not have brain damage or some genetic disorder. The individual differences in the general population are just too slight for these important abilities to emerge as factors. We've only discovered them when the modules underlying them have been neurologically damaged, resulting in conspicuous malfunctions, such as perceptual distortion, lack of recognition memory, or various aphasias (the inability to use or to understand speech, or specific components of language, such as numbers or written words).

Miele: Then what do you think the modules are?

Jensen: They are distinct, innate brain structures that have developed in the course of human evolution, characterized by the various ways that information or knowledge is represented by the neural activity of the brain. The main modules involve specific functions we'd class as linguistic (verbal/auditory/lexical/semantic), visuo-spatial, object recognition, numerical-mathematical, musical, and kinesthetic. Although these modules generally exist in all normal people, they are striking by their absence in people with highly localized brain damage, whereas their presence is highlighted in savants.

The various modules have distinct functions, but they are all affected by brain characteristics such as chemical neurotransmitters, neural conduction velocity, amount of dendritic branching, and degree of myelination of axons. And factor analysis shows that the specialized mental activities associated with different modules are correlated to some degree.

Miele: Okay, let's accept the reality of the g factor and that it is the single best predictor of how well you can get along and advance in a modern technological society. But what does g have to do with the abilities and skills that were needed for that 99 percent of human evolutionary history before we developed agriculture? How could evolution select for the ability to do factor analysis, solve verbal analogies, or mentally rotate a matrix?

Jensen: That is one of the really big questions for behavioral genetics, evolutionary psychology, and psychometrics. Why are there such great individual differences between humans in the abilities to learn mathematics, compose music, play the violin, write poetry, draw pictures, hit baseballs, shoot baskets, and so on? And how can there be a genetic basis for these differences? These abilities are all so recent in human history that they couldn't have been subjected to selection, natural or otherwise, over the course of human evolution.

The only answer psychology has offered is that the genetic and neurological basis for these specialized abilities was originally developed by natural selection for other activities that were important for survival in our prehistoric past. In historic times, elements of these traits could be applied to new tasks. Modern abilities like the ones you mentioned were never explicitly selected, but they have been able to utilize many of the same neurological structures that were selected for other purposes in our remote past. This may not be provable, but it appears entirely plausible.

For some reason that you might guess, *g* is a less popular idea than "multiple intelligences" or these other rival views.

Miele: Maybe Gardner's naturalistic, spiritual, and existential intelligences are somewhat airy-fairy concepts, but aren't spatial, musical, bodily-kinesthetic, intrapersonal, and interpersonal also important? I certainly would play a lot better flute if I had perfect pitch and win a lot more racquetball matches if I had better eye-hand coordination.

Jensen: I'm sure that's true. But if you had to be in the lowest 10 percent of the population in *g* or in musical ability, athletic ability, artistic ability, or any of those other skills and abilities, which would you choose? How many points off your IQ score based on the Raven's Progressive Matrices (one of the purest measures of *g*) would you be willing to trade for a commensurate increase in your score on the Seashore Measures of Musical Talents or a test of eye-hand coordination?

Why do most parents and teachers show only a modest amount of concern when a child with average or above-average IQ shows little aptitude for music, sports, dancing, or drawing, but are quite concerned when a child has a very low IQ? It's because g predicts school achievement, employment, and much more. It does no good to belittle the reality of g or its far-reaching consequences. Studies comparing the lives of people in the lowest 3 percent of the population in IQ with those in the top 3 percent have shown the differences are greater and more far reaching than you might imagine. If you were free to do so, you'd have no difficulty choosing between having a high or a low IQ. We don't like to think about this issue, but that makes it no less real. Our character is tested by how we deal with it.

Miele: Our character is tested by how we deal with what? What is it we don't like to think about?

Jensen: We are hesitant and reluctant to recognize, at least openly, the existence of large individual differences in general mental ability. It's a sensitive issue, especially with respect to group differences in IQ and scholastic achievement, which have many important personal, social, and economic consequences.

When people are asked about their own IQ, nearly everyone considers himself or herself average or above, which is statistically impossible. Few people mind admitting they have poor musical ability or artistic ability. But no one says this about their intelligence, and people generally avoid discussing the relative intelligence levels of other people.

People look for all kinds of reasons except IQ level to explain poor scholastic performance. Often there are other reasons that have nothing to do with intelligence, but by far the most frequent basis for very poor scholastic achievement is below-average general mental ability. Dealing with these sensitive issues kindly and charitably requires wisdom as well as intelligence. Wisdom implies intelligence, but the converse is not necessarily true.

Miele: Can you provide any biological evidence for the existence or importance of g?

Jensen: Yes, that's easy. I developed the "method of correlated vectors" for that purpose. (See Appendix A of my most recent book, *The g Factor*, for a detailed explanation of this method.) It shows that g is more highly correlated with a greater number of biological and other nonpsychological measures (including heritability estimates, the electrical activity of the brain in response to an external stimulus, overall brain size, inbreeding depression, PET scans of the brain's glucose metabolic rate during mental activity, and nerve conduction velocity in the brain) than any other mental factor that is statistically uncorrelated with g.

Inbreeding depression is a well-documented genetic phenomenon. It is the reduction in any measurable trait (height is a good example) that occurs in the offspring of parents who are very closely related genetically, such as siblings or close cousins. When the children of cousin marriages are compared against the children of parents with similar intelligence and background but who are not related, the children of cousin marriages are shorter and they also average five to seven points lower in IQ. Of all psychometric measures, the g factor shows the most inbreeding depression. Inbreeding depression occurs on brain size as well.

All of this evidence and more shows that g is not the result of any mathematical legerdemain associated with the process of factor analysis, but is a real physical and natural phenomenon.

Miele: The method of factor analysis does, however, require measuring or ranking people and that's the source of an argument against the g factor and the whole London School of psychology that has both a scientific and a larger philosophical part.

The scientific part is that unlike learning, which we can demonstrate in one individual, or gravity, which we can describe mathematically based on the observation of one cannon ball, the concept of g is based on measuring and comparing people. All the statistics you use involve the mathematical manipulation of relative standings, not absolute measures with a true zero and equal intervals.

The broader philosophical argument is that underlying the whole London School of psychology is some hidden agenda of measuring and inevitably ranking of people, if not groups—and the individual or group doing the ranking always comes out on top. So even if it's scientifically valid, doesn't the underlying philosophy of the Galton-Spearman-Jensen tradition run counter to our notions of democracy and even the marketplace? Most Americans believe we're all equal, if not now, then with a little more effort—or one of those many training courses you see on TV infomercials, or another government program, or the help of God—we will be. So isn't the viewpoint of the London School anti-American in that sense?

Jensen: Your question requires a four-part answer, at least.

First, recognizing individual differences is neither anti-American, anti-democratic, nor anti anything else. The statement of the nation's founding fathers—"all men are created equal"—refers to equality before the law and this now includes equality of all civil rights. Individual differences in all kinds of human traits—physical features, mental abilities, personality—have been obvious to everyone as far back as anyone knows in recorded history. Individual differences were no doubt important in prehistoric times as well.

Second, equality of talent is not characteristic of any "marketplace" I have ever heard of. Can every pianist in the musician's union play like Paderewski or Horowitz and command the same kind of fees that they got? Are all employees of, say, General Motors, equally qualified to be its CEO? What percentage of the population could make it through medical school, or sing at the Met, get into big league baseball, or win a Nobel Prize? Because the abilities or talents demanded by these kinds of performance are very scarce in the general population, they can command greater rewards in an open market. There are more people willing to pay to hear Horowitz in concert or buy his recordings than there are people willing pay the same amount to hear a performance by their local piano teacher.

Third, because everyone sees all this human variation in many different behavioral traits, and because psychology is the science of behavior, it is the job of psychology to study the nature of individual and group differences in all aspects of behavior, including those regarded as mental abilities.

Fourth, of course people can study and practice and learn new things, and can acquire new knowledge and skills, or improve their existing skills with further practice. That's what training and education are all about. But there are also individual differences in predisposing factors that are largely dependent on genetics and the physical structures that they control in the brain and nervous system. These result in individual differences in the ease and speed with which training, education, practice, and experience produce certain behavioral outcomes. A number of individuals all highly motivated to succeed in the acquisition of some knowledge or skill, and all given the same opportunities for learning and practice, will show marked differences in accomplishment assessed after X months or Y years of effort. The performance level of each individual will have improved in absolute terms, but the differences between individuals in performance will also have increased over the period of learning and practice. And there are some things that some individuals can never achieve with any amount of training, practice, and effort.

The best single predictor of these individual differences in the rate of learning and the level that can be attained in a great many areas of knowledge and skills that people regard as being of a mental nature is the g factor that we have been talking about. And we know that individual differences in the g factor not only have a genetic component but other biological correlates such as the brain's overall size, electrical activity in response to a stimulus, glucose metabolism during mental activity, and nerve conduction velocity. As for group differences, whether the groups are races, or social, or economic classes, if the groups live in the same culture and have similar educational opportunities, then any group differences in g are really just aggregated (or accumulated) individual differences. That is, psychometrics has found no causal factor that makes racial differences or social class differences any different than individual differences.

To speak of "ranking" individuals or groups, as I emphasized earlier, makes no scientific sense unless you can specify a specific dimension or trait on which the individuals or groups differ. One of the aims of factor analysis is to delineate the dimensions (called factors) in a given domain of measurements.

Miele: So the Galton-Spearman-Jensen viewpoint has no hidden agenda?

Jensen: I don't know of any agenda other than advancing our scientific understanding of human behavioral differences. And there's certainly nothing in the least "hidden" about it. Both Galton and Spearman, and I too, have written a lot about what we think on these topics—about our theories and research. We've all been rather extraordinarily outspoken in our many publications. One of the tenets of my own philosophy is to be as open as possible and to strive for a perfect consistency between my thoughts, both spoken and published, in their private and public expression. This is essentially a Gandhian principle, one that I have long considered worth striving to live by.

Further Reading

The inability of psychologists to reach a definition of intelligence is discussed in: The Editors (1921). Intelligence and its measurement: A symposium. *Journal of Educational Psychology, 12*, 123–147, 195–216, and 271–275; and Sternberg, R. J., and Detterman, D. K. (1986). *What is intelligence? Contemporary viewpoints on its nature and definition.* Norwood, NJ: Ablex.

The classic statement of the theory of general mental ability is: Spearman, C. E. (1927). *The abilities of man: The nature and measurement.* New York: Macmillan. See also Jensen's articles on Spearman and Sir Francis Galton in: Sternberg, R. J. (Ed.) (1994). *Encyclopedia of intelligence.* New York: Macmillan.

For a detailed explanation of factor analysis, the *g* factor, and the statistical and biological evidence for the existence of *g*, see Jensen's most recent book: Jensen, A. R. (1998). *The g factor: The science of mental ability.* Westport, CT: Praeger. More conversational, less technical descriptions appear in: Jensen, A. R. (1981). *Straight talk about mental tests.* New York: Free Press; Herrnstein, R. J., and Murray, C. (1994). *The bell curve: Intelligence and class structure in American life.* New York: Free Press; as well as: Miele, F. (1995). For whom the bell curve tolls: Charles Murray on IQ, race, class, Gould, Gardner, and the Clintons. *Skeptic,* 3 (3), 34–41.

Gould's criticism of Jensenism and the London School appears in: Gould, S. J. (1996). *The mismeasure of man.* (Revised and expanded edition.) New York: Norton.

For Sternberg's Triarchic Theory of Intelligence, see: Sternberg, R. J. (1988). *Beyond IQ: A triarchic theory of human intelligence.* New York: Cambridge University Press; as well as: Miele, F. (1995). Robert Sternberg on "the bell curve." *Skeptic,* 3 (3), 72–80.

The Theory of Multiple Intelligences is described in: Gardner, H. (1983). *Frames of mind.* New York: Basic Books; and in: Gardner, H. (1993). *Creating minds.* New York: Basic Books.

Evolutionary Psychology's Modular Theory of the Mind is described in: Cosmides, L., Tooby, J., and Barkow, J. (Eds.) (1992). *The adapted mind.* New York: Oxford University Press; and more conversationally in: Mithen, S. (1996). *The prehistory of the mind: The cognitive origins of art, religion, and science.* New York: Thames and Hudson. For an introduction to this emerging discipline, see: Miele, F. (1996). The (im)moral animal: A quick and dirty guide to evolutionary psychology and the nature of human nature. *Skeptic,* 4 (1), 42–49.

For the currently most-accepted factor-analytic models of mental abilities and personality, respectively, see: Carroll, J. B. (1993). *Human cognitive abilities: A survey of factor-analytic studies.* Cambridge: Cambridge University Press; and Wiggins, J. S. (1996). *The five factor model of personality: Theoretical perspectives.* New York: Guilford Press.

For more on Jensen's work, see the bibliography of his publications in Appendix A.

3

NATURE, NURTURE, OR BOTH?

Can Heritability
Cut Psychology's Gordian Knot?

What do baseball stars Barry Bonds (who set a new major-league record by hitting 73 home runs in one season), Cal Ripken, Jr. (who surpassed Lou Gehrig's record of consecutive games played), Roberto Alomar, Sandy Alomar, Jr., and Ken Griffey, Jr., have in common? Each is the son of a former major league player or manager. Johann Sebastian Bach, one of the greatest composers in the history of Western music, was the father of Carl Philipp Emanuel, Johann Christian, Johann Christoph Friedrich, and Wilhelm Friedmann Bach, who also were composers, though none as illustrious as their father. Wolfgang Amadeus Mozart was the son of Leopold Mozart, also a composer, but not of his son's caliber. And there are the Bernoullis in science and the Bolyais in mathematics, and the novelists Alexandre Dumas *père et fils*. Actress Drew Barrymore comes from a theatrical family that includes her grandfather John Barrymore and his sister Ethel, brother Lionel, and son John Drew Barrymore. And then there are the Fondas: Henry, Jane, Peter, and most recently, Bridget.

We all know there are "dynasties" in sports, music, science, and mathematics. The question is, why? Are genes for athletic, musical, or intellectual ability passed from parents to children, like those for hair color or blood type? Or are these abilities acquired, the way a child learns his or her parents' language or religion? Or perhaps the genetically gifted children of genetically gifted parents are doubly endowed by being reared in home environments that foster their inborn talents?

Is it nature, or nurture, or both? That is psychology's Gordian knot. *Heritability* is the sword that Jensen believes has cut the knot.

In this chapter we discuss the second of the three pillars of Jensenism—*individual differences in IQ are more the result of the fact that we inherit different genes than of the fact that we grow up in different environments*—and the political and scientific controversies that have swirled around it. In Jensen's definition, "environment" encompasses every cause of individual or group differences that is not genetic. It includes biological factors (such as exposure to toxic chemicals, mother's age and health, problems during childbirth, and even incompatibility in blood type between the mother and fetus) and quantifiable factors linked with socioeconomic status, or SES (such as family income, number of books in the home, and time spent by parents with their children) as well as qualitative cultural factors (such as growing up in a poor, Black, inner-city neighborhood versus an affluent, mostly White suburb).

Jensen does not deny that environment affects IQ. But, he says, not only are genes more important than environment, but the biological environmental factors are more powerful than cultural and socioeconomic factors. The average difference in IQ between siblings reared in the same household (where family SES and culture are pretty much the same) is greater than the average difference in IQ between families from different SES and cultural groups.

Contrary to the hopes and expectations that have shaped social policy since the days of the Great Society, genes play by far the biggest role in producing differences in IQ, followed by environmental differences (especially biological ones) between siblings who grow up in the same family. Differences in SES between families finish dead last. Therefore, even the most extreme government policy that made all families exactly equal in income, number of books in the home, quality of schools, time spent with parents—even providing professionals to assist disadvantaged parents in child rearing—could not eliminate or even substantially reduce IQ differences. Or so Jensen says.

Jensen supports his conclusions by citing studies of IQ that use the methods of quantitative genetics, especially a statistic called heritability.

Placing the case of *Nature v. Nurture* before the Court of Quantitative Genetics means that we must treat it like a civil suit, rather than a criminal case. For a specific criminal charge, say vehicular homicide, the defendant is found either 100 percent not guilty (and walks free) or 100 percent guilty. In civil suits such as auto accidents due to faulty original equipment or subsequent repair work, negligence can be apportioned. The judge can find each of the defendants 100 percent liable, 0 percent liable, or any-where in between. For example, the judge may decide that the auto manu-facturer is 60 percent liable and the repair shop 40 percent liable for the faulty brakes that caused the plaintiff's accident. Likewise, quantitative genetics renders its decision by apportioning the relative roles of genes and environment in producing individuals' differences through a statistic called heritability.

For any measurable trait—height, the age at which teeth erupt, intelli-gence, or blood pressure—heritability is defined as the proportion of the total variance in the trait that is due to genes, and not to the environment (including the biological environment described earlier). We can even determine the heritability of traits like charisma or sex appeal, provided we can reliably and accurately rate individuals on those traits.

To understand heritability and the controversies that have swirled around it, it is necessary to understand just what that term does and does not mean. When Jensen states that the heritability of IQ in a particular group of people is 0.75, he is not saying that someone with an IQ of 100 got 75 IQ points from his genes and the remaining 25 from his environ-ment. What he is saying is that 75 percent of the *individual differences*—the variation or the *total variance* in IQ—in that group is because of differences in their genes, and the remaining 25 percent of the total variance is due to differences in their environment (including the biological environment).

Quantitative genetics grew largely out of the work of Sir Ronald A. Fisher in which varieties of plants were grown in different types of soil and given different amounts of fertilizers or nutrients. Suppose that we are measuring differences in oil yield of genetically different corn seeds grown in the same soil and given the same amount of nutrients. Any significant differences that we find must be the result of genetic differences between the seeds. Conversely, differences between genetically identical seeds of corn grown in different soils or given different amounts of fertilizer must be the result of environmental differences. In the case of genetically diverse seeds grown in different soils and given different amounts of fertilizer, a heritability of 0.60 would mean that 60 percent of the measured differences in oil yield were the result of genetic differences between the seeds, and 40 percent of the differences were due to the different environments (soil and fertilizer) in which they were grown.

Jensen and other hereditarians applied this same reasoning to the study of differences in IQ and other human behaviors. Ethically, our society does not allow behavioral scientists to place children in different homes, give them different nourishment, or manipulate any other factor simply for research purposes. Nor would behavioral geneticists want to do so. Instead, they rely on "natural experiments" in which the resemblance in any trait between different degrees of kinship (that is, twins, siblings, unrelated children reared together) is compared with the degree of similarity predicted by genetic theory. By definition, however, these natural experiments lack the control of laboratory plant or animal studies.

One of the most informative natural experiments compared identical twins reared apart. Identical (also called monozygotic, or MZ) twins develop from a single egg fertilized by a single sperm that divides and then develops as two embryos. Sometimes the division is not complete and we get conjoined twins (commonly called "Siamese twins"). But in most cases, MZ twins are two (or more) genetically identical individuals—in effect, natural human clones. Just about everyone has known at least one pair of twins who look—and even act—alike. But again the question is *why?* Identical twins are often dressed alike by their parents and treated alike by others. To unravel the Gordian knot of nature versus nurture, we need to look at the rare cases of identical twins separated early in life (the earlier the better) and reared in different homes (the more different the better). These are often termed MZA (monozygotic twins reared apart) in human behavior genetic studies.

The correlation between the IQs of MZA twins (who inherited the same genes but were then reared in different environments) provides the best single estimate of the heritability of intelligence. The average correlation in IQ from the various studies of MZA twins is about 0.78. Working from the opposite direction, the fact that the correlations in IQ between parents and their adopted children (about 0.19) and between adopted children and the natural children of the adopting parents (about 0.32) are low also argues for a high heritability of IQ. At least for the White population of the United States and Europe, heritability studies of various degrees of kinship consistently show that different genes are responsible for about 75 percent of the total differences in IQ. This is true even for brothers and sisters in the same home (remember, they share only about 50 percent of their genes—to be technically precise, 50 percent of their genetic variance—on average). (See Table 3.1 on page 94.)

Another result from these studies that is predicted by Jensen and those who attribute a major role to genes but that poses a problem to anti-Jensenists is that the heritability of IQ increases with age, while the correlation between adopted children and their adoptive parents and also the correlation between adopted children and the natural children of their adoptive parents both decrease with age. In this respect, IQ acts like height, obesity, tooth size, or any number of physical traits for which environment plays a major role early in development but for which genes—and usually several genes acting together—increasingly steer the course of development. Consider how the environmental factor of severe malnutrition or illness in infancy can permanently impair a person's general health for the rest of his or her life, but may cause less devastating though still adverse effects if experienced later, when the body is more fully developed. And those of us who reach middle age become painfully aware of how much our family's medical history becomes increasingly pertinent to our own probability of encountering such diseases and conditions as high blood pressure, cataracts, diabetes, stroke, cancer, or heart disease.

But the devil—and to many anti-Jensenists, a quite literal and evil one—is in the details. They argue that when identical twins are separated and placed in different homes, their environments are really not that different in terms of the critical factors. Rarely, they argue, is one identical twin placed with poverty-stricken parents on Skid Row while the other grows up in the lap of luxury on Park Avenue. They also question whether twins are even representative of the population as a whole. As an environmental factor tending to make twins more alike, anti-Jensenists point to the fact that twins share the same womb. In the case of adoption, they question whether adoptive parents really treat their adopted children exactly as they do their biological offspring. And they point out that in many cases the fact that these children are being placed for adoption may be evidence of early environmental problems, such as the use of drugs or alcohol by the mother (Jensen concedes that such biological problems are important).

The most powerful attempt to topple the second pillar of Jensenism was the notorious Burt Affair. The late Sir Cyril Burt, a founder of the hereditarian London School of psychology, had published a number of studies showing that the correlation in IQ for identical twins reared apart was 0.77. Jensen, in his 1969 *Harvard Educational Review* article, cited this figure and other similar findings by Burt on the inheritance of mental ability. After Burt's death, a number of anti-Jensenists carefully scrutinized Burt's published research. They noted that the correlations between twins hardly changed even after Burt claimed he had added new sets of twins to his database. Then similar discrepancies were uncovered in Burt's other publications. Not only the anti-hereditarians but Burt's biographer as well concluded that the aging scholar had begun to lose touch with reality and not only had cooked up the correlations but even invented nonexistent co-authors to support his claim of having conducted new research. Jensen counters that the work of two subsequent authors seems to have vindicated Burt, and more importantly, that even disregarding Burt's results the preponderance of evidence supports the conclusion that about 75 percent of the variation in IQ is because of genes, not environment—a figure very close to Burt's 0.77. Jensen then describes the state-of-the-art research that recently has identified some of the specific genes for IQ.

A PRIMER ON VARIANCE AND HERITABILITY

The methods of quantitative genetics allow us to determine the proportion of the variation in any measurable trait that is due to heredity and the proportion that is due to environment.

The easiest way to get some idea of the variation within any group of people and in any measurable trait—whether IQ, blood pressure, height, or weight—is to subtract the lowest figure from the highest. Statisticians refer to the difference between these two figures as the "range." But even if there are many people in the group, as there are in most social science experiments, a single extreme case can distort this value. For example, if we were measuring variations in income, home runs hit in a season, or books sold, the inclusion of just one person at the top of the scale (e.g., Bill Gates, Barry Bonds, or Danielle Steele) would really inflate the range.

The next thing we might try would be to calculate an average (termed the *mean*) for the group and then to subtract the mean from each person's score. The result would be a series of values that statisticians call "deviations from the mean." For a score above the mean, the deviation would be a positive number; for a score below the mean, a negative number. To get some idea of the *average* deviation from the mean, we might just add all these deviations and then divide by the number of people we measured. But the sum of all the positive and negative deviations has to equal zero, and so the result would not tell us anything at all.

Since we're interested in how much variation there is in the group, we're really not concerned with whether the deviations from the group mean are positive numbers or negative numbers. Either way, they represent variation. The simplest and most direct approach in this case would be to ignore the signs (whether positive or negative), add up all the deviations from the mean, and then divide by the number of people in the group to get a value that represents the average deviation from the mean.

Statisticians have done essentially this, first squaring each deviation from the mean (that is, multiplying the number by itself), which makes all the values positive numbers. The squared deviations from the mean then are added together, and the sum is divided by the number of people in the group under study. The result is called the *variance*. (The widely used statistic known as the *standard deviation* is the square root of the variance.) Variance has a very important characteristic statisticians call "additivity," which means that the total variance is always equal to the sum of its components.

There are complex mathematical reasons for using the squared deviations from the mean rather than simply ignoring the plus and minus signs. For the purposes of the present discussion, it's enough to note that using the squared deviations allows us to compute the variance, which we can then break down into the percentage of the total variance due to genes and the percentage due to environment; and that these two percentages must add up to 100 percent (the total variance). As a very rough analogy, think of asking a financial advisor to go over your family budget. He breaks down your total monthly income into the percentage you must spend on necessities such as taxes, rent or mortgage, utilities, and car payments versus the percentage that you can either save or spend as you wish.

Analysis of variance is central to the way quantitative genetics estimates the relative roles of heredity and environment. The total variance in any trait is broken down into the proportion due to genes—called "heritability," and represented by the symbol h^2—and the proportion due to the environment, termed "environmentality," and represented by the symbol e^2. Both h^2 and e^2 can be further broken down into their components (just as the percentage of spending on necessities and on niceties could be broken down further in the family budget analogy). The sum of these components must always equal the total variance.

An Example

Suppose we were testing a group with only four subjects. (Real studies use many more.) Let's call them A, B, C, and D.

Their systolic blood pressure readings (or their tested IQs) are:
A = 100; B = 120; C = 90; and D = 90.

The mean is:

$$(100 + 120 + 90 + 90 = 400)/4 = 100$$

The deviations from the mean are:

$$A = 100 - 100 = 0$$
$$B = 120 - 100 = 20$$

$$C = 90 - 100 = -10$$
$$D = 90 - 100 = -10$$

Note that the sum of these deviations equals zero:

$$0 + 20 + (-10) + (-10) = 0$$

The squared deviations from the mean are:

$$A = 0^2 = 0$$
$$B = 20^2 = 400$$
$$C = -10^2 = 100$$
$$D = -10^2 = 100$$

The variance in our group, then, is:

$$(0 + 400 + 100 + 100)/4 = 600/4 = 150$$

So the standard deviation in our example is equal to the square root of 150, which is approximately 12.25.

The Important Things to Remember About Variance and Heritability

- The proportion of the total variance in any trait that is due to genes is termed the *heritability of the trait* and is represent by the symbol h^2.

  For example, if we find that differences in genes explain 80 percent of the variation in blood pressure in a group of people, the heritability of blood pressure in that group is 0.80 ($h^2 = 0.80$).
- The heritability of 0.80 refers to the variation in blood pressure in that group—not the percentage of the blood pressure reading for any individual in the group—that is due to genes rather than environment.

- Further, $h^2 = 0.80$ is the heritability in that group. Blood pressure (or IQ or any trait) could have a different value if we tested a different group.
- However, heritability studies of IQ have been largely consistent in reporting values of h^2 from 0.50 to 0.80, even for different countries or different races or ethnic groups.
- Whatever proportion of the variance is *not* due to genes $(1.00 - h^2)$ is due to the environment.

  The proportion of the total variance in any trait that is not due to genes is termed the *environmentality of the trait* and is represented by the symbol e^2. In our example, 20 percent (that is, 100 percent − 80 percent) of the variation in blood pressure would be due to the environment. (To be technically precise, $1.00 - h^2 = e^2 +$ measurement error. For IQ and other psychological tests, the error is usually between 5 and 10 percent. Medical measures such as cholesterol level, blood pressure, and X-ray interpretation often have higher measurement errors. Even reading length from a ruler involves some measurement error.)
- In human research, the environment includes not only socioeconomic factors such as income, quality of schools, and years of education, but also biological factors such as exposure to toxic chemicals, and injuries during pregnancy.
- Both heritability and environmentality can be broken down further into components. But no matter how detailed the breakdown, the components must add up to the total variance (that is, the total variance must equal the sum of its parts).

Miele: Well, if the first tenet of Jensenism—the *g* factor, which we talked about in Chapter I—isn't controversial, I hope you're not going to tell me that the second tenet—that the differences in *g* are more the result of heredity rather than environment—isn't controversial either.

Jensen: The fact that g is more strongly genetic than most other psychological variables is not really controversial among empirical researchers in this field. It is highly controversial only in the popular media. Just try to find any real controversy among the experts who know the research on this issue. There's always a handful of dissenters regarding any body of empirical knowledge, of course, even in the scientific community. Unfortunately, the mass media have presented the views of this small number of highly vocal dissenters as the prevailing position.

Miele: No matter which side I talk to on issues like this I find there's only one thing the two sides agree on—blaming the media that their side isn't accepted and the other side is given any voice at all. Can you provide any solid evidence to support your claim of media bias?

Jensen: Anyone who wants a thorough presentation of expert opinion among behavior geneticists and psychometricians on the subject and a scholarly analysis of the popular media's distortion of it should read *The IQ Controversy: The Media and Public Policy* by Mark Snyderman and Stanley Rothman.

Miele: Again, I've found that both sides in any controversy point to books that they claim set the record straight. What makes Snyderman and Rothman's book the definitive statement? It wasn't published by the American Psychological Association (APA) or the Behavior Genetics Association (BGA), was it?

Jensen: No, but they came to their conclusions after surveying those best qualified to judge, the members of the Behavior Genetics Association and the Tests and Measurements Division of the American Psychological Association. And an article summarizing their findings and conclusions was published in *American Psychologist*, the APA's house journal.

Miele: Are you telling me that if I did a content analysis on the most popularly used Psych 101 textbooks or polled the members of the APA, I'd get a paraphrase of what you just told me?

Jensen: I'm not sure what you'd get from a random poll of the APA membership. But if you polled experts in biological psychology, comparative psychology, behavioral genetics, and psychometrics, you would find a solid consensus that individual differences in IQ and the *g* factor have a large genetic component. The APA itself has published an introduction to the genetics of individual differences, *Nature, Nurture, and Psychology*, edited by Robert Plomin and Gerald McClearn, which also agrees with that consensus.

Miele: And is that consensus reflected in psychology textbooks?

Jensen: I'm afraid it is not. I recently examined the chapters on intelligence and individual differences in a sample of introductory psychology textbooks. The conceptual errors and misinformation in their discussions of the heritability of IQ are appalling, even in some of the most widely used textbooks. There are a few exceptions, but on the whole, undergraduate psychology textbooks are misinforming hundreds of thousands of college students on this subject every year. This has gone on for at least 30 years. The disparity between specialist books in this field and the treatment of the subject in most undergraduate texts is scandalous. Students might as well read pop psychology articles in the Sunday newspaper supplements.

Miele: You seem to have little but contempt for introductory psychology texts and to get awfully worked up about them. Why?

Jensen: I'd rather have students read William James's *Principles of Psychology*, originally published in 1890, than to read the pabulum now passed off on undergraduates as "Introductory Psychology." And the introductory course has a considerable influence on who will and who won't major in psychology. I still read James for pleasure now and then, but it almost sickens me even to thumb through most of the introductory psychology books published in recent years. They represent a dumbing-down of the whole field! I doubt that textbooks of this ilk exist in the biological or physical sciences, because they wouldn't be tolerated by either the students or the faculty. Of course there are a few perfectly respectable introductory texts in psychology. It is up to instructors to be discriminating and search for them.

Miele: Perhaps part of the problem comes from the origins and associations of the words. Before the scientific term "heredity," we had the word "hereditary." "Hereditary" can mean "genetic, not environmental"; but it can also mean "by right of birth," as in "the hereditary Duke of Northumberland." The term "genetic" is easily confused with "eugenics." Do you think the origins and associations of the words "heredity" and "hereditary" with aristocracy, and later, of "eugenics" with Nazism, have cast a dark cloud over the scientific study of mental ability?

Jensen: They shouldn't, but I'm sure they have cast a shadow, if not your dark cloud. And hopefully our increase in scientific knowledge is clearing the skies. "Heredity" simply refers to the transmission of genes from parents to their offspring; genes are the physical units of heredity. "Hereditary" means about the same thing, but often implies the passing on of parental genes that affect some observable characteristic of one or both parents to one or more of their offspring. A "hereditarian" is someone who holds that some part of the variation in mental and behavioral as well as physical traits is attributable to genetic variation within the species. The word "genetic" pertains to genes, or to characteristics known to be influenced by genes.

Miele: And "eugenics"?

Jensen: When Sir Francis Galton coined the word "eugenic," which literally means "good beginning" or "good genes," he meant the hereditary basis of characteristics such as good health, longevity, the absence of birth defects or physical or mental handicaps, personally and socially advantageous mental abilities, and favorable personality traits.

To dispel any Third Reich or Holocaust guilt by association implied in your question, let me quote exactly what Galton said about eugenics in his autobiography, *Memories of My Life*:

> Man is gifted with pity and other kindly feelings; he has also the power of preventing many kinds of suffering. I conceive it to fall within his province to replace Natural Selection by other processes that are more merciful and not less effective. This is precisely the aim of Eugenics.

Even if we don't use the term, eugenics is practiced throughout the civilized world today through genetic counseling, amniocentesis, and DNA testing for various genetic diseases such as Tay-Sachs, Huntington's chorea, and many other genetic anomalies. And it is the prospective parents who are requesting these family planning procedures. Government is not ordering them. What opposition there is these days comes from a few on the political left and many more on the religious right.

Miele: You still haven't answered the second part of my question— Do you think all this talk of genes and heredity, and its association with aristocracy, eugenics, and even Nazism, have forever bedeviled the scientific study of the nature of mental ability?

Jensen: No, I don't believe that the scientific study of the inheritance of mental ability is really bedeviled by these wrong or evil things from past history. I don't put the Galtonian conception of eugenics, as stated in the quote I gave you, in that category. Nor do I see any intrinsic relationship between aristocracy or Nazism and the scientific study of the g factor, behavior genetics, and individual or group differences.

There are those, however, who for whatever reason deny the reality of individual differences or the evidence that individual differences have genetic as well as environmental causes. Some have tried to link psychometrics and behavioral genetics with Fascism, Nazism, Hitler, or whatever and hereditarian psychologists have been subjected to such defamatory propaganda. The *New York Review of Books* review of my 1980 book *Bias in Mental Testing* (whose findings were subsequently confirmed by a special committee of the National Academy of Sciences) ran with a cartoon of me in what looks like a Nazi storm trooper uniform! And a Canadian psychologist who studies the evolutionary basis of racial differences in mental ability was caricatured in a newspaper cartoon as shaking hands with Hitler. That abysmally low level of criticism merely shows their desperation. They aren't worth recognizing.

Miele: Okay. Then let's get back to the technical term used in behavior genetics, "heritability."

Jensen: Here we have to shift gears drastically, because "heritability" means something very different from the terms "heredity," "hereditary," and "inherited." I'm willing to bet that only a minority of Ph.D.'s in psychology know the definition of "heritability." So let's get its meaning straight right now.

Technically, "heritability" is defined as the statistically estimated proportion of the population variance in a given trait that is attributable to genetic factors. Variance (Var.) is calculated as the arithmetic average (or mean) of all the squared deviations of each individual measurement from the overall mean of all the measurements. [See the Primer on Variance and Heritability that begins on page 74, after the introduction to this chapter.]

Here's the key point: The heritability of any trait is the proportion of the total trait variance due to genetic variance. As a very rough analogy, think of the pie charts showing federal revenue you see in the newspaper that show, say, 25 percent comes from corporate income tax, 70 percent from individual income tax, and the remaining 5 percent from excise taxes, tariffs, and inheritance tax.

Geneticists make a further distinction between *narrow heritability* and *broad heritability*. Technically, narrow heritability is the proportion of total variance due to the additive effects of genes only. Broad heritability consists of the narrow heritability plus the variance resulting from genetic interactions whose effects are not simply additive (that is, not $2 + 3 = 5$, but $2 \times 3 = 6$); from assortative mating (the tendency of like to marry like, which increases total variation); and from a very special component called genotype-by-environment ($G \times E$) covariation. $G \times E$ *covariation* refers to cases in which genes and the environment are both favorable (or unfavorable) for the development of a particular trait, as in the case of a child who is genetically gifted musically and also grows up in a highly musical environment, like Mozart.

Miele: So are you saying that heritability can cut the nature-nurture Gordian knot? What about the classic example of the same seeds sown in different soils that goes back to Charles Cooley, the founder of the American Sociological Association? Or maybe back even further, to Jesus in the Parable of the Sower and the Seeds:

> Behold the sower went out to sow. And as he sowed, it happened one indeed fell by the roadside; and the birds of heaven ate it. And another fell on the rocky place where it did not have much earth. And it sprang up at once, due to not having deepness of earth. And the sun rising it was scorched. And through not having root, it was dried out.
>
> And another fell among the thorns, and the thorns grew up and choked it, and it did not yield fruit. And another fell into the good ground and yielded fruit, going-up and increasing; and one bore thirty, and one sixty, and one a hundred-fold. (Mark 4:3–8)

Jensen: I love your apt quotation from the New Testament. Its poetic language offers a welcome relief from all my technical terminology. And today's behavior genetic research pretty much tells us the same thing.

Essentially, heritability estimates do cut the nature-nurture Gordian knot for any measurable traits by separating the total variation into the part due to variation in genes and the part due to variation in environment. I prefer the terms "genetic influences" and "nongenetic influences" because so many people think environment means just the psychological, social, and cultural milieu in which a person grows up. These nongenetic influences begin virtually at the moment of conception. They have direct effects on the brain's development and are probably the most important of all environmental effects on g. They include intrauterine conditions related to the mother's age, health, and blood type; incompatibility between mother and fetus; nutrition; certain medications; and substance abuse. Then there are perinatal conditions such as anoxia, birth trauma, and extreme prematurity. And also postnatal conditions—mainly early nutrition and the various childhood diseases. My analysis of IQ differences in MZ (monozygotic, or identical) twins, who have the same genes, suggests that nearly all these effects are disadvantageous.

Miele: But does that mean that factors like home environment, parent-child interaction, schooling, and family income have no effect on a person's g?

Jensen: No, later environmental influences have their effects largely on what a person does with his or her level of g rather than on the level of g itself. These effects are fully recognized by geneticists—the sources of environmental variance are every bit as interesting to them as the genetic variance. The important point is that by means of quantitative genetic analysis, such as the calculation of heritability, we are able to get good estimates of the relative strengths of the environmental and the genetic influences on a given characteristic in a given population at a given time. And by the same means we can look at the relative effects of genes and environment on a particular trait over the course of development, from infancy to later maturity.

Miele: That all seems so contrary to everything we've come to believe about the importance of education. Do you have any evidence to support those statements?

Jensen: Consider the heritability of height. In our population, height has a heritability of about 0.30 in infancy, which gradually increases, up to about 0.95 in early adulthood. IQ shows a similar developmental increase in heritability, going from about 0.40 in early childhood to about 0.70 in adulthood, then up to about 0.80 in older adults. If environment and experience were the chief determinants of mental growth throughout our life span, you would predict that the longer we have lived, the lower the heritability of IQ, because the difference between our life experience and those of our kin should accumulate. But just the opposite is found to be true. IQ behaves like height and other physical traits in that the resemblance between genetic relatives increases with age, despite their differences in cumulative life experience.

Miele: But critics point out that heritability estimates are dependent on the population studied and the conditions under which that population developed. Don't those qualifications dull the edge of the behavior genetic knife? Rather than cleanly cutting the nature-nurture Gordian knot, what we see is a fuzzy and frayed tangle.

Jensen: Those critics write as if behavioral geneticists weren't aware of these points. The basic genetic model is that the total variance we see in any trait, termed the phenotypic variance ($var.P$), is composed of the genetic variance ($var.G$) plus the nongenetic variance ($var.E$), also called the environmental variance, or

$$var.P = var.G + var.E$$

Heritability (h^2) is simply the ratio of the genetic variance to the total variance:

$$h^2 = (var.G)/(var.G + var.E.)$$

So by definition, heritability can vary over some range of values depending on the degree of genetic variation in the population ($var.G$) and the amount of environmental variation ($var.E$). If you look at the second equation, you can see that the smaller $var.E$ becomes, the higher h^2, until you reach the point at which there is no environmental variation at all (that is, $var.E. = 0.00$), at which point $h^2 = 1.00$. As $var.G$ gets smaller, h^2 also decreases, until $h^2 = 0.00$ and $e^2 = 1.00 - h^2 = 1.00 - 0.00 = 1.00$. If everyone's environment is pretty much the same, heritability will be very high because the only thing that really varies is the genes. Likewise, if there is very little genetic variation, as for example in highly inbred strains of corn or laboratory mice, heritability will be very low. In a country where part of the population suffers from malnutrition while others are well fed, the heritability of height is lower (because of greater environmental variation) than in a country where everyone is reasonably well nourished.

The other point about heritability follows as a corollary—a heritability estimate is not a constant like the speed of light, nor is it meant to yield some single, constant value. Rather, heritability is an inherently inconstant population statistic, like the average birthrate, the average mortality, or the average height of adult men or women. The heritability of IQ estimated in different studies varies as a function of the test used, the age of the subjects, and the degree to which the subjects vary in socioeconomic status and educational level. The heritability of IQ fluctuates somewhat from sample to sample and study to study from about 0.40 to 0.80, with the average for all studies falling somewhere between 0.60 and 0.70. But such an overall average isn't really as informative as knowing the heritability in a particular population under specified conditions.

Miele: But I've heard Jerry Hirsch, a distinguished psychologist who's done some pioneering work in behavior genetics, say that heredity is a fact but heritability estimates are just hand waving that implies greater certainty than really exists. And he quotes no less an authority than Sir Ronald A. Fisher, who developed many of the methods of quantitative genetics, to support his criticism.

Jensen: I just explained why uncertainty is inherent in any heritability estimate. No one who knows anything about Fisher's views could imagine that he would disagree with anything I've said on this subject. Fisher merely pointed out that a properly estimated heritability coefficient is a population statistic, and, like any population statistic, it has a clearly definable probable error—that is, its likelihood of being off the mark by a given amount. The same thing is true for just about every scientific measurement, say a statistical determination of the birthrate in the U.S. population in the year 2002. Would you then echo Jerry Hirsch and say that a newborn child really exists, but the birthrate is just hand-waving?

Miele: Since we can't and wouldn't want to perform controlled breeding experiments with humans, our knowledge about the roles of heredity and environment and the heritability of mental ability comes from comparing identical twins, nonidentical twins, other relatives, and adopted children.

Before summarizing the results of those studies, could you sketch the logic behind those studies?

Jensen: I covered this material in depth in the courses on behavior genetics and on theories of intelligence that I taught at the University of California at Berkeley. It says something about the social sciences in contemporary America that after my retirement no one was hired to teach these courses in either the psychology or the education departments.

Most of the statistical methodology was originally developed to solve problems in genetics, especially as applied to agriculture. But it's just as applicable to the field of behavior genetics, which came into its own in the 1970s with the formation of the Behavior Genetics Association (of which I was a charter member) and their journal *Behavior Genetics,* in which I have published a number of articles.

Miele: Okay. Let's try a really short course, for now.

Jensen: Well, the essential ideas did indeed come from Sir Ronald A. Fisher's elaboration of the basic principles of heredity discovered by

Jensen's favorite photo of himself because "it shows me in my most typical setting and activity" — in his study at home, working on another article or book. (Taken but never used by Life *magazine)*

Gregor Mendel, which we call Mendelian genetics. Mendel dealt entirely with traits in which variation is due to a single gene locus that can take two distinct forms—like his wrinkled peas or smooth peas, or red flowers or white flowers. If you grow these flowers in a uniform environment (which Mendel did) you get either two or three distinct variants, depending on whether the trait manifests either *genetic dominance* (where the offspring appear just like the dominant parent but show no trace of the *recessive* parent) or *genetic additivity* (where the offspring display a blending of the two parental forms).

Let's say we have a gene with two possible forms (termed "alleles")—and let's call one *R* (for Red) and the other *w* (for White)—that determine the color of the flowers. Each flower has two alleles for color (*R* and *w*), with one allele coming from each of its two parents. Then each flower must have one of the following four possible allele combinations (technically termed "genotypes"): *RR* (Red-Red), *ww* (White-White), *Rw* (Red-White), or *wR* (White-Red). The *RR* genotype is pure red (technically termed "homozygous"), and its phenotype (that is, what we observe) is a red flower. The *ww* genotype is pure white (again homozygous), and its phenotype is a white flower. The *wR* and *Rw* genotypes (technically termed "heterozygous") are the same; their different designations simply indicate that a different parent provided the allele to the offspring (which for our present purposes doesn't matter).

Now, the genotypes of the offspring of one of our pure red *RR* flowers and a pure white *ww* flower can be either *RR*, *Rw*, *wR*, or *ww*. Let's suppose flower color has genetic dominance and red is dominant over white. Then the *RR*, *Rw*, and *wR* genotypes all result in the Red phenotype (that is, a red flower). Only the pure white *ww* genotype produces the phenotype for a white flower. Given sufficient numbers, about three fourths of the offspring of pure red flowers and pure white flowers will be red flowers and the remaining one-fourth or so will be white flowers—the 3:1 ratio Mendel described. Many blood types in humans also show genetic dominance.

But now suppose we're dealing with a different trait, say, stem height at maturity. We again have two homozygous, or pure, strains. Let's call them *TT* (homozygous tall) and *tt* (homozygous short). Now, the genotypes of the offspring of one of our homozygous tall *TT* flowers and a homozygous short *tt* flower can be either: *TT*, *Tt*, *tT*, or *tt*. Unlike color, stem height has *additive inheritance*—that is, neither *T* nor *t* is dominant or recessive, but instead they blend. The homozygous tall *TT* genotype produces the tall phenotype. The homozygous short *tt* genotype produces the short phenotype. The heterozygous *Tt* and *tT* genotypes, however, produce plants that are intermediate in height between the two parental strains. So for stem height, the offspring would display three phenotypes, not two as was the case for color. About one fourth would be tall, one-half would be intermediate, and one fourth would be short. Important human traits such as height and IQ show polygenic, rather than simple Mendelian, inheritance.

Miele: The ratios you've given are statistical. They're what you see with sufficiently large numbers. If I start breeding a couple of pea plants out on my balcony I'm not going to see these exact ratios in each and every generation. Right?

Jensen: Of course. That's one of the defining properties of quantitative genetics—its predictions are probabilistic. That means that our experiments in human behavior genetics require statistical inference. And this often makes the results harder to explain and harder for nonspecialists to understand. But it also means—and this is important in relation to a lot of your earlier questions about the historical and political associations of the nature-nurture problem—that the antiquated ideas about trying to breed a master race and so on just don't make any scientific sense in terms of modern genetics. What we can do genetically, even when and if we would want to, is really rather modest.

And there are always trade-offs, even when we do apply selective breeding. Consider the "green revolution" that developed grains with higher yields. They've been achieved by selecting for only one or two genetic characteristics, such as kernel size or oil content, in very standardized environments. But human behavior is the result of thousands of genes and develops in all sorts of environments, including environments our individual genetic tendencies lead us to select or create for ourselves. The human genome has about at least 30,000 and perhaps twice that many genes. The central mechanism of behavior is the brain, and at least half of all the genes in the human genome are involved with the brain, and the effects of about one third of all the genes are entirely unique to the brain.

Miele: Anything more in your short course in genetics?

Jensen: Yes, one more thing, about genetic dominance. The genes for the characteristics that prove to be advantageous to survival over the course of natural selection are usually dominant genes, while the characteristics that prove disadvantageous are usually recessive. The two mechanisms that cause this are spontaneous mutation and natural selection. Most mutated genes confer undesirable characteristics (that is, phenotypes) in their homozygous (that is, "pure") combination. They remain recessive, and selection very gradually reduces their frequency until it is nearly at the rate of spontaneous mutations for that gene. Mutations that confer some selective advantage, or Darwinian fitness, increase in frequency over successive generations and are dominant over the less advantageous alleles at the same locus, which are therefore said to be recessive.

For some traits, however, it is most advantageous to maintain intermediate values. So selection favors the preservation of alleles with additive effects, producing more intermediate phenotypes (like the peas of intermediate height in the previous example). Physical size, or stature, is an example of this; the average for a given species generally has a biological advantage over either extreme. Another example is the heterozygous condition for sickle-cell anemia. The homozygous condition produces a genetic disease, but the heterozygous condition confers a relative immunity to malaria. That isn't important in modern technological society, but when slash-and-burn agriculture was spreading through Africa there was probably selection favoring the heterozygous condition. This example also points out how complex the interplay between heredity and environment can be.

Miele: Let's get back to intelligence and mental ability. As you said, it's obvious that a simple inheritance model based upon two alleles— smart and dull—just doesn't fit.

Jensen: Right. Most of the human traits of greatest interest to psychologists are not Mendelian. Individual differences and group differences in these traits are not attributable to a single gene with two alleles. The variation in these traits does not consist of only two or three discrete types, as in Mendelian characters (like blood type), but of continuous, quantitative gradation throughout the whole range of variation, from the lowest to the highest. The genetic underpinning of continuous or quantitative traits is *polygenic*, which only means that more than one gene is involved in the trait variation. The number of genes for a polygenic trait may range anywhere from two genes on up into the hundreds. For most polygenic traits, the number of genes is not known, but there are ways theoretically to make a rough estimate of this number for a given trait.

Miele: So how can genetic models deal with the human behavioral traits you've just said were so complex?

Jensen: This problem was also solved by the British geneticist and statistician Sir Ronald Fisher in one of the landmark papers in the history of genetics. "The Correlation Between Relatives on the Supposition of Mendelian Inheritance," published in 1918, laid the foundation for quantitative genetics (the genetics of continuous, polygenic traits as contrasted with single-gene or Mendelian traits).

Fisher proposed that quantitative traits are determined by a whole set of genes (that is, they exhibit *polygenic variation*) and that the alternate alleles for each gene in the set slightly increase or slightly decrease the observed phenotype from the population mean of that trait, but the simple Mendelian laws hold for each of these genes. For example, suppose that stem height was not the result of just the two alleles for one gene (T and t, as in the model above), but three genes with two alleles each: (S and s), (T and t), and (U and u). The alleles S, T, and U each slightly increase stem height from the population mean, while the alleles s, t, and u each slightly decrease it.

Given these explicit conditions and a set of mathematical formulas (known as "Mendelian algebra"), Fisher calculated the theoretical genetic correlation between any degree of kinship (for example, parent-child, identical twins, fraternal twins, siblings, first cousins, and so on) for any polygenic trait in any species of humans, or any sexually reproducing plants or animals. To take the simplest case, MZ (that is, monozygotic or identical) twins share the exact same set of genes because they both develop from the division of a single fertilized egg. So according to Fisher's formulas, their theoretical correlation on any heritable, quantitative trait (such as height or IQ) is +1.00, as it would be for any individual with themselves or with their clone. The theoretical correlations for DZ (that is, dizygotic or fraternal twins, whether of the same sex or opposite sexes), parent-child, and full siblings are all +0.50 because these kinships all share, on average, half of their genes. The correlations predicted by Fisher's formulas continue to decrease as the degree of kinship decreases. For unrelated individuals, the predicted correlation is 0.00, though this would not hold for remote, small villages whose members are all related or in pure breeds of dogs, thoroughbred horses (who all derived from a handful of ancestors), laboratory mice, or inbred strains of corn, rice, or other plants.

Those are the theoretically predicted correlations based on genetic similarity. The actual correlations we find when we test pairs of MZ twins or DZ twins, or groups of siblings, cousins, or unrelated individuals, can vary continuously from −1.00 (that is, exact opposites—the higher one member of the pair scores or measures, the lower the other does) to 0.00 (no greater resemblance in their scores than between pairs of random numbers) to +1.00 (perfect parallel—the higher one member of the pair scores or measures, the higher the other does, as well).

Table 3.1 compares the predicted correlations for the various degrees of genetic similarity against the actual correlations found by behavioral genetic research.

Miele: And how do these figures help us to resolve the nature-nurture uncertainty?

Jensen: By comparing them against the correlations we actually find in behavior genetic studies of mental ability and other psychological traits to see how well they fit. It turns out that they closely fit the genetic predictions and do not fit predictions we would make from a purely environmental theory. There is no valid environmental explanation, for example, for why identical twins reared apart should be almost as alike as identical twins reared together and much more alike than fraternal twins or ordinary siblings reared together; or, on the other hand, why unrelated adopted children reared together should be so unlike. There are all sorts of statistical tests you can use to validate

TABLE 3.1 Predicted and Actual Correlations in IQ for Various Degrees of Kinship

Degree of Kinship	Predicted:	Actual:
Identical (MZ) twins reared together (Same genes in same home environment)	1.00	0.86*
Identical (MZ) twins reared apart (Same genes in different home environments)	1.00	0.78*
Fraternal (DZ) twins reared together (50% same genes in same home environment)	0.50	0.60*
Full siblings reared together (50% same genes in same home environment)	0.50	0.47*
Full siblings reared apart (50% same genes in different home environments)	0.50	0.24*
Natural parent–child in same home (50% same genes in same home environment)	0.50	0.42*
Natural parent–child adopted by other home (50% same genes in different home environments)	0.50	0.24*
Adopted siblings reared together (Different genes in same home environment)	0.00	0.32†
Parent–adopted child (Different genes in same home environment)	0.00	0.19†

* These correlations, which contain a genetic factor, increase with age.

† These correlations, which contain only an environmental factor, decrease with age.

SOURCES: The predicted correlations are those derived from the simplest genetic model and taken from: "How Much Can We Boost IQ and Scholastic Achievement?" *Harvard educational review* 39, Winter 1969, p. 49. The actual correlations are those summarized from various sources and reported in Robert Plomin, et al., *Behavioral genetics* (4th edition), (New York: Worth Publishers, 2000).

the genetic model, but I've given you the big picture. The genetic model, which also takes account of environmental factors, fits the observed facts, while a purely environmental model fails.

Miele: So then is the best estimate of the heritability of intelligence the average of all these studies, about 0.60?

Jensen: No, not really, because the average estimate of heritability is based on the combined heritability estimates of IQ for every age group, and it is now known that the heritability of IQ increases with age, going from about 0.30 in very early childhood to about 0.70 in early maturity and up to about 0.80 in later maturity. The older we become, the more the phenotype reflects the genotype. A strictly environmental theory would predict just the opposite, so the increase in the heritability of IQ with age is another case where the genetic model fits the facts and the purely environmental model fails.

When we talk about a best estimate of heritability, we have to specify an age group. Various mental tests do not yield equivalent heritability estimates, either. Virtually all IQ tests are highly g loaded, but some are purer measures of g than others. Generally, the more a mental test measures the g factor, the higher is its heritability. This fact also provides evidence for the biological, rather than merely statistical, reality of g.

Miele: So how do we best estimate the heritability of IQ, and what is its value?

Jensen: From studies of identical twins reared apart. In all the published studies of pairs of MZ twins separated in infancy, put out for adoption, and reared entirely apart, the average correlation between the IQs of the twins in adulthood is 0.75. Since the twins did not share a common environment but do have identical genes, this correlation provides a fair estimate of the heritability of IQ for people in the normal range of environments for our population. At the other extreme from MZ twins reared apart are unrelated adopted children who are reared together like full siblings. In early childhood their IQs correlate about 0.25, but by late adolescence the correlation drops to nearly zero. This shows that the shared environment in which they both were reared has virtually no lasting effect on their IQs. The IQs of full siblings reared together, however, correlate about 0.47, which is close to their theoretically expected genetic correlation of +0.50.

Miele: Don't these figures show that environmental factors are also important?

Jensen: Yes, but the most powerful environmental effects are not part of the shared family environment. These effects occur within families, not between families, and make up what is often referred to as the "nonshared environment." I prefer to call it "nongenetic," because I believe it has much less to do with the psychological or social environment than with what I call the "biological microenvironment." It consists of all environmental effects that have biological consequences, particularly on the neural basis of mental development, beginning at conception. They are largely accidental or random. Each single effect is usually too small to be detected, but if they accumulate over the course of development from conception to maturity they can become evident.

These microenvironmental effects may contribute as much as 20 or 25 percent of the total variance in IQ in the population. Because they are more or less random, they are difficult to remedy or control. Their occurrence has probably been reduced in recent decades by improved nutrition of mothers and children, advances in obstetrical techniques, inoculation against the common childhood diseases, and improved health care in general. Most of the population in Third-World countries and in some small subpopulations in the United States and other industrialized countries have not had the benefits of these nutritional and health-care measures, and this probably affects their mean IQ. The reduced occurrence of these unfavorable microenvironmental elements in the industrialized countries is probably one of the causes of the gradual rise in mental test scores in these countries during the last 60 or 70 years.

Miele: In theory, identical twins share 100 percent of their genes. We can usually tell they're identical just by looking at them. So the physical traits are largely genetic. But doesn't the fact that they look so much alike also mean that they're treated more alike by their parents, by schoolteachers, by society at large? Doesn't the self-fulfilling prophecy factor confuse the effects of heredity with those of environment?

Jensen: There is no evidence at all that people looking alike makes their IQs more alike. Dizygotic (DZ) or fraternal twins are genetically no more alike than ordinary siblings; their genetic correlation is 0.50. However, like other siblings, some same-sex DZ twins look much more alike than others. In some cases their parents even wrongly believe that their DZ twins are identical twins, and they treat them as such by dressing them alike and giving them the same hairstyles, and so on. But DZ twins whose parents and others had mistaken them for MZ twins are no more alike in IQ than other DZ twins or ordinary siblings who don't look much alike.

If those who really believe that the IQ correlation between MZ twins is better explained in terms of their physical similarity than in terms of their genetic correlation, they should go out and find unrelated people who look alike, such as movie stars and their doubles, and determine the correlation between their IQs. That would put this theory to the acid test. The safest bet imaginable would be that the correlation comes much closer to the correlation between pairs of people picked at random (that is, about 0) from the general population than the correlation between MZ twins reared apart (that is, about 0.75). Of all the failed attempts I've ever heard to explain away the importance of genetics in individual differences in intelligence, the look-alike theory is the most absurd.

Miele: Some of the studies of identical twins reared apart that you and other hereditarians use to estimate the heritability of IQ were conducted by the famous British psychologist Sir Cyril Burt. A number of scholars carefully scrutinized Burt's published research. They questioned how the correlations between twins changed so little even though Burt claimed that he had added new sets of twins to his database and concluded that Burt just "made up" the correlations. Did you ever question Burt's twin studies? Do you think he "faked" his twin data? Hasn't the Burt Affair cast a shadow over twin studies?

Jensen: Because of these suspicions, Burt's twin correlations are no longer cited in any summaries or discussions of the heritability of IQ. Two extremely thorough independent investigations of the accusations against Burt, however, have found these claims of faked or fraudulent data to be wholly unsubstantiated. To the best of our knowledge, the charges against Burt are false. For a time they seemed plausible because there are a considerable number of numerical errors in Burt's later published reports. Virtually all of Burt's errors are in articles he published when he was in his late 70s and 80s (he died at age 88) and are probably inadvertent, careless errors because about the same rate of numerical errors, things like transposed page numbers and the like, occur in the reference citations in his articles.

Miele: So that lets Burt off the hook? How about the way the correlations remain so constant, even though the articles show different numbers of twins were examined?

Jensen: The fact that the MZ twin correlation was 0.77 in three different reports is not too surprising for cumulated, overlapping data sets. Burt's value of 0.77 is very close to our best estimate for this correlation. A number of other studies of MZ twins reared apart have reported correlations of 0.76 and 0.78, and no one claims those studies were "faked" or the numbers were "cooked."

No one with any statistical sophistication, and Burt had plenty, would report exactly the same correlation, 0.77, three times in succession if he were trying to fake the data. One noted scientist laughingly told me that when he and his colleagues found a correlation of

0.78 for the IQs of MZ twins reared apart, they were grateful as hell that the correlation didn't turn out to be 0.77! In view of these recent findings, if Burt did fake his data, we'd have to credit him with clairvoyance.

During Burt's long and influential but controversial career, he seemed to have made more enemies than friends, and I believe that was probably part of his problem. His autocratic and egocentric personality hardly endeared him to people. His most vociferous detractors included both those who disliked him personally and those who disliked the idea that human mental ability is so highly heritable as Burt had claimed. However comforting it seemed for Burt's opponents to suggest, and perhaps even believe, that Burt "cooked" his data, more recent research has proved Burt to be correct and his detractors flatly wrong. One commentator likened the latest phase of the nature-nurture IQ debate to "a stomping match between Godzilla [that is, genes] and Bambi [that is, environment]." Much has been written about the Burt scandal for those who may be interested in the details.

Miele: Leon Kamin, one of the principal critics of Burt's work, yours, and hereditarian research in general, once claimed that you only admitted that Burt's twin correlations were faked—an admission you've now told us you've taken back—and took credit for finding the fraud, after he [Kamin] called you on it in a debate. That's a pretty serious challenge to your scientific integrity and competence! Any comment?

Jensen: Here are the details. You decide.

After Burt died, I went to London and obtained from Burt's secretary reprints of all of the papers Burt ever wrote on twins and other kinships in his studies of the heritability of IQ. As these were scattered in many different journals, I thought it would be of value to behavioral geneticists to have all of Burt's data summarized in a single article. In preparing this article, which consisted of listing Burt's correlation data for each type of kinship in separate tables, the numerical errors in his reports became clearly apparent; I found some 20 such errors, including the three correlations of 0.77 or 0.771 that Kamin suspected were fraudulent because they all had the same value. I wrote a detailed article on Burt's errors and submitted it to the *British Journal of Psychology*. After a long delay, they rejected it and I submitted it to *Behavior Genetics*, which published it the same year that Kamin's book came out. When I learned that Kamin, in an address given I believe at a meeting of the Eastern Psychological Association, had mentioned three of Burt's errors as the basis of his claim of fraud, I credited Kamin for this observation in a footnote in my paper in *Behavior Genetics*.

If I have behaved in any way dishonorably with respect to the Burt affair, I'd like to know just how. If anything, I was too quick to come to accept that Burt's data were "cooked" based on the information given in Hearnshaw's biography. When further, more careful investigations revealed the lack of any solid evidence of fraud, I, of course, reversed my opinion.

Miele: Returning to the science involved, why doesn't your estimate of the heritability of intelligence of about 0.76 agree with the estimate of about 0.50 that appeared in the prestigious British journal *Nature*? Surely that isn't a case of media bias. It still indicates a significant genetic factor, but it's substantially lower than the figure of 0.75 to 0.76 that you and other hereditarians keep repeating. And there are also arguments that the only really conclusive estimate of the heritability of intelligence comes not from Thomas Bouchard's Minnesota Twin Project or the other similar studies but from the work of geneticists C. R. Rao and Newton Morton. It used a method known as path analysis, which the authors say is the only way to take cultural factors properly into account. So who's right?

Jensen: Setting up a genetic model that encompasses all of the various degrees of kinships on which there exists suitable IQ data always involves certain assumptions. Different models that use different assumptions result in somewhat different estimates. The more detailed and fine grained the model, the more equations and assumptions it requires. The technical disagreements largely concern these assumptions, rather than the actual data per se.

The analysis in *Nature* that you mentioned hypothesizes a maternal effect that would make MZ twins more alike because they share the mother's womb during the nine months of pregnancy. Since it is an environmental, not genetic, effect, it reduces the estimate of heritability. But other behavior geneticists argue that most of what happens during pregnancy makes twins more different, rather than more alike, and thus causes us to underestimate the true heritability.

But even if the heritability of IQ is 0.50 rather than 0.78 (or 0.70, 0.75, or 0.77), it still shows that there is a significant genetic component to individual differences in mental ability. That is a far cry from saying that IQ differences are largely the result of social, economic, and cultural factors.

Miele: But some critics question whether twins provide a fair representation of the entire population. Don't you need other evidence?

Jensen: Yes, and further incontrovertible evidence comes from looking at the other side of the coin. Adoption studies allow us to compare genetically unrelated children who have been reared together from infancy against full siblings reared together. And adoption studies require fewer assumptions than any other method of estimating the effects of genetic factors and shared family environment on IQ. The IQ correlation between unrelated children reared together decreases with age, going from about 0.30 in early childhood to almost zero in late adolescence, showing that the effect on IQ of being reared together in the same family is virtually washed out by the time people reach maturity.

The Texas Adoption Project with 300 adoptees, conducted by a team of behavioral geneticists at the University of Texas, is the largest data bank of this kind and has the highest quality of data, with IQs of all family members. A path model analysis of these data, consisting of IQs for the mother, father, their biological offspring, and the adoptees, was recently performed by the Texas team when the adopted children had an average age of 17 years. The population value of the heritability derived from these data is 0.78, which is not significantly different from the heritability of 0.75 estimated from the correlation between MZ twins reared apart or even Sir Cyril Burt's allegedly "cooked" heritability of 0.77! The strong agreement between the two most direct lines of evidence—identical twins reared apart and unrelated children reared together—provides the best estimate we now have of IQ heritability.

The most important and unarguable point in all of these studies is that no one has been able to explain the pattern of the various kinship correlations without recognizing the substantial effect of genetic factors. If it could have been done, it certainly would have been done by now, because many technically competent scientists have tried. Even if heredity turns out to be King Kong and not Godzilla, would that make you switch your bet to Bambi in the hypothetical stomping match?

Miele: Well, the Human Genome Project is in the process of trying to map every human gene. That should provide the most direct evidence imaginable. So far, the Project has identified the specific genes for various diseases, including mental and behavioral ones like Alzheimer's. But no one has found a gene for intelligence. If the heritability estimates are accurate as you claim they are, shouldn't finding the IQ genes be relatively easy? After all, your theory says that there are many genes that contribute to IQ. Why hasn't anyone stumbled onto at least one of them?

Jensen: One doesn't merely stumble onto these things. One has to search for them. But you're wrong. At least four genes or DNA segments that affect IQ have been identified by behavior geneticist Robert Plomin of the Institute of Psychiatry of the University of London. And his investigation continues. These experiments have to be replicated at least two or three times to rule out chance findings, and the genes identified have held up in repeated studies.

The method Plomin uses is known as quantitative trait loci, or QTL. What he and his research team do is to get two groups of subjects, one group with average IQs and another group with very high IQs. Using blood samples from these two groups, they extract DNA and examine a strand of DNA from a particular chromosome (in this case, chromosome number 6) and search for a significant difference in the DNA between the average and high IQ groups. A significant difference in the DNA could be a marker of one of the genes that influence IQ. The research team then has to look at the same DNA in a new set of average and high IQ groups to see if the same significant difference in DNA shows up. To rule out any "chance" effect, you have to repeat the study with new groups. It is certainly not easy to do this research, as you seem to believe it should be. It is extremely laborious and painstaking, but is getting somewhat easier as the technology of molecular genetics develops more efficient methods of DNA analysis.

And because intelligence is polygenic, each gene contributes only a small part of the total variation in IQ. The first few genes discovered, for example, account for only about 3 or 4 percent of the total IQ variance. The genes with the largest effects will most likely be found first. The task of finding the next ones will probably become more difficult, because each one's effect will likely be smaller than that of those found earlier in the search. From all the evidence of the high heritability of IQ, however, we know that genes are involved. But finding the specific genes is much like looking for needles in a haystack, even when you know for sure that there actually are needles in the haystack.

Miele: Then if it's so difficult to look for the specific genes, why bother if we already know from heritability studies that IQ is partly genetic?

Jensen: For the same reason that geneticists look for the specific genes for, say, a particular form of cancer, or for a type of Alzheimer's disease, or Huntington's chorea, or Tay-Sachs disease, cystic fibrosis, muscular dystrophy, and many other genetic conditions. Identifying the gene or genes is the first step in uncovering the processes by which some individuals develop lower or higher IQs than others. Merely knowing that something is genetic doesn't explain much of anything; it only tells us where to look for the explanation, or at least some part of it. A good example is a type of mental retardation known as phenylketonuria, or PKU, which we now know is caused by a double recessive gene. Possession of this particular gene was found to result in a failure to metabolize properly a certain protein. This faulty metabolism yields biochemical products that damage the growing brain, thereby retarding mental development. Eliminating this protein (phenylalanine) from the diet, in fact, usually allows mental growth to proceed fairly normally. We want to discover the chemical modus operandi for the most influential genes that are involved in human intelligence.

At the same time, neuroscientists are directly studying the brain structures and the neural and metabolic processes that underlie intelligence. For a complete understanding, we have to explore in both directions, from the genes and from the brain. Like digging a tunnel, you excavate from both ends. That's how I see the advancement of our knowledge of the physical basis of intelligence as taking place.

Miele: Is there anything to be gained by more heritability studies of the Whites in North America and Europe? What about other groups, especially Blacks? Can heritability studies ever tell us anything about the cause of the Black-White difference in average IQ?

Jensen: By now, heritability studies of g in White populations have probably reached the point of diminishing returns. There have been a few studies of IQ heritability in the Black population and there seems to be no statistically significant difference from the White heritability of IQ. But the heritability within each group alone tells us virtually nothing about whether the average difference between the groups is heritable. If the group means differ markedly, and if the heritability of IQ within each group is very high, and if the environmental factors known to affect IQ do not differ very much between the groups, it would be surprising if the groups did not actually differ genetically to some extent. But such evidence by itself is insufficient to support any serious argument on this point. Other lines of evidence are needed for studying the causes of the observed average IQ difference between different racial populations. I have discussed this whole issue in considerable detail in my book *The g Factor*.

Miele: Then let's take it up in the next chapter.

Further Reading

For excellent introductions and summaries by experts in behavior genetics and psychometrics, see: Plomin, R., and McClearn, G. (Eds.) (1993). *Nature, nurture, and psychology*. Washington, DC: American Psychological Association; and Rowe, D. C. (1994). *The limits of family influence: Genes, experience, and behavior*. New York: Guilford Press. Contributions by Jensen and other hereditarians and nonhereditarians, and cognitive psychologist Earl Hunt's concluding essay (the source of the "Godzilla versus Bambi" one-liner), are in: Sternberg, R. J., and Grigorenko, E. (Eds.) (1997). *Intelligence, heredity, and environment*. New York: Cambridge University Press. Generally more environmentalist contributions appear in: Sternberg, R. (1997). Special issue: Intelligence and lifelong learning. *American Psychologist*, 52 (10), 1025–1168. An overview of the last two and other related publications can be found in: Miele, F. (1997). IQ in review: Getting at the hyphen in the nature-nurture debate. *Skeptic*, 5 (4), 91–95.

The kinship correlations predicted by genetic theory are reported in: Jensen, A. R. (1969). How much can we boost IQ and scholastic achievement? *Harvard Educational Review*, 39 (Winter), 1–123. The actual correlations found by researchers are adapted from: Plomin, R., et al. (2000). *Behavioral genetics*. (4th ed.) New York: Worth Publishers.

The evidence of media bias on the race-IQ issue cited by Jensen is in: Snyderman, M., and Rothman, S. (1987). Survey of expert opinion on intelligence and aptitude tests. *American Psychologist*, 42, 137–144; and their 1988 follow-up book, Snyderman, M., and Rothman, S. (1988). *The IQ controversy: The media and public policy*. New Brunswick, NJ: Transaction. When I interviewed Robert Sternberg, he also faulted the media, but for a different reason—giving unwarranted attention to Herrnstein and Murray's hereditarian best-seller *The Bell Curve*. See: Miele, F. (1995). Robert Sternberg on "The bell curve." *Skeptic*, 3 (3), 72–80.

Perhaps the earliest and harshest book attacking the credibility of Sir Cyril Burt and his research on twins and the inheritance of mental ability is: Kamin, L. J. (1974). *The sci-*

ence and politics of I.Q. Potomac, MD: Erlbaum. The biography of Burt that also concluded that he had "cooked" his numbers is: Hearnshaw, L. (1971). *Cyril Burt: psychologist.* New York: Random House. Countering this view, Fletcher, R. (1991), *Science, ideology, and the media,* New Brunswick, NJ: Transaction; and Joynson, R. B. (1989), *The Burt affair,* London: Routledge, dismissed the charges against Burt as "not proven" (Joynson) or "false" (Fletcher). For Jensen's own retrospective on the Burt Affair, see: Jensen, A. R. (1992). Scientific fraud or false accusations? The case of Cyril Burt. In Miller, D. J., and Hersen, M. (Eds.), *Research fraud in the behavioral and biomedical sciences,* 97–124. New York: Wiley. A number of pro and con essays can be found in: Mackintosh, N. J. (Ed.) (1995). *Cyril Burt: Fraud or framed?* Oxford: Oxford University Press. This book includes an essay by Jensen (Burt was framed) and one by Jensen's late mentor Hans J. Eysenck, who also knew Burt very well (Burt's research was a fraud).

For more on Jensen's work, see the bibliography of his publications in Appendix A.

4

WHAT IS RACE?

Biological Reality
or Cultural Construction?

Jensen's 1969 *Harvard Educational Review* article probably would have set off little or no controversy if he had made only two points (the failure of compensatory education, and the role played by the genes in IQ), and the word "Jensenism" might never have been uttered were it not for the third component—*race*. That one four-letter word has bedeviled not just American history but also the social sciences from their beginning. In the minds of many, it is inextricably linked with a record of violence, slavery, prejudice, hatred, and all that we hope not to be.

When I ask him why he took up so controversial a topic in the first place, Jensen replies that the Black-White difference in average IQ was *the* big question in education at that time. So it was only natural that an educational psychologist try to answer it using IQ tests. Further, he insists that race has never been his main interest. His research has been directed at understanding the nature of mental ability. At the time of the *HER* article, he, like most social scientists, believed that test scores simply measured bits of knowledge or skills acquired in White, middle-class homes and schools. As he probed deeper into the nature of mental ability, he began developing tests of reaction time and simple decision making instead of IQ tests, and applying genetic methods to study both individual differences and group differences.

I then ask how he, an educational psychologist, defines the word "race" and responds to an official statement by the American Anthropological Association (AAA) that "the concept of race is a social and cultural construction" that "simply cannot be tested or proven scientifically." According to the AAA statement, "it is clear that human populations are not unambiguous, clearly demarcated, biologically distinct groups," and therefore "the concept of 'race' has no validity . . . in the human species."

The cultural constructionist view opposes the concept of race both for presuming to establish fixed categories out of the flux of nature and for any further tendency to attach racial stereotypes to those categories once they are established. According to the constructionist position, the carving up of the continuum of human variation into races is not a scientifically valid pursuit but an arbitrary activity constrained by cultural conditioning. Just how many races one distinguishes, and where and how one draws the boundaries between races, depend on one's purposes. Further, cultural constructionists believe, the use of what may be insignificant physical features as criteria for classifying people into distinct, fixed categories encourages the faulty assumption that particular, shared physical traits are accompanied by particular, shared mental abilities and behavioral attributes, and that the categories can be ranked accordingly.

Jensen responds by giving two definitions of "race" that, he says, differ only in the perspective that they take. In the taxonomic definition, races are subspecies or varieties of a species that differ in their physical characteristics and may also differ in their behavior. The concept applies to animals and plants as well as to humans, and no qualitative ranking is implied. For example, the wolf species, *Canis lupus,* includes various subspecies typically found in different parts of North America, Europe, and Asia. In the second definition, which comes from population genetics, subspecies or races are breeding populations that differ in the frequencies of one or more genes. It is these genetic differences that produce the physical and even some of the behavioral differences among animal subspecies. Jensen dismisses the American Anthropological Association's characterization of "race." Neither of the definitions he offers assume the existence of the "unambiguous, clearly demarcated, biologically distinct groups" described in the AAA caricature. Because subspecies or

WHAT IS RACE? III

races can and do interbreed, Jensen says, they are by definition "fuzzy sets"—that is, they lack the distinct boundaries that demarcate species, and instead show a continuous blending of characteristics. He argues that modern DNA studies generally confirm the traditional racial classification schemes of anthropologists as well as of the man on the street, although many human geneticists use the more neutral term "population" instead of the emotionally laden "race."

Of course, the flash point is the linkage of "race" with "genes" and "intelligence." Jensen's research and the race-IQ debate in general have centered around Black-White difference in average IQ because most of the relevant research has focused on these groups and because the race issue has long been seen as America's major social problem. Jensen presents the data and analyses that he believes support what he terms his Default Hypothesis regarding racial differences in the g factor (that is, in general intelligence):

- The causes and consequences of race differences in intelligence are the same as the causes and consequences of individual differences within either group—both environmental and genetic factors are involved, and the importance of the genetic factor is no different for Blacks than for Whites.
- There is no evidence for some special cultural factor (such as the legacy of slavery) that lowers the average IQ scores of Blacks.
- Therefore, both the difference in adult socioeconomic status (SES) between members of the same race and the difference in average SES between Blacks and Whites are causally related to differences in the g factor. But genetic differences in the g factor are a more significant cause of differences in adult SES than are differences in childhood SES of differences in g.

When I challenge Jensen to support these bold assertions, he presents three lines of evidence and reasoning that he believes favor the Default Hypothesis against any nongenetic, culture-only hypotheses:

- First, when culture-only explanations have been tested, they have been disproved.
- Second, evolution tells us that if subspecies, or races, have physical differences, they have some behavioral differences as well.
- Finally, Jensen's research has confirmed Spearman's observation that the more a test measures the g factor, the greater the Black-White difference on that test. Both the g factor and Black-White differences correlate with direct biological and physiological measures, including heritabilities, inbreeding depression, gains produced by outbreeding, and the size, electrical activity, and glucose metabolism of the brain.

I cross-examine Jensen on each of his three lines of evidence, starting with ten of the best-known culture-only theories that many social scientists say disprove his Default Hypothesis. We end with the report of a special committee appointed by the American Psychological Association to look into the race-IQ question, which concluded that "there is certainly no such support for a genetic interpretation" of the Black-White difference in average IQ.

Miele: Please don't tell me that race isn't a controversial topic. Even among experts it's a four-letter word, and among ordinary citizens it's best avoided. Discussion of race can end friendships, derail careers, or set off riots, as well you know from your own personal experience!

Jensen: Race isn't just a controversial topic—it is the *most* controversial topic. In academic circles, race differences in mental ability are the most tabooed research subject. The only runner-up—at a great distance behind in this respect—is the topic of sex differences in behavioral traits.

Miele: Why then did an educational psychologist interested in how we learn, how everyone learns, get involved in the race issue? In retrospect, wouldn't you have done better to have stuck to the concept of general intelligence, the evidence for genetic factors within groups, and just bypassed the whole race-IQ issue by saying that it can't be resolved? Instead, you've had to spend your last 30 years contesting this issue?

Jensen: Well, there are two points here.

First, the big question in education has long been conspicuous— why do Black children, on average, have quite markedly lower scholastic achievement as compared with any other racial or ethnic group in the U.S. population? The popular media have devoted considerable attention to this question for the last 30 years. It has been the subject of presidential commissions and countless discussions among school officials, from the federal to the local level. Now wouldn't it seem strange if a psychologist, especially an educational psychologist, didn't ask himself that question? And even stranger if he didn't then try to find the answer, using the tools of his profession, namely, empirical research based on psychometric and statistical methods?

When I got into this area, all informed persons knew that both individual differences and racial group differences in scholastic achievement could be predicted by IQ. And we had long known of the average Black-White difference of about 15 points in IQ, based on nationwide norms. So naturally one would suspect that the Black-White IQ difference is probably an important factor in Blacks' average shortfall in scholastic performance. And since various causal theories of the Black-White IQ difference, often contradictory theories, were being propounded, wasn't it logical to ask which theories were valid and which were not, in light of whatever empirical evidence could be sought on this question? Well, that pretty much summarizes my thoughts and my motivation regarding these questions over 30 years ago when I was teaching educational psychology in Berkeley. They are questions that were then, and still are, of great national concern, not just academic curiosity.

Miele: And your second point?

Jensen: I haven't spent 30 years researching *only* the race question. I've never lost interest or run away from it, but my primary interest was and is the more basic question of the nature of mental ability itself and the causes of individual differences. It was these questions, more than the race question, that led me first into behavioral genetics and then experimental cognitive psychology. I have devoted two decades to research on mental chronometry, using reaction time to measure speed of processing information by individuals of different IQ levels.

Miele: Why is that important?

Jensen: Because the people who studied the race question a generation or so ago didn't realize that underlying the race question were more fundamental psychological and psychometric questions. There's the question of cultural bias in mental tests, whether test scores reflect anything other than bits of knowledge or skills that could be acquired by children brought up in a White, middle-class cultural environment—the kind of environment that affords the opportunity to learn the kinds of knowledge that mental tests are devised to measure. If racial differences are not explainable in terms of test bias, other explanations must be considered, including biological and genetic causes. I researched these questions in depth and stated my conclusions in my 1980 book *Bias in Mental Testing*.

It is my position, based on the available research, that racial group differences in *g* are essentially no different from individual differences with respect to their causes and consequences. I see average group differences simply as aggregated individual differences. This is the best conclusion I have been able to reach so far, but I am not dogmatic about it. I am still researching this aspect of group differences.

Miele: Race was certainly the organizing concept of nineteenth-century anthropology, but it's hardly even mentioned these days. Many, including the experts, say race is, not a biological reality, but a mere cultural construction in which a few insignificant physical features are seized upon, for some nefarious purpose, to classify people into distinct, fixed categories, all of whose members supposedly share not only physical but behavioral characteristics as well. So, before we go any further, what is your definition of race?

Jensen: There are two definitions of race. They are simply different ways of viewing the concept, and both of them are completely compatible.

First, in biological taxonomy, a given species typically has a number of distinguishable subspecies or varieties. In the human species, *Homo sapiens*, the subspecies are called "races." Species are highly and clearly differentiated in a large number of physical and even behavioral characteristics, and different species are not interfertile, although in very rare cases matings between certain closely related species can produce offspring. Therefore, one does not see blending, or continuous intermediate gradations of physical characteristics, between different species. Within any species, however, there are subspecies that are truly interfertile, and their offspring show a blending of the characteristics of both subspecies.

In the course of evolution, subspecies or races have developed as a result of genetic isolation and natural selection. The isolation of one group from another occurs because of migration of some part of a population to another location, and because of natural barriers to intermingling of populations, such as mountain ranges, deserts, oceans, and the like. For humans, isolation may also occur because of man-made social barriers to the intermixing of groups, such as religious prohibitions and caste systems. Natural selection occurred because different environments made different demands on relatively isolated groups as they struggled to survive. Certain traits favor survival under one environment, and other traits favor survival in other environments. There is natural selection for the traits that favor survival in each specific environment.

There is also the effect known as "genetic drift," which refers to the fact that any relatively small subgroup randomly selected from its parent population will not have exactly the same gene frequencies as the parent population. So if this subgroup migrates to a new geographic location, it will differ to some degree from its parent population, and these genetic differences will be passed on to its descendants.

All these forces act together to produce the anatomical, biochemical, and behavioral differences that allow us to distinguish subspecies within a species, which in the case of our own species, *Homo sapiens*, we term "races." Because isolation of groups is not 100 percent and because races are interfertile, they are not distinct categories, or pure types, as exist in other species. Races have been called "fuzzy sets" because, rather than their having distinct boundaries, we see a continuous blending of the characteristics that, on average, distinguish the different groups as races.

The relative geographical isolation of Africa from Europe and of both of these continents from Asia, combined with the hazards of prehistoric migration over such long distances, produced the three largest and most clearly distinguishable groups: sub-Saharan Africans, Caucasians, and Mongoloids. There is considerable variation within these broad groups, of course, and there are many other derivative or blended groups that could be called races. The number of races one wishes to distinguish by certain criteria depends on the criteria used and on how fine-grained the distinctions are. The precise number of races is an open-ended and arguable issue. By certain blood-group criteria, for example, one can even distinguish between North Chinese and South Chinese, and between North Europeans and South Europeans.

Miele: Isn't saying that the precise number of races is an open-ended matter of dispute equivalent to the cultural constructionist position that "race" is a subjective (sociological) rather than an objective (biological) concept?

Jensen: No, not at all, because the criteria for all of the classifications are genetically based. The same types of arguments go on between "lumpers" (who like to lump the categories together to reduce their number) and "splitters" (who like to split the categories into a greater number of smaller groups) among taxonomists, who study species and subspecies of plants and animals; among paleoan-thropologists, who study human evolution and classify fossils; and even among dinosaur hunters. The important point is that the aver-age difference between individuals *within* a group is less than the average difference *between* groups on the relevant physical characteris-tics, whether at the molecular level or the gross physical level of measurement.

Miele: And the second definition of race?

Jensen: In population genetics, races are defined as breeding popu-lations that differ in the frequencies of one or more genes. The number of genes in which various population groups differ serves as an index of the genetic distance between them. And the world's population can be divided up into subpopulations based on their genetic distances. Again, the number of subpopulations will be rather arbitrary, depending on how finely one wishes to divide the virtually continuous scale of existing genetic distances. Various experts have distinguished anywhere between 2 and 70 subpopula-tions, and theoretically one could even increase the upper bound. For example, there are probably different breeding populations within a city like London. They are associated with different neigh-borhoods and social classes. Of course, the genetic distances would be very small compared to those between, say, the indigenous pop-ulations of sub-Saharan Africa, Europe, and Asia. Here is where recent attempts to produce a politically correct, "races don't exist" terminology produce confusion. To be precise, I should say north-ern or northeastern Asian populations, since the genetic distance between the population of India, which also is Asian, and that of Northern Europe, is surprisingly small, in fact hardly more than between, say, those of England and of those of Southern Europe. But if I just used the older and no longer politically acceptable ter-minology of the Mongoloid race, everyone would know which populations I was talking about and which ones I wasn't, whether they lived in Asia or anywhere else.

Miele: You've given me those definitions, but how can you square them with the policy statement of the American Anthropological Association in 1998, which says, "The concept of race is a social and cultural construction," that "race simply cannot be tested or proven scientifically," and that "it is clear that human populations are not unambiguous, clearly demarcated, biologically distinct groups" so "the concept of 'race' has no validity . . . in the human species."

Why believe Arthur Jensen, emeritus professor of educational psychology, and not the American Anthropological Association?

Jensen: Well, I don't know why the official position of the American Anthropological Association is wrong, but it is, if your characterization of their position is accurate. Perhaps they think that denying the reality of race will make racial problems disappear or help combat racial prejudice, or they have other well-intentioned motives that have more to do with social ideology than with science. Perhaps they merely wish to be politically correct, which I think is less forgivable for any group that wishes to be viewed as a scientific organization. Further, I don't think scientific organizations should make official pronouncements on issues that can only be answered in terms of empirical research. The AAA does not speak for all anthropologists, and probably not even for a majority of physical anthropologists, on this matter.

The majority of physical anthropologists, evolutionists, geneticists, and specialists in human biology probably take a position similar to my own. However, I am in complete agreement with one important point in the AAA statement, and I don't know anyone who is up on this subject who would disagree. *Races are not biologically clear-cut categories or distinct groups.* I've already said that races are "fuzzy" groups with clines, or blends, at their blurry boundaries. That's the difference between a subspecies or a race as contrasted with a species. Ask any zoologist. The fact that I'm a psychologist rather than an anthropologist is not relevant. The consensus of expert opinion and the evidence itself support my position.

Miele: Well, the most extensive, state-of-the-art book on human genetic variation, *The Geography of Human Genes* by L. L. Cavalli-Sforza, reaches pretty much the same conclusion as the AAA. In the popular volume Cavalli-Sforza co-authored with his son, *The Great Human Diasporas*, which summarizes his tome for the layman, he states that the stability over time of the various physical markers we use to distinguish races is just "not high enough to support the current definition of race."

Jensen: I have studied the tome by Cavalli-Sforza and his co-authors. His position on this issue is substantively no different from my own. In fact, his work has shaped my own view of the concept of race as much as, or more than, anything else I've read. The book is a mine of information about genetic variation between populations. While the term "race" is assiduously avoided, the authors use the term "population" to mean the same thing as the second definition of race I gave you earlier.

The visible characteristics—such as skin color, hair texture, and facial features—used by physical anthropologists in earlier studies of racial variation, which serve as the basis of the first definition of race I gave, are usually polygenic (that is, they are determined by the net effect of many genes, each causing a slight quantitative variation in that trait). Cavalli-Sforza's research, which corresponds to the second definition of race, examines genetic polymorphisms such as blood groups, enzymes, immunoglobulins, and antigens that have rather simple Mendelian patterns of inheritance. Perhaps the best-known example of a genetic polymorphism is the familiar ABO blood system. The different populations around the globe differ in the frequencies of the ABO genotypes and many other blood types and other polymorphisms. For example, people of unmixed Native American ancestry generally have type O blood. Since O is recessive to both A and B, this could be because their ancestors were under strong selective pressure for some characteristic either conferred by or associated with blood type O. But it's more likely an example of genetic drift, because the Native Americans probably all derive from a small number of ancestors who crossed the Bering land bridge.

Cavalli-Sforza's research team has gone far beyond the ABO blood group and calculated the frequencies of over 100 genes in 42 different populations from all around the world that have lived in their home territory since 1492. The difference between the frequency of each of the 100+ genes in one population and in any other provides a measure of the genetic distance between the two groups. The team calculated the genetic distance between each one of the 42 populations and the 41 others—a total of 861 paired-comparisons. (As an analogy, we can use longitude, latitude, and elevation above sea level [rather than 100+ gene frequencies] to measure the geographic [rather than genetic] distance between any two places on the earth. If we have longitude, latitude, and elevation [gene frequencies] for 42 places [populations], we can then calculate the geographic distance between each place [population] and the 41 others, again giving us a total of 861 paired-comparisons.)

Miele: Okay, you can measure the genetic distance between populations, but how does that produce any "races"?

Jensen: The races appear when you feed these genetic distance measures into a statistical procedure called principal components analysis (PCA), which groups the individual measures that share some common features into a smaller number of clusters, termed principal components. Psychometricians regularly use PCA to determine which mental tests in a large battery cluster together.

Cavalli-Sforza performed a PCA to see which populations would cluster together based on how far apart they were on the 100+ genetic markers. I performed the same kind of analysis on a different set of genetic distance data obtained by geneticists A. K. Roychoudhury and Masatoshi Nei. Of course, there is genetic variation within the clusters. Nevertheless, PCA does sort the various populations into genetically similar clusters. Both analyses came out with the same seven population clusters based on their degree of genetic resemblance: African, Caucasoid, Northeast Asian, Arctic Asian, Native American, Southeast Asian, and New Guinean/Australian. For the most part, so did William W. Howells's analysis of the type of cranial measurements used by classical anthropology. I've also used different types of statistical analysis. All these different methods of analysis and the different data sets to which they have been applied produce essentially the same picture, which pretty much agrees with the racial classifications of the old-time anthropologists and of the man on the street. It is highly unlikely that a "mere cultural construction" would show such consistency across time, characteristics studied, and methodology. (See Table 4.1.)

Cavalli-Sforza has graphically summarized his results by a linkage tree diagram in which the genetic distance between any two of the seven population clusters is depicted by the length of the line connecting them—the longer the line, the greater the genetic distance. (See Figure 4.1.)

As a rough analogy, suppose you could measure a number of languages in terms of the similarity of their basic vocabulary and their grammatical structure. You could then calculate the "linguistic distance" between them. A PCA would then group them into clusters of related languages. And the result would pretty much correspond to what our ears and history both tell us—that Spanish and Portuguese are closely related to each other. And they are related, but not so closely, to Italian and French, and more distantly to English, German, and even very distantly to Russian and Polish. In other words, you'd get clusters that correspond to the familiar Romance language family, Germanic language family, and Slavic language family, and that while all these families were related to each other, they showed little if any relation to many other languages of the world.

As you can see from Figure 4.1, on Cavalli-Sforza's analysis of genetic polymorphisms, the largest genetic distance lies between the cluster of African populations and all of the others. Among the non-African clusters, the largest distance is between the aboriginal New Guinean/Australian cluster and the other clusters. In Howells's analysis of cranial measurements, however, the African cluster and the New Guinean/Australian cluster lie close together. This is probably because natural selection would select for similar head shapes in sim-

TABLE 4.1   Comparison of Population Clusters or Races Produced by
Different Investigators and Methodologies

Cavalli-Sforza's Tree Diagram of Genetic Frequencies	Howells's Tree Diagram of Cranial Measurements	Jensen's PCA of Genetic Frequencies
African	African	Negroid
Australia and New Guinea	Australia and New Guinea	Australia and New Guinea
Pacific Islands	Polynesia	Pacific Islands and Southeast Asia
Southeast Asia	Southeast Asia	
Northeast Asia	Japan Northeast Asia	Mongoloid
Arctic North Asia	Eskimo, Ainu, and Guam	
Amerind	Amerind	Amerind and Eskimo
European Caucasoid Non-European Caucasoid	Caucasoid	Caucasoid

SOURCES: L. L. Cavalli-Sforza, P. Menozzi, and A. Piazza, *The history and geography of human genes* (Princeton, NJ: Princeton University Press, 1994); W. W. Howells, *Getting here: The story of human evolution* (Washington, DC: Compass Press, 1993); and A. R. Jensen, *The g factor: The science of mental ability* (Westport, CT: Praeger, 1998).

ilar climates. Hot climates select for a narrower head shape to maximize surface area and thereby maximum heat radiation to protect the brain from getting too hot; cold climates select for a more spherical head shape to minimize surface area and thereby minimize heat loss to protect the brain from getting too cold.

Miele: So that's your evidence for biological reality? Given the associations with those older ideas of distinct, Platonic types that you

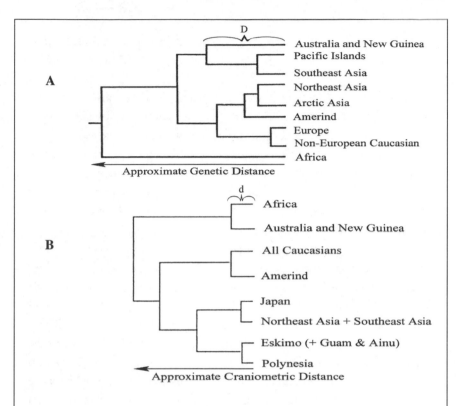

Figure 4.1 Approximate Major Population Clusters (Races) based on: (A) Cavalli-Sforza's Analysis of Genetic Polymorphisms; and (B) Howells' Analysis of Cranial Measurements.

The horizontal axis in both A and B shows the approximate genetic distance between the population clusters—the longer the horizontal line, the greater the genetic distance between the two population clusters. This implies that they separated earlier in human evolutionary history than clustersthat have less genetic distance between them. (The vertical dimension is only used to provide spacebetween the cluster names. It does not represent genetic distance or anything else.) The analyses of genes (A) and skulls (B) identify more or less the same clusters or races. One major difference is in the distance between groups and, therefore, implied time of their separation. The analysis of genetic polymorphisms (A) shows the greatest distance is between the African cluster and the Australia–New Guinea cluster (D), while the analysis of cranial measurements(B) places them close together (d). This is probably because the cranial measurements were shaped by the similar selective pressure of hot climates, rather than evidence of a recent common ancestry.

SOURCES: (A) — L. L. Cavalli-Sforza and F. Cavalli-Sforza, *The great human diasporas: The history of diversity and evolution* (Reading, MA: Addison-Wesley,1995); (B) — Howells, W. W. *getting here*: *The story of human evolution* (Washington, DC: Compass Press, 1993)

dismissed earlier, can "race" really be used in any legitimate, scientific way?

Jensen: The biologically significant point is that various human groups differ genetically. Whether you call these groups subspecies, population clusters, breeding populations, varieties, or races is only of semantic, not scientific, importance. The groups traditionally referred to as the major races differ, on average, in many genetically controlled phenotypic physical characteristics. You can find at least three or four dozen of them listed in physical anthropology textbooks.

These average differences in physical traits and genetic polymorphisms are real, and they have real-life consequences. They allow forensic specialists to identify the racial background of individuals with a high degree of accuracy. Then there is the new specialty called "racial medicine." It is based on the recognized fact of racial differences in the frequencies of certain diseases, medical conditions, birth defects, and the like. There are now a number of textbooks on the subject of racial medicine, and its findings can be critical because the optimal dosages of certain drugs differ between certain racial groups.

Miele: Okay, but you're talking mostly about blood groups and enzymes here. No one gets turned down for a job, denied housing, or discriminated against in any way based on what blood type they have. How can you make the leap from these simple genetic markers to a complex behavior like the *g* factor, which, as you explained in the previous chapter, is based on a large number of genes?

Jensen: Given that perhaps as many as 50 percent of the genes in the human genome are involved with the structural and functional aspects of the brain, it would be surprising indeed if populations that differ in a great many visible characteristics and in various genetic polymorphisms did not also differ in some characteristics associated with the brain, the primary organ of behavior. Carefully controlled

studies of infant behavior in the first days and weeks after birth have
revealed unmistakable behavioral differences between infants of
African, Asian, and Caucasian descent. So we shouldn't be surprised
if these races, or population clusters if you prefer, differ in a number
of behavioral characteristics, including abilities, both physical and
mental as well. It's as legitimate and necessary for differential psychology to study psychometric differences between these groups as it
is for forensic anthropology to study their skeletal and dental differences, geneticists to study their blood group and immunological differences, or research physicians and pharmacologists to determine
their dosage curves.

Miele: Again, the most direct and state-of-the-art evidence we have
now comes from the Human Genome Project. Maybe Robert
Plomin's research, which you described earlier [in Chapter 3], has
identified one or more genes for high IQ. But certainly no one has
found the gene for race (or population cluster). Please don't tell me
that there is a gene for being "Caucasian," "Mongoloid," "African,"
"Polynesian," or "Italian," that determines your physical traits and
genetic markers, let alone your behavior.

Jensen: Of course, there is no single gene for "race." As I've already
explained, races are defined as breeding populations that differ in the
frequencies of a number of genes— note my use of the plural.
Nearly all of these genes are present in all biologically normal members of the human species, and in many other species as well. But
many of the particular alleles that differ between different individuals of the same race also have different frequencies in the different
races. Racial differences are simply aggregated individual differences
in the allelic frequencies at a number of particular genetic loci. Only
rarely are there extreme, all-or-none, racial differences in the frequencies of any particular gene. One example is the Duffy blood
group gene, which has a frequency of about 40 percent in Europeans
and of near zero in indigenous West Africans. But an intermediate
frequency for Duffy gene is found among African Americans, which

is one of the ways genetics has confirmed what we know from history about that group's ancestry.

From the time the first Africans arrived in North America in 1619 until the present, a real but relatively low number of interracial matings have taken place that have produced a steady infusion of Caucasoid genes into the African American gene pool. Virtually all of today's African Americans have some degree of White ancestry. The average for the entire United States is around 25 percent, but it runs from as low as 10 percent in some areas of southern states, to as high as 40 percent in some northeastern and northwestern states. There has also been a smaller percentage of African genes, estimated at less than 1 percent, that have entered the White American gene pool. Similar analyses of genetic markers have helped unravel the racial origins of the peoples of the Indian subcontinent, Latin America, and other areas.

If the Human Genome Project progresses apace for the next decade or so, I expect we will find direct DNA evidence that some behavioral characteristics, including mental abilities, have a genetic basis and are correlated with race.

For more than 30 years I have made an extensive study of the nature of Black-White differences in mental abilities and their correlates with psychometric and biological variables. The most comprehensive and direct explanation for the totality of evidence is what I have termed the Default Hypothesis—both individual differences and the average Black-White difference in the g factor arise from the same genetic and environmental causes and in about the same proportions. In other words, there are no special factors that systematically depress the IQ of Blacks that do not also affect IQ in Whites. The environmental and cultural differences between Blacks and Whites explain some of the race difference in average IQ, but they cannot explain all or even most of it.

Miele: Well, now we've come to what's really been the issue all along, from Jensenism to the Bell Curve Wars. What is the evidence for your

Default Hypothesis that the mean Black-White IQ difference has any genetic, rather than purely social, economic, or cultural, cause?

Jensen: Three main lines of evidence and reasoning argue in favor of the Default Hypothesis and against any nongenetic, culture-only hypotheses:

- First, the culture-only explanations that could be tested have been, and they have been disproved.
- Second, what we know about human evolution and evolution in general makes it likely that if subspecies (or races) show physical differences, they have some behavioral differences as well.
- Finally, there is now a mass of research confirming Spearman's hypothesis that the more a test measures the g factor, the greater the Black-White difference on that test.

After some 30 years of my examining this question, I have found that the Default Hypothesis more consistently explains all of the relevant data regarding the Black-White differences in a wide variety of psychometric test data and all their real-life correlates—educational, social, and economic—than any entirely nongenetic explanation.

Miele: There are hundreds if not thousands of articles and books that say exactly the opposite. We can't examine every nongenetic or culture-only explanation for the Black-White difference in average IQ, but I'd like to present ten of the best-known, one-by-one, and have you respond with the evidence you believe disproves them.

Jensen: Go ahead.

Miele: Culture-Only Theory#1—Blacks and Whites differ significantly in their average socioeconomic status (SES), and since SES is a determinant of IQ, it explains the average Black-White IQ difference.

Jensen: Racial differences in SES cannot explain the average IQ difference. When statistical procedures are used to remove the effect of the difference in SES or when Blacks and Whites are simply matched on measures of SES, the Black-White IQ difference is reduced, but only from 15 to 12 points. And not all of that three-point reduction is due to SES, because SES differences within each racial group also have some genetic component. Therefore matching Blacks and Whites on SES to some extent also matches them genetically in terms of the *g* factor.

Miele: Culture-Only Theory #2—School facilities of Blacks are well below those of Whites.

Jensen: Educational inequality can't explain away the average IQ difference either. In the last 30 years or so many school systems have been racially integrated and now provide the same facilities and instructional programs for Blacks and Whites alike, yet the average differences of about one standard deviation in IQ and scholastic achievement remain.

Miele: Culture-Only Theory #3—IQ only measures knowledge of the "core culture" and therefore the tests are inherently biased against minorities.

Jensen: The claim that the Black-White IQ difference is a result of culturally biased tests has been disproved. A detailed explanation, which requires a working knowledge of psychometrics, is presented in my 1980 book *Bias in Mental Testing*. But you need not take my word on it. Following publication of my book, a special committee of the National Academy of Sciences and the National Research Council examined the question and reached essentially the same conclusions, which I'll try to summarize as simply as I can.

The most widely used mental tests today have the same reliability for Blacks and Whites, which means that if you give the test to a group of people and then test them again at a later date, they get about the same scores. The important point is that there is no evidence that the test scores for Blacks are unstable or erratic. Whatever the tests measure, they measure it just as reliably for Blacks as for Whites.

Mental tests also have the same predictive validity for Blacks as they have for Whites. This means that they predict other important real-life criteria, such as school grades and job performance, with the same accuracy for both groups. If you're trying to predict how well someone will do in college and they have an IQ of 125, it makes no difference whether they are Black or White, or anything else.

Tests also have the same factor structure in both groups. So if you factor analyze the test scores of either Blacks or Whites on a battery of mental tests, you will still find the g factor at the top, followed by the group factors, and then the special factors. The g factor is just as real and just as important for Blacks as it is for Whites, and indeed, for any group.

The item-to-item correlations are the same for both groups, and so is the rank order of item difficulties. Simply stated, the items that are hardest for Whites are also hardest for Blacks, and the items that are easiest for Whites are also the ones that are easiest for Blacks. This is important because it would not be true if some types of items were specially biased against Blacks—the way vocabulary items, for example, are biased against recent immigrants who are unfamiliar with English. Blacks and Whites even make the same types of errors and get fooled into picking the same distractor items in multiple-choice tests.

The evidence on each of these points is so overwhelming that no one in the field any longer argues the point.

Miele: Culture-Only Theory #4—African Americans *are* being tested in a language other than their own.

Jensen: Insufficient familiarity with standard English and the use "Black English" was a popular claim in the 1960s and '70s. But the Black-White IQ differences are as large or larger on a variety of nonverbal tests that make no use of alphanumeric symbols as on verbal tests. And children who were born deaf and hence have had virtually no exposure to spoken language do not show any deficit on nonverbal IQ tests.

Miele: Culture-Only Theory #5—Nutrition plays an important role in mental development, as does exposure to toxic chemicals and Blacks and Whites differ on these measures also.

Jensen: I've never claimed that the Black-White difference in average IQ is 100 percent genetic, only that both genetic and environmental factors are involved, just as with individual differences within each race, and probably to around the same degree. Nutritional factors do account for some part of the average racial IQ difference. Even when there is no evidence of poor nutrition, however, there is still a Black-White IQ difference.

In the Black underclass, nutrition does have a measurable effect on IQ. On a per-capita basis, prematurity and low birth weight are much more prevalent among Blacks than among Whites. The difference between mother's milk and baby formulas also makes a significant difference in the IQs of low-birth-weight infants of either race by the time they reach school age. Unfortunately, at this point in history, a smaller percentage of African American mothers breast-feed their babies. Fortunately, that's one thing that could probably be changed at relatively little cost by making the information better known in communities, Black or White, that are at highest risk for low-birth-weight babies.

Miele: Culture-Only Theory #6—Blacks and Whites differ markedly in their historical experience.

Jensen: To my knowledge, no one has demonstrated that a group's past history, independent of its earlier genetic history, affects their present-day average IQ. Some racial and ethnic minorities that historically have been victimized by discrimination and persecution, such as Jews in Europe, East Indians in Africa and in Britain, and Chinese and Japanese in the United States, actually have higher average IQs than the White or other majority population they live among.

Miele: Culture-Only Theory #7—The totality of these cultural, environmental, and nutritional factors interact step by step, from conception to adolescence, to construct our entire cognitive structure.

Jensen: This hypothesis could be tested by rearing Black children from infancy in middle-class or upper-middle-class White families. That is what was done in the Minnesota Transracial Adoption Study. The researchers compared infants with two Black parents (*BB* or Black in everyday parlance), infants with a White mother and a Black father (*WB*, or mixed race), as well as a control group of White children (*WW*), all adopted into two-parent White upper-middle-class homes. The adoptive parents were mostly college graduates with managerial and professional jobs.

All of the adoptees, Black (*BB*), mixed race (*WB*), and White (*WW*), were given IQ tests and scholastic achievement tests at age seven years and then again at age 17. When tested at age seven, average IQs for the *BB* and *WB* children were several points higher than the average for Black children reared in the same community, indicating a beneficial effect of the middle-class, White home environment on the IQ of these adoptees. By age 17, however, the average IQ for the Black adopted children was about 16 points below the White average. This is not significantly different from the national average IQ for Black youths. So even growing up in a White middle-class home did not produce a lasting reduction in the familiar one standard deviation Black-White difference in average IQ.

Miele: Culture-Only Theory #8—The lower average IQ of Americans of African ancestry is the result of racist America's "self-fulfilling prophecy" of discrimination against Blacks and even supposedly "scientific theories" about "genetic inferiority" based on the color of their skin, not the level of their g factor.

Jensen: To some extent, you can test that hypothesis as well by a more detailed analysis of the results of the Minnesota Transracial Adoption Study. The average IQ of the mixed race (*WB*) adoptees, when they were tested at age seven and again at 17, was just about halfway between the average IQs of the *WW* adoptees and of the *BB* adoptees. Yet there was no mistaking the African ancestry of the mixed-race children from their appearance. In fact, a *WB* child would probably be considered "Black" in America today, as are well-known individuals of mixed racial ancestry such as Halle Berry and Tiger Woods. It's hard to explain the intermediate position of the average IQ of the *WB* adoptees in purely environmental terms, including the consequences of societal racism, but it is what you would predict beforehand from the Default Hypothesis. The complete results of the Transracial Adoption Study showed no evidence that, by age 17, being reared from infancy in an upper-middle-class White family raised the Black adoptees' average IQ or their overall level of scholastic performance above that of Black children reared by their biological parents.

Miele: Culture-Only Theory #9—Experimental programs of intensive early cognitive intervention such as the classic "Miracle in Milwaukee" successfully increased the IQs of Black children.

Jensen: The results of these experimental attempts to raise the IQs of Black infants at risk for low IQ are quite consistent with the results of the Transracial Adoption Study. In the highly publicized Milwaukee Project, a trained staff gave Black children from poor homes intensive all-day environmental enrichment and training in mental skills from infancy to age six, at which time they entered regular public schools. The special training raised IQ scores quite markedly above those of a control group of similar children who did not receive the training. But the training did not significantly raise the scholastic achievement and other kinds of performance that are typically correlated with IQ. So the gains in test scores were "hollow" with respect to the g factor. The most likely explanation is that the results came from "teaching the test," and not really raising the level of g.

Miele: Culture-Only Theory #10—The Milwaukee Project was an early attempt at experimental cognitive intervention and naturally had its limitations. But the more recent Abecedarian Project produced lasting gains in the IQ and school achievement of at-risk Black children. So both the claim in your 1969 *HER* article that "compensatory education has been tried and apparently it has failed" and your Default Hypothesis about intelligence, race, and genetics have now been disproved.

Jensen: You're correct that the criticisms of "teaching the test" and "hollow gains" cannot be made of the more recent Abecedarian Project, which involves intensive and prolonged educational training of children at risk for low IQ. The project raised the IQ of the children who received it about five points, on average, above a control group, who did not. You're also correct that this gain still held up when the children were retested at age 15 and that it was accompanied by a comparable gain in scholastic performance. And this is all well and good. But it should also be noted that even the most intensive cognitive intervention program yet devised provided during all of the children's preschool years only reduced the national Black-White difference in average IQ by about one third (that is, 5 out of 15 IQ points). This is the best evidence we have of the extent to which improving the cognitive environment of at-risk groups can increase their IQ. The results of the Abecedarian Project in no way disprove the Default Hypothesis of genes and environment; they are fully consistent with it.

Miele: Then let's briefly run through the second line of evidence supporting your Default Hypothesis that the Black-White IQ difference has a genetic component.

Jensen: The second line of evidence looks at the question of human differences from a broad evolutionary and genetic perspective. Race differences in physical traits (like skin color, hair color and form, body build, and so on) and in biochemical and genetic traits (like blood group frequencies and DNA markers) are the result of geographic separation, adaptation to different climates, as well as any "genetic bottlenecks" they passed through as the earliest humans migrated out of Africa, eventually reaching every continent except Antarctica.

Contrary to what some would have you believe, the major races (as I defined and listed them earlier) differ, on average, in virtually every anatomical, physiological, and biochemical characteristic that also exhibits differences between individuals within any racial group. It is, therefore, highly unlikely that there would be no race differences at all in the 50 percent or more of the total human genome that is involved in brain functions, especially in those parts of the brain—the cortical areas of the cerebrum, the frontal and temporal lobes—that evolved most recently and most clearly distinguish *Homo sapiens* from all other primates.

Daniel G. Freedman's studies of Black, White, and Chinese American infants in the first days and weeks after birth show that they differ in behavior as well as in their physical appearance. All the neonates were born in the same hospital under the same obstetrical conditions. The Black babies were the most precocious in motor activity and development, the Chinese American babies took the longest to develop in this respect, and the White babies were intermediate.

Miele: That's fine for simple motor behavior. The Out-of-Africa theory of human evolution says that racial differentiation took place 100,000 or at most 200,000 years ago, long before any population developed what we would call civilization. So there simply hasn't been enough time or genetic isolation for the different races to develop significant differences in the types of things that IQ tests measure.

Jensen: From an evolutionary standpoint, there is really no question of whether races differ in virtually all physical attributes in which we find individual differences within each race. And of all physical characteristics, none has evolved so rapidly as the human brain, the physical basis of mental abilities. If 200,000 years has been enough time for the major racial groups to differentiate in their physical features, it was also enough time for some degree of racial differentiation in certain features of the brain. The existence of racial differences is not in question, only the direction and magnitude of the difference in any given trait.

Miele: That's a theoretical argument. Do you have evidence of race differences in the anatomy or physiology of the brain?

Jensen: Racial differences in average brain size are well established, as is the fact that head size, cranial capacity, and total brain size correlate with g. Head size, which provides an estimate of brain size in many older studies, correlates about +0.20 with IQ; actual brain size, as measured by volume in cubic centimeters, has a much higher correlation of about +0.40 with IQ.

Miele: You're sure of this? Gould's best-selling *Mismeasure of Man* and just about every psychology textbook dismiss this "smart people have big heads" stuff as nineteenth-century pseudoscience.

Jensen: Well, here's the evidence from the latest research. You decide which is science and which is pseudoscience. There are now at least a dozen independent studies, performed in different laboratories around the world, all published in peer-reviewed scientific journals, in which brain size was measured in living persons by magnetic resonance imaging (MRI). In almost every study brain size—total volume in cubic centimeters—was significantly correlated with IQ. The average correlation from my analysis of the ten different studies then available is about +0.40. In one study I found that head size was specifically correlated with the g factor extracted from a battery of 17 diverse tests. Furthermore, the degree to which each of the 17 tests correlated with head size within each racial group predicted the size of the average White-Black differences on these 17 tests, with a correlation of 0.51, because head size provides an estimate of g, and Black-White differences are primarily on the g factor.

Evidence from a number of independent studies of racial differences in cranial capacity and in autopsied brain volume and brain weight show approximately 100 grams difference between the average autopsied brain weights of Blacks and Whites matched for sex, age, and overall body size. Also, East Asians are found to have somewhat larger brains than European Caucasians, and their average IQ is about six points higher.

Miele: But even if IQ is directly dependent on brain size and Whites, on average, have higher IQs and bigger brains than Blacks, couldn't this be because, on average, Whites enjoy a more enriching environment? There are classic studies that show that, even among laboratory rats, an enriched environment directly influences the development of the brain.

Jensen: Research on children in the Third World who during certain critical periods in their early development have been severely deprived nutritionally—for example, by a famine—grow up to have somewhat smaller bodies and smaller heads and brains than children who did not suffer this deprivation. The vast majority of the Black population in the United States, however, has the same level of nutrition as Whites. The estimates I have seen of the largest possible effects of nutritional factors on the average IQ of American Blacks some 25 years ago was one or two IQ points, and in the poorest parts of the Deep South, possibly as much as four IQ points.

Yet the correlation between head size—and by inference, brain size—and IQ exists independently of the kinds of nutritional or other environmental differences associated with differences between families in socioeconomic status or racial origin. In a study of 14,000 full siblings, every pair of sibs reared together, I found that the sibs differed from each other in both head size and IQ, and their difference in head size correlated positively with their difference in IQ—the sib with the higher IQ, on average, having the larger head. Because it compared siblings within the same family, the correlation could not be the result of any differences between families in their SES or home environment.

The correlation between head size and IQ of siblings was found in both the White and the Black samples, each having about 7,000 individuals. There was a significant difference between the Black group and the White group in average head size and in average IQ. But when Blacks and Whites were matched for IQ, we found that they didn't differ in head size at all. Matching on IQ controls for all the brain variables related to IQ, including brain size, but matching for head size controls only some small part of all the variables that relate to IQ.

Miele: You've covered your first two lines of evidence that argue for some part of the Black-White difference in average IQ having a genetic component—the failure of culture-only theories to hold up when they have been tested, and the general evolutionary reasoning which says that if subspecies or races show physical differences, there is some behavioral difference as well. No doubt your third line of evidence relates to the *g* factor.

Jensen: Yes, it involves what I have called "Spearman's hypothesis." In his book *The Abilities of Man*, Spearman made a casual observation that the size of the average White-Black difference on ten diverse tests was directly related to his subjective impression of how much each test reflected the *g* factor—the more *g*, the greater the Black-White difference. I turned Spearman's offhand conjecture into an empirically testable hypothesis by calculating the average Black-White difference for a number of diverse mental tests, obtaining the *g* loading for each test (that is, how much each test measures *g*), and ranking the average W-B differences and the *g* loadings. If the rank order of the Black-White differences and the *g* loadings are pretty much in the same order, Spearman's hypothesis is confirmed.

I've now tested Spearman's hypothesis on 25 large independent samples and it has been confirmed on every one. It has held up for many different test batteries, and at every age level from three-year-olds to middle-aged adults. Nor did matching Blacks and Whites for SES diminish the effect. It even shows up in reaction-time tests that have different g loadings but require no cultural knowledge and can be performed in less than one or two seconds by elementary school children. Based on all these studies, the overall probability that Spearman's hypothesis is false is less than one in a billion!

Miele: I'm sure that's interesting to psychometricians, but how does it show that genes are responsible for the Black-White average difference in IQ?

Jensen: Because g is significantly related to many other variables that fall outside the realm of psychometrics and factor analysis. Some of these variables are genetic, some are anatomical and physiological, and some are occupational and social. And many have important real-life consequences.

Miele: Let's take the genetic variables first. What have you found out about g, other than the fact that the twin and kinship studies show that mental ability is to some extent heritable within each race?

Jensen: I have discovered something much more specific. The more a test measures the g factor, the higher is its heritability. In various studies that compared a diverse set of tests, their respective g loadings and heritabilities correlated between 0.60 and 0.80.

Next is the phenomenon of inbreeding depression, which we discussed earlier—the weakening or diminution of a metric trait in the offspring of parents who are closely related. [See Chapter 3.] Inbreeding depression of IQ has been found in at least 14 independent studies around the world. Inbred children born to first-cousin matings average about seven to ten IQ points lower than children born to comparable parents who are not genetically related to each other.

The connection to the g factor that you've been waiting for is that the more g-loaded the test is (that is, the more it measures g), the more inbreeding works to decrease scores on that test. For the offspring of cousin matings, the correlation between g loadings and the effect of inbreeding depression on those tests is about 0.80. The opposite of inbreeding depression—the effect known as *heterosis*, or hybrid vigor—is due to outbreeding between people whose genetic distance from one another is greater than the average genetic distance in the general population (in other words, mating between people of quite different racial ancestry). A study of the effects of outbreeding on mental abilities found the converse of the inbreeding depression studies: the larger a test's g loading, the greater the enhancing effect of heterosis on outbred children's scores on that test. I know of no environmental, cultural, or attitudinal factor that can account for these findings, but they are all not only explainable but even predictable from a genetic hypothesis. The g factor specifically reflects a large genetic component.

Miele: Then let's go on to the physiological correlates of the g factor. What are they?

Jensen: There are two kinds of physiological measurements that show a relationship to g. The first are brain-wave measurements—the amplitude and the complexity of the average evoked potential (AEP), which is the electrochemical response of the brain to a brief external stimulus, such as an audible click or a flash of light. The amplitude reflects the brain's activity level in response to the stimulus. The person being tested has a recording electrode attached to his or her scalp and doesn't have to do anything more than sit in a chair and relax while 200 clicks (or flashes) are presented in series, every two seconds. The amplitude and the complexity of the AEPs to the 200 clicks (or flashes) are averaged just as you would average 200 paper-and-pencil test scores.

Once again, the important point is that the size of the correlation between the AEP measurements and a variety of mental tests is highly predicted by the tests' g loading. High-g subjects have more complex wave-forms and a lower amplitude. If you use statistical methods to remove the effect of the g factor from the test scores, their correlation with the brain's electrical activity disappears. So the brain-wave measurements are specifically related to the g factor.

Another measure of brain physiology that has been found to be related specifically to g is the brain's glucose metabolic rate (GMR) during mental activity, such as taking an IQ test. The GMR is measured by means of a PET-scan (Positron Emission Tomography) procedure. Just as higher-IQ subjects show less amplitude of the AEP, they also show a lower GMR in response to the same test items. That is, the brain response of high-g subjects is more efficient because they require less "fuel" [that is, glucose] to do the same amount of "brain work" as a person who is lower in g.

Miele: You've mentioned the Spearman Effect, but you haven't mentioned the Flynn Effect. There is also evidence that average IQs are increasing all around the world and most of the increase is because people at the lower end of the socioeconomic spectrum have been doing better. Doesn't that show that IQ test performance is a function of the modern technological cultural complex and African Americans and Third World peoples are simply the last ones to be allowed to enter? So does the Flynn Effect trump the Spearman Effect?

Jensen: The raw scores on several widely used standardized IQ tests have been gradually rising by about the equivalent of three IQ points per decade for the past five decades. The causes of this effect are still a mystery. My hunch is that the gain in test scores over time is a combined result of four trends that have taken place in the industrialized nations over the past few decades: (1) a greater use of standardized tests and a resultant increased familiarity with test taking, (2) improvements in education and more years of schooling for more people, (3) improved nutrition and health care, and (4) advances in obstetrical practices and in inoculations of most children against the formerly common childhood diseases.

However, a PCA performed by J. P. Rushton, similar to those used for the racial classifications I described, has shown that the increase in IQ scores over time is on the tests' specific knowledge content and skills and not on the *g* factor. He found that *g* factor forms a cluster with biological factors such as inbreeding depression and heritability, but the Flynn-Effect increase in scores does not. In brief, neither a theoretical nor an empirical connection has been established between the Flynn Effect and the average Black-White IQ difference.

Miele: You've presented a great deal of evidence to support what you've termed the Default Hypothesis that both environmental and genetic factors are involved in causing the average Black-White difference in IQ and especially in *g*. Some of that evidence was also presented in *The Bell Curve*. In response to the controversy surrounding that book, the American Psychological Association appointed a special commission to look into the question. It was headed by cognitive psychologist Ulric Neisser and included Thomas Bouchard, who conducted some of the twin studies you referred to earlier; Nathan Brody, who has written the most widely used textbook on intelligence; Diane Halpern, an expert on sex differences in cognitive ability; Robert Sternberg, editor of *The Encyclopedia of Intelligence*, to which you have contributed; and several other experts.

Here are their conclusions regarding race, intelligence, and genetics:

> The mean differential between the mean intelligence test scores
> of Blacks and Whites (about one standard deviation, although
> it may be diminishing) does not result from any obvious biases
> in test construction and administration, nor does it simply
> reflect differences in socioeconomic status. Explanations based
> on factors of caste and culture may be appropriate, but so far
> have little direct empirical support. *There is certainly no such support
> for a genetic interpretation.* At present, no one knows what causes
> this difference. [The emphasis is mine.—*F.M.*]

So was the committee clueless as to all you have told me in this chapter? If not, how could a number of scholars, including noted psychometricians and hereditarians, put their names and the APA imprimatur on the conclusion I just quoted?

Jensen: I can't answer that, but I do think they should have spelled out in more detail why they think it so unlikely that genetic factors are involved, and how they would interpret, in purely environmental terms, the kinds of evidence I have presented. If they had done that, we could get a grip on their reasoning. I think they were much too cavalier in dismissing genetic factors with so little consideration.

As I read the APA statement, however, I didn't feel it was contradicting my position, but rather was merely sidestepping it. It seems more evasive of my position than contradictory. The committee did acknowledge the factual status of what I have termed the Spearman Effect, the reality of g, the inadequacy of test bias and socioeconomic status as causal explanations, and many other conclusions that don't differ at all from my own position. Remember, it was the report of a committee, so I suspect the joint statement went about as far as they all were willing to agree or would commit themselves to regarding this socially and politically sensitive issue. Considering that the report was commissioned by the APA, I was surprised it went as far as it did. Viewed in that light, I am not especially displeased by it.

Miele: Then let me read you one more quotation:

> With the encouragement of Christianity, people had disseminated the doctrine of the equality of all men. Gypsies, Hottentots, Botocudos, and Teutons are all said to be equal. Unfortunately Nature . . . teaches us otherwise—there are higher and lower races. To equate that racial hotchpotch, the Chandalas, with the Aryans, those human aristocrats, is to commit a crime against mankind, for to attain higher development, mankind needs leaders as well as leading nations. Of all the races on this earth, it is the Teutonic . . . which is called upon to play that leading role.

That's not from the APA, but from the *Völkischer Beobachter,* the Nazi party newspaper. Some people would say that everything you've told me in this chapter is nothing but the old, disproven, and dangerous idea of an immutable, eternal hierarchy of races, simply recycled with contemporary references and repackaged in more palatable terminology. Any comment?

Jensen: I haven't said a word about any "hierarchy of races," "higher and lower races," "aristocrats," or a "master race." Those concepts are nonsense in terms of what we know about racial variation. Racial differences are not at all unidimensional or unidirectional, and it's meaningless to speak of a difference without specifying a particular dimension, characteristic, or trait. What I've investigated is the distribution of individual differences in one particular dimension, namely the *g* factor, both within groups and between groups, and their probable genetic and environmental causes. How is that scientifically different from looking at the distribution of height, blood pressure, visual acuity, or any other metric characteristic in those or other groups, and inquiring about environmental and genetic factors influencing those variables?

Your quotation from the Nazi party newspaper reflects a typological, essentialist view of individuals and races as distinct Platonic types—an outmoded view that has long been known to be wrong. There is no single gene that causes "black" skin, a mean IQ of 85, dark hair, or hypertension; nor is there any other single gene that causes "white" skin, a mean IQ of 100, blond hair, and myopia. Each of these particular phenotypes is separately the result of a number of genes, and their effects become manifest during the course of development, with environmental factors certainly playing a role. The statistical correlations among these variables at this point in time doesn't determine their possible distribution and statistical correlations at some future point in time. If we had, say, ten generations of racial interbreeding, all these statistical associations would diminish to the point that we'd simply be talking about individual differences.

Moreover, I never said anything about preserving the genetic "purity" of any race or group. Rather, I explained in some detail the negative effects of inbreeding and the positive effects of outbreeding both on physical measurements and on IQ. And I also explained why they provide some of the best evidence for the influence of genetic factors on those traits within each group and for genes playing a part in the difference between groups.

As to the implied charge of racism or neo-Nazism, I absolutely disavow any association whatsoever between my views and those you quoted from that Nazi party newspaper. I have always rejected that kind of thinking, ever since I was a child, and so did my parents and all my other relatives. So I hope we can turn to the important question of why the scientific issue of average race differences in mental ability has been so badly misrepresented not only by the popular media but even by some in the scientific community. We need to discuss how society can best use scientific information in formulating public policy.

Miele: Then we shall in the next chapter.

Further Reading

The literature on the concept of race is so voluminous that only the most directly relevant books and articles can be cited here. For a complete and technically detailed discussion of the evidence and arguments Jensen presents in this chapter, see: Jensen, A. R. (1998). *The g factor: The science of mental ability.* Westport, CT: Praeger (especially chapter 11, Population differences in *g*, and chapter 12, Population differences in *g*: Causal hypotheses).

I have summarized the history of the nature-nurture debate and its relation to the race-IQ question in: Miele, F. (2001). The shadow of Caliban: an introduction to the tempestuous history of anthropology. *Skeptic*, 9 (1), 22–35. The 1998 Statement on Race by the American Anthropological Association was reported in a number of newspapers, my own source being: *The San Francisco Chronicle* (1998). (23 February), A1. The argument that race is a social construction rather than a biological reality is made most strongly by: Smedley, A. R. (1999). *Race in North America: Origin and evolution of a worldview.* (2nd Ed.) Boulder, CO: Westview. The diametrically opposite view that race is an extremely important concept in explaining not only intelligence and brain size but over 60 other variables including neonate behavior, speed of maturation and longevity, personality and temperament, family stability and crime, sexual behavior and fertility is summarized in: Rushton, J. P. (2000). *Race, evolution, and behavior: A life history perspective* (2nd special abridged edition). Port Huron, MI: Charles Darwin Research Institute; and is presented in depth in: Rushton, J. P. (2000). *Race, evolution, and behavior: A life history perspective* (3rd unabridged edition). Port Huron, MI: Charles Darwin Research Institute. The definition of races as "fuzzy sets" appears in: Sarich, V. M. (1995). In defense of the bell curve: The reality of race and the importance of human diversity. *Skeptic, 3* (3), 84–93. Although it was published more than 25 years ago, the following is worth consulting for its breadth and evenhandedness in covering this contentious issue: Loehlin, J. C., Lindzey, G., and Spuhler, J. N. (1975). *Race differences in intelligence.* San Francisco: W. H. Freeman.

The tome on genetic polymorphisms in human populations is: Cavalli-Sforza, L. L., Menozzi, P., and Piazza, A. (1994). *The geography of human genes.* Princeton: Princeton University Press. It is summarized for the layman, along with a criticism of Jensen and Jensenism, in: Cavalli-Sforza, L. L., and Cavalli-Sforza, F. (1996). *The great human diasporas: The history of diversity and evolution.* Reading, MA: Addison Wesley.

The issue of test bias was explicated in all its psychometric detail in: Jensen, A. R. (1980). *Bias in mental testing.* New York: Free Press. His findings were largely confirmed in: Wigdor, A. K., and Garner, W. R. (Eds.) (1982). *National Academy of Science report: Ability testing: uses, consequences, and controversies.* Washington, DC: National Academy Press.

The study of race differences in infant behavior is: Freedman, D. C., and Freedman, N. C. (1969). Behavioral differences between Chinese-American and European-American newborns. *Nature, 224,* 1227.

The report issued by the American Psychological Association on the race-IQ question in response to *The Bell Curve* is: Neisser, U., et al. (1996). Intelligence: Knowns and unknowns. *American Psychologist, 51,* 77–101.

For more information on these subjects, see the bibliography of Jensen's publications in Appendix A.

5

FROM JENSENISM
TO THE BELL CURVE WARS

Science, Pseudoscience, and Politics

In this chapter our conversation moves from the science of the race-IQ issue to the larger political issues that lurk behind it and make it so inflammatory. I cite the contradiction between Jefferson's words in the Declaration of Independence that "all men are created equal" and his derogatory statements about the mental ability of Blacks in his *Notes on Virginia,* as well as similar remarks made by American presidents from the Great Emancipator, Abraham Lincoln, to Richard Nixon, who assigned his staff to report to him on Jensen's famous *HER* article. When I offer these as evidence that anti-Black racism has been central to American political history, Jensen responds that such statements have no scientific value, nor should they prevent science from looking into the subject. In fact, he says, the only intelligent way to resolve the age-old conflicting theories of human nature that are an integral part of politics, religion, and philosophy is through behavioral science.

Jensen's defense of academic freedom and scientific inquiry leads to a discussion about the controversial Pioneer Fund, the small foundation that has supported hereditarian research, including Jensen's. I ask Jensen to respond to the charges by two of his and the Pioneer Fund's severest critics. Psychologist Jerry Hirsch, who, ironically, had studied genetics with UC Berkeley geneticist Everett Dempster, as did Jensen, and like Jensen, is a member of the Behavior Genetics Association, described Jensen as a "charlatan" and his work as "science without scholarship." Barry Mehler, who worked with Hirsch, charged that from its very beginning the Pioneer Fund not only supported "race science" but helped fuel race conflict in the United States.

Mehler also claimed that Jensen was "recruited" for the Pioneer Fund by the late William Shockley. Shockley had shared the 1956 Nobel Prize in Physics with John Bardeen and William Brattain, his coworkers at Bell Labs, for the development of the transistor. Then in 1965 *U.S. News & World Report* published an interview with Shockley entitled "Is the Quality of the U.S. Population Declining?" in which he drew attention not only to the Black-White difference in average IQ but also to the higher birthrate among Americans with lower IQ, even more prevalent among Blacks than among Whites. Shockley also suggested possible corrective policies including elite-contributor sperm banks (he and three other Nobel laureates would later contribute to one such bank set up in California) and what he called a "thinking exercise." He proposed that, as an alternative to the existing welfare system, society consider a Voluntary Sterilization Bonus Plan under which low-IQ non-taxpayers who agreed to be sterilized would have the sum of $1,000 per IQ point below 100 paid into a trust account on their behalf. (Shockley emphasized both the heuristic nature of the plan and its restriction to non-taxpayers.) Coupled with his contentious style in debates and lectures, these proposals made Shockley an increasingly controversial figure on college campuses in the late 1960s and early '70s.

Jensen emphatically dismisses the statements by Hirsch and Mehler as ad hominem vituperation and contends that those who have valid, scientific criticism of his work should submit their critiques to the appropriate peer-reviewed journals. When they have done so, Jensen has replied.

Jensen commends the relatively small Pioneer Fund for having the intellectual courage to support psychometric research on the nature of intelligence, and behavior genetic studies of individual and group differences in ability (especially the race-IQ question), which government and large private foundations have been afraid to touch. Jensen has received grants from other foundations and government agencies during his career and has reviewed articles for leading journals, and he says the Pioneer Fund's review process is just as thorough. Indeed, he says, Pioneer follows a "no strings attached" policy, which many other foundations or government agencies do not.

We also discuss the question of why, if the evidence in its favor is as strong as Jensen says it is, Jensenism is often treated as "fringe science," like creationism or homeopathic medicine. Jensen totally rejects that characterization, countering that Jensenism is regarded as mainstream science by experts in the relevant disciplines. As evidence, he cites Snyderman and Rothman's survey of the members of the Behavior Genetics Association (BGA) and of the American Psychological Association's (APA) Division 5—Tests and Measurement (each APA division being composed of specialists in that area), and a statement by 50 behavioral scientists printed in the *Wall Street Journal* (which has not, on the whole, given favorable coverage to Jensenism) under the headline "Mainstream Science on Intelligence." If that is so, I ask, why have organizations such as BGA, APA Division 5, and the Educational Testing Service (ETS) remained silent?

While critical of most mass media coverage of the issue, Jensen has the highest praise for the presentations by some of the "quick studies" who have interviewed him—Joseph Alsop, Lee Edson (*The New York Times Magazine*), Morton Hunt (*Playboy*), Dan Seligman (*Fortune*), and Mike Wallace (for two episodes of CBS's *60 Minutes*). But, Jensen says, media pieces should not and cannot decide what is scientifically correct. What is important is that readers and viewers understand how behavioral scientists approach such questions.

Miele: The Declaration of Independence says "all men are created equal" and "endowed by their Creator with certain unalienable Rights." Though the Declaration carries no binding legal weight, it has been an inspiration to the abolitionist, suffragist, and civil rights movements, and even the UNESCO Declaration of Rights. The U.S. Constitution, on the other hand, which is the supreme law of the land, contains no such words and severely restricted those it originally defined as citizens—women were not guarantanteed the vote, slavery was accepted, the Native Americans were pretty much written off, and so on.

So from the very first, hasn't there been a tension, indeed a contradiction, between what we preach about human rights and what we practice based on our beliefs about human nature?

Jensen: Yes, of course, there have been tensions, contradictions, ambivalence, and outright disagreements about the nature of human nature throughout history, not just American history. This is why it is so important for science to get into the picture, to try to find out what is and isn't true about apparently conflicting notions of human nature. This is the task of the behavioral and biological sciences. The job is uphill, not only because of the strictly scientific problems, but also because of the entrenched beliefs and prejudices from the past. If our faith in science is too weak to overcome these obstacles, we might as well give up, because there is no other means for obtaining reliable knowledge.

Miele: Well, contrast those oft-quoted words of Jefferson, a slave owner, in the Declaration with these much less often quoted words from his *Notes on Virginia:*

> Comparing them [Blacks] by their faculties of memory, reason, and imagination, it appears to me that in memory they are equal to the whites; in reason much inferior, as I think one could scarcely be found capable of tracing and comprehending the investigations of Euclid; and that in imagination they are dull, tasteless, and anomalous.

Abraham Lincoln, the Great Emancipator, in his 1858 debates with Stephen Douglas, declared:

> there is a physical difference between the white and Black races which I believe will forever forbid the two races living together on terms of social and political equality. And inasmuch as they cannot so live, while they do remain together there must be the position of superior and inferior, and I as much as any other

man am in favor of having the superior position assigned to the white race.

Theodore Roosevelt, hero of the Progressive Era in American politics, said, "The Negro, for instance, has been kept down as much by his lack of intellectual development as anything else," and "in the mass, the Negro [is] altogether inferior to whites."

According to John Ehrlichman, Richard Nixon told him that he believed that America's Blacks could only marginally benefit from federal programs because they were genetically inferior to Whites. All the federal money and programs we could devise could not change that fact. Though he believed that Blacks could never achieve parity in intelligence, economic success, or social qualities, we should still do what we could for them, within reasonable limits, because it was "right" to do so.

Don't quotes like that prove that anti-Black racism is as American as apple pie?

Jensen: Your examples and quotations are political history, and are interesting from that standpoint. But they have no scientific value and so hold no fascination for me at all. There are many scientific subjects that incur this kind of liability. Darwin feared the consequences of publishing his theory of evolution by natural selection, but in his day this liability came from religion rather than politics.

My own interest is not at all political, but if anyone thinks there are political overtones in any of my work, I hope they take the trouble to understand me correctly. I myself don't feel inclined or properly qualified to think through what others may consider the "politics" of my work.

Miele: The most recent incarnation of Jensenism has been *The Bell Curve* wars. That book was co-authored by the late Richard Herrnstein and Charles Murray, who has served as a domestic policy advisor for the Reagan administration and for Republican and conservative politicians. Don't the critics who claim Jensenism and

The Bell Curve undermine public support for progressive or egalitarian programs have a point?

Jensen: It's debatable whether these academic issues actually undermine or even influence public actions. I wish there were some way of knowing. However, it should be a realistic concern for such critics if "progressive" and "egalitarian" social programs, to use your words, are actually contradicted by solid evidence. Good intentions must be backed up by evidence that the prescribed means for achieving them actually work.

The marked individual differences and average race and sex differences in abilities are real and important in relation to education, employment, and other social and economic variables. It is presently not within our power to materially reduce these differences by purely psychological or educational means, or any other means yet known. If so-called progressive programs depend on the egalitarian notion that such differences are only a superficial effect of unequal social privilege or lack of opportunity and can be changed easily by psychological and educational interventions or measures such as Affirmative Action, they are in conflict with the evidence and need to be seriously reconsidered.

Miele: Well, those who argue for the political implications, if not inherent nature, of your work and similar research by behavioral scientists always point out that it has been generously supported by the Pioneer Fund. What is the Pioneer Fund?

Jensen: It's a small foundation as compared with a great many others, such as the Ford, Rockefeller, Carnegie, Guggenheim, and Mellon Foundations, for example. Its area of interest is mainly research in differential psychology, or the study of individual and various group differences in behavioral traits relevant to education, employment, and other socially significant aspects of the human condition, such as population growth, immigration, welfare dependency, delinquency, and crime. I believe it has supported research projects in all these areas. It accepts and reviews grant proposals from anyone who submits them, and it also invites established scholars to submit research proposals in any of these areas. The research typically concerns the basic science relevant to the study of human variation, such as psychometrics, behavioral genetics, and cognitive abilities. For a small foundation, its record of accomplishments is remarkable. It has a high batting average for sponsoring research that has had high impact in the field.

Miele: Do you have any second thoughts, misgivings, or qualms about accepting Pioneer Fund support, for this or any other work you've been involved in?

Jensen: Not in the least. I have had many grants from various federal agencies and private foundations, and I can say that the Pioneer Fund's grants have never had any strings attached, as have grants made by some funding sources. The Pioneer Fund's support of research on the genetics of intelligence and particularly on the subject of racial differences in educationally and socially important human traits is the only basis I have been able to find for the criticisms I have seen made of the Pioneer Fund. It has been willing to support research on socially sensitive issues at a time when few, if any, other agencies were willing to fund such research. The name "Pioneer" is indeed very apt.

Miele: Are you familiar with all the work the Pioneer Fund has supported and do you have any concerns or criticisms of any of it?

Jensen: No, I haven't made a study of all the research sponsored by Pioneer. That would virtually preclude doing my own work. But I am very familiar with studies they have sponsored that are related to my own research, naturally. I judge each piece of research on its own merits, and of course one can often find points in the work of others and in one's own work that can be criticized in some respect. Analysis, search, skepticism, and criticism are all part of the scientific enterprise. No research is exempt from such scrutiny, regardless of who funded it. As a member of the editorial boards of five psychological journals during the past 35 years, I have critically reviewed hundreds of articles submitted to these journals. I have seen no reason to believe that the standard met by Pioneer-funded research differs significantly from that sponsored by other private foundations or federal granting agencies.

Miele: One of the Pioneer Fund's principal critics, Barry Mehler, has charged that it has funded academics whose work on "genetically based race differences" could be used in support of eugenics and to oppose integration and immigration and to support other right-wing causes. In a backhanded acknowledgment that its impact far exceeded its size or the size of its grants, he credits the Pioneer Fund with "being at the cutting edge of almost every race conflict in the United States since its founding in 1937."

Any comment?

Jensen: The notion that the Pioneer Fund has had anything at all to do with race conflict in the United States or anywhere else is utterly ridiculous as well as totally false. The rhetoric of the passage you quoted sounds as if it was crafted to be as defamatory as possible. I used to see a lot of such rhetoric directed at me personally, in pamphlets and placards produced by demonstrators from various radical student groups in the 1970s, most of them now defunct. That quotation is of the very same ilk.

Miele: In the same article, Mehler says that your *HER* article claimed that because Black children had an average IQ of 85, no amount of compensatory education could improve their performance. And that since you were "recruited" for the Pioneer Fund by William Shockley, the Fund has provided you with more than a million dollars in grants over the past three decades.

Jensen: That is so exaggerated and full of falsehoods and inaccuracies that it would be otiose to give a detailed critique. If anyone has legitimate scientific criticisms of my research, they should submit them to the same respectable peer-reviewed journals in which my research appeared. Many scholars have done this, either on their own initiative or by an editor's invitation, and, as is the custom, I have been allowed to reply in the same journal. That is the way of science. The intemperate and slanderous propaganda pieces masquerading as criticism that you have mentioned are something else again, and are worthy of contempt from the scientific community.

Miele: Mehler began criticizing you and the Pioneer Fund as part of Jerry Hirsch's program studying "Academic Racism." Like you, Hirsch is a psychologist who then became interested in behavior genetics. In fact, he told me at a meeting of the Behavior Genetics Association that both of you had studied the subject with Everett Dempster of the University of California Berkeley genetics department.

Having started from the same research question at the same point in time, how and why do you think you and Hirsch arrived at such opposite and adversarial positions that he felt compelled to write papers entitled "To Unfrock the Charlatans" and "Jensenism: The Bankruptcy of 'Science' Without Scholarship."

Jensen: I have no way of fathoming Hirsch's attitudes and actions, and I doubt that it would be worthwhile for me to attempt to do so.

Miele: Well, how about his use of the term "charlatan"?

Jensen: It's just more of the purely ad hominem vituperation I just described.

Miele: While Stephen Jay Gould did not indulge in any such personal attacks, he did strongly attack all three tenets of Jensenism—the existence of the g factor, the heritability of differences in g, and especially that part of the cause of the Black-White IQ difference is genetic.

The Mismeasure of Man won more awards and sold a lot more copies than *The g Factor*. Even if you combine the sales of all the books written for a general audience that take a more or less "Jensenist" point of view—such as your own *Straight Talk About Mental Tests* (which is out of print) Dan Seligman's *A Question of Intelligence*, and Hans Eysenck's posthumously published *Intelligence: A New Look*—they've sold nowhere near as many copies. I'd like your evaluation of the impact and scientific merit of *The Mismeasure of Man*.

Jensen: I wrote a lengthy review of the book, titled "Debunking Scientific Fossils and Straw Persons." Gould's *Mismeasure of Man* is engaging and entertaining, but virtually worthless as scholarship, and it has almost nothing to do with the current picture in the study of human mental abilities. Gould was an excellent writer, and I was sorry that he applied his talents to producing such a misleading book.

The Mismeasure of Man did receive the accolades in the popular media and among the literati you mentioned, but mine was not the only critical review. The book was also panned in the specialist journals by reviewers with a technical background in psychometrics and behavioral genetics. Gould claimed that the *g* factor, which he called the "rotten core" of Jensenism, is a chimera, a fantasy, just an artifact of psychometrics and factor analysis. This argument is thoroughly refuted by the evidence of the biological reality of *g*, which I present in detail in *The g Factor* and which I summarized in our earlier discussions. [See Chapters 2, 3, and 4.]

Outside the sphere of psychometrics and differential psychology, my attitude toward Gould was largely positive. I admired and supported his battle against creationist efforts to demote Darwinian thinking in high school biology courses and textbooks. When it comes to human variation in psychological or behavioral traits, however, Gould himself seemed to be a creationist rather than an evolutionist. I regard differential psychology as a branch of human biology, and I would have hoped that that Gould did also. Too bad he never wrote an autobiography, which might have explained the origins of his antipathy toward psychometrics, the *g* factor, and their relevance to advancing the scientific study of human differences. That would have been most interesting.

Miele: But in most social science texts Jensenism is likened to creationism or flat-earthism. Are you telling me that there's some Inquisition going on to stamp out the Jensenist heresy?

Jensen: To liken the behavior-genetic view of human variability and *g* theory to creationism or anything like that is of course ridiculous. I can't think of any biologically oriented psychologist who is actually informed on the issues connecting biology to psychometrics, individual differences, and genetics who would believe that.

Some people may fear there is a kind of inquisition going on. For new Ph.D.s, the inquisition against the so-called hereditarian position is perceived as consisting of narrowing the range of their employment opportunities—particularly in college teaching. Mid-career psychologists are concerned about prospects for promotion and rising in the profession via being elected to offices in their professional organization, being appointed to influential committees, getting research grants, and winning awards. There's no doubt this happens.

Miele: Can you give me specifics, naming names, of any serious scholars having a problem publishing competent articles in the best peer-reviewed journals today?

Jensen: I won't name names, because that would require my getting permission from the named persons and would also violate the confidential nature of my role as a journal referee. I presently serve on the editorial boards of four psychological journals and am frequently a consulting editor for at least half a dozen more. I actually don't know of a case within the past two or three years where a technically competent article that is considered controversial because it dealt with racial differences in mental abilities has been denied publication in a reputable journal on spurious grounds. However, there is no doubt that a double standard of review still exists; articles dealing with the race-IQ-genetics nexus when the results have not come out in the politically correct direction have to pass a much more critical review process than if the results were in the opposite direction.

However, I will give examples from my own publishing experiences in the 1970s and 1980s. One quite key article submitted to an APA journal, for example, showed a racial difference on certain tests that was practically impossible to explain in terms of culture bias or any other environmental or motivational factors anyone could think of. The study was technically impeccable. But the review process took about three times as long as usual for that journal. The editor eventually accepted the article as is, and apologized for the long delay, which resulted from the fact that the article had to be sent to seven reviewers rather than the usual three in order to get three real reviews of the paper itself. The other four supposed reviews were merely ad hominem diatribes; the editor said it would be too embarrassing to the journal for me to be allowed to see them.

My first article on Spearman's hypothesis was also submitted to the APA's house journal, which claims to take no more than ten weeks to make an editorial decision on unsolicited manuscripts. They took eleven months with my manuscript, and responded only after I had written to them asking for a decision. Though two of the referees wrote highly favorable comments on the article, the third one did a hatchet job on it, making utterly trivial criticisms, and the editor rejected the article without option to resubmit. I figured it must have taken the editor about ten months to find someone willing to provide the trivial and spurious reasons for rejection. I have saved this whole correspondence as of possible historical interest, because it is such prima facie evidence of bias by APA's house journal. The article was then submitted to *Behavioral and Brain Sciences* (1985), was critically reviewed by no fewer than 11 referees, and was accepted and published along with commentaries by 30 experts in the relevant fields. I received over 1,500 reprint requests for that article, and it has been highly cited. I could easily go on and on with other examples from my own experience, but they are much the same. I am glad to say that I have seen considerably less of this sort of thing within the last few years.

Miele: The anti-Jensenist position is presented in workshops for teachers by the National Educational Association (NEA) and similar groups. Are they afraid of losing government funds if the public starts to believe that education is not omnipotent?

Never afraid to challenge sacred cows, here Jensen in New Delhi, India, feeds some. (Fall 1980)

Jensen: I know too little about the NEA's leadership and their motivation to make any informed comment. But I do know that after the publication of my book *Bias in Mental Testing*, the NEA sponsored lectures and workshops that denounced my book and promoted the notion that IQ and scholastic aptitude tests are culturally biased against Blacks and certain other minorities in the school population. This has been the politically correct position, and perhaps the NEA is merely following that line on all the issues in its purview.

Miele: Well, do you think the race-IQ question should be studied and discussed in high school or introductory college courses at all or should it be left for upper-division college and graduate classes?

Jensen: It shouldn't be explicitly made a topic for silence in high school or lower-division courses in college, but students should be told that a proper understanding of the issues depends upon a good deal of prior background in some of the technical aspects of psychology. You can only discuss these matters before an uninformed group the limited way you could discuss, say, quantum mechanics in front of a group with no background in physics and math. For stu-

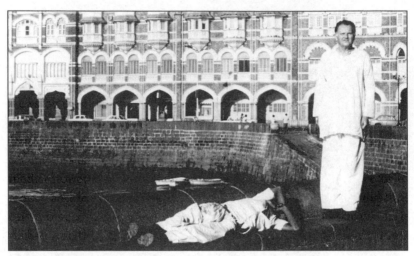

Dressed in a kurta, *Jensen stands in front of the Taj Mahal Hotel in Bombay, India, while on a 33-lecture tour of Indian universities. (December 1980)*

dents without sufficient background, time is better spent providing the background knowledge long before ever getting into its application to the race-IQ issue. But there's also no need to tell beginning psychology students things that are not true.

Regardless of the subject, I don't like to tell students bare facts or conclusions without their having knowledge of the kinds of evidence and reasoning required either to support or to disconfirm a particular hypothesis. Scientific psychology is best taught in terms of empirical hypothesis testing. Students should know clearly the hypothesis, the methods for testing it, and the results of the test. Without those minimum requirements, they are left with no real knowledge of the subject, only prejudices on whichever side of the issue.

Miele: Do you think students could handle the subject or would even want to listen?

Jensen: Absolutely, provided they are given the background information necessary to understand it. College freshmen and sophomores are very eager to learn more about things discussed by the media. One year while teaching at Berkeley I had heard some things from a couple of students who were taking an introductory psychology course that led me to suspect their class was being ill informed by the instructor on such things as the nature of intelligence, and the evidence for its heritability. Based on their input, I complained to the department and it resulted in my being invited to give the lectures for the unit specifically dealing with the genetics of IQ. What impressed me most was the level of interest in this subject and the open-mindedness and high quality of the questions that were asked. Interestingly, students were most interested in the subject of assortative mating (the tendency of like to mate with like), its degree in human matings, and its genetic and psychological consequences for the population at large.

In my last year of teaching at Berkeley, I had a freshman class in an introductory course. I was again struck by the students' open-mindedness and spontaneity in asking intelligent questions about virtually every aspect of the IQ controversy. It seemed very different from the doctrinaire and opinionated attitudes of the students I encountered 20 or 25 years earlier. I believe that students today, provided they haven't been in college too long or haven't taken many courses in the social sciences, are more curious and fair-minded than were students of an earlier generation.

Miele: Earlier we discussed the special APA committee report on *The Bell Curve*. I believe there were earlier APA resolutions that circulated around APA about your *HER* article and the whole issue of Jensenism. What's your opinion of the APA, specifically Division 5, Testing and Measurement?

Jensen: My *HER* article was harshly denounced by one Division of the APA called the Society for the Psychological Study of Social Issues (SPSSI) in the APA's house journal, *American Psychologist*, which also published my reply to this quite inept critique. My complaint with APA's Division 5, which represents psychological measurement and quantitative psychology, is that they never, or hardly ever, defend this branch of psychology against those who criticize it. As far as I'm aware, for example, only two members of Division 5, Lloyd Humphreys and myself, ever published a critique of Gould's *Mismeasure of Man*, which attacked not only Jensenism but psychological testing and measurement in general. And our critiques were not published in any journal controlled by Division 5. Too many measurement psychologists have, in my opinion, been negligent in defending their own field against attacks by patently incompetent critics from outside the field and ideologues who oppose the whole idea of studying human variation in behavioral traits. Most academicians, of course, speak up on controversial issues only after they are no longer controversial. If it weren't so disheartening, it would be amusing to see so many of them run for cover when threatened by ideological criticism.

Miele: Well, perhaps the Behavior Genetics Association has been more willing to take up the race-IQ issue?

Jensen: Not only has it not done so, it has conspicuously avoided doing so. Don't ask me why. I don't really know; you'll have to ask them. One speculation that is common, and probably true to a large extent, is that getting into the race-IQ issue in terms of genetics would threaten one's receiving research grants from federal agencies, and many behavioral geneticists' research is supported by federal grants. It would be a true loss if support for this research, which is generally excellent and essential for advancing the science, were cut off. The appropriations to the federal granting agencies are controlled by Congress, which is, of course, a political body. So when it comes to much of the scientific research done in the United States, politics rules. And some research topics are more at the mercy of Political Correctness than others. There are also more subtle personal reasons for distancing oneself from viewing the race question in a genetic context. Anyone who does so risks getting called a racist and is often misunderstood and even shunned by friends or colleagues. It puts one in a difficult position socially and professionally, which not everyone can tolerate. I myself don't like it, but I sometimes wonder why I seem to tolerate it. I believe one has to have relatively little need to be liked. I suppose it's a kind of eccentricity to be willing to risk strong disapproval.

Miele: The Snyderman and Rothman poll of APA Division 5 and BGA members, which we discussed earlier, found that the majority agreed with the three tenets of Jensenism. [See Chapter 1.] Why haven't they come out with resolutions to that effect?

Jensen: Personally, I don't think that a scientific organization as such should pronounce resolutions and the like dealing with questions of a substantive and empirical nature. In science these questions are not answered by a show of hands.

However, self-selected individuals or research teams should be free to publish their analyses and conclusions about a book such as *The Bell Curve*. This has been happening to some extent, although most of the critiques of *The Bell Curve* are pretty pathetic from a scientific standpoint. You may know that some 50 experts in the branches of the behavioral sciences most relevant to the subject matter of *The Bell Curve* published a statement in the *Wall Street Journal* called "Mainstream Science on Intelligence." It contained a list of 25 points that they regard as scientifically well established and most generally accepted involving the basic issues involved in the controversy surrounding *The Bell Curve*. Your readers might well appreciate having this list, as an appendix to this book. I think it would be worth including, as I was among those who signed that statement. [See Appendix B.]

Miele: The organization with the greatest stake in the reality and importance of g is the Educational Testing Service. Has ETS made any official statement concerning your work, either on g or in behavior genetics, or on Jensenism and *The Bell Curve* wars?

Jensen: None at all, as far as I know. However, ETS did sponsor a two-day Spearman Symposium at the University of Plymouth,

England, and I was invited to give the opening Spearman Lecture. I talked about Spearman's hypothesis that the Black-White difference on various psychometric tests is directly related to how well each test measures the *g* factor. [See Chapter 4.]

The race question, however, is not a research topic at ETS. Their research mission lies strictly within the realm of ensuring the reliability, validity, and fairness of their tests. They have no reason to do research on the genetics of mental ability or to make pronouncements about it.

ETS concentrates its efforts on developing the best tests possible for predicting scholastic performance. They have long employed some of the world's top experts in psychometrics who have done important research on detecting and eliminating cultural bias from tests. Their tests stand up well for the claims that ETS makes for them.

Miele: Let's turn to book publishing. *The Bell Curve*, no matter what the mass media may have said about it, was a best-seller and a commercial success. How do you think the success and controversy of *The Bell Curve* affected the publication, sales, or media coverage of your book, *The g Factor?* Please be specific. Did the fact that Chris Brand, a controversial figure for a number of reasons, came out with a book with the same title somewhat earlier, sour people on the "*g* factor" in general?

Jensen: I think *The Bell Curve* had a salutary effect in bringing the scientific issues before a large segment of the American public, regardless of one's agreement or disagreement with the public policy ideas in its final chapter. *The Bell Curve* gave general currency to Spearman's concept of the *g* factor. But there were many scientifically uninformed people in the book-publishing world who were easily led to believe that *The Bell Curve* was wholly unsound scientifically. So when I discussed the prospects of my book *The g Factor* with the psychology editors of several large publishing firms, including one that had published *The Bell Curve* as well as two of my earlier books (*Bias in Mental*

Testing and *Straight Talk About Mental Tests*), I discovered an unusual wariness about anything having to do with the *g* factor. One editor told me his firm regarded *The Bell Curve* as pseudoscience and said they would have no interest in a book that was consonant with the psychometric and substantive aspects of *The Bell Curve*.

The psychology editor at another large publishing house, who read most of the manuscript of my book, was quite enthusiastic about it. The same firm first published and then withdrew a book also titled *The g Factor* by Christopher Brand, a well-known psychologist at Edinburgh University, which was already in print and about to go on the market. A demonstration by dissident students and a bad press provoked by Brand's press conference caused the publisher to de-publish Brand's book immediately. The publishers said they found Brand's book "repugnant" (their exact word), although they were never willing to state specifically what they considered repugnant about it. About two weeks later, the manuscript of my book with the same title, *The g Factor*, was returned to me via Federal Express with a brief letter from the editor saying they decided this wasn't the right kind of book for them to publish. I immediately sent the manuscript off to another publisher, who kept it for about five months and then returned it, without a letter, totally without any comment at all. Finally, my book was accepted and published, after rejection by eight other publishers. This would be of no interest if it were a crummy or incompetent piece of work, but the experts in this field who were asked by the publishers to review the manuscript expressed highly favorable opinions of it and urged publication.

The reviews of *The g Factor* in the professional journals so far have been highly favorable. I think it was the two chapters (out of 14) that discussed racial differences in *g* that caused so many publishers to decide against acceptance. My experience, however, was not unique. I know of two publishers that were willing to relinquish a huge advance on royalties for solicited and contracted books when they found that they touched on racial differences, even in the most minor way. It has been my experience that if a book doesn't denounce or completely dismiss the idea that genetics may have anything to do with racial differences in any behavioral trait, especially intelligence, most publishers will not touch it.

Miele: Let's discuss the gatekeepers of the zeitgeist—the mass media. Your *HER* article got a rather good treatment by *The New York Times Magazine. The Bell Curve* received good coverage in *Newsweek* and *Forbes. Skeptic,* for which I write, devoted part of two issues to *The Bell Curve* controversy, much of the coverage unfavorable, but not all of it.

So is there really a special hostility on the part of the mass media to Jensenism, or is it just getting mixed treatment, depending on who is doing the story and where it's being published, just like any other issue? Do you have any evidence of any special hostility to you or your views by the major news magazines, newspapers, or radio and TV?

Jensen: What you are saying is generally correct. It's usually a mixture of favorable and unfavorable treatment. The power of the mass media, however, is more evident in what they choose to notice or to ignore and leave unmentionable. Also, as you suggest, a lot depends on who gets the assignment to cover a particular topic. But you have picked out the very best examples that immediately come to mind. *The New York Times Magazine,* for example, asked one of the top popular science writers (Lee Edson) to do the story on my 1969 *Harvard Educational Review* article, and I know he took pains to get the story right. The science part of the *Newsweek* story about *The Bell Curve* was very well done, because the staff writer who was assigned to work on this article also took the trouble to understand the issues and explain them simply but correctly. However, the typical level of objectivity and accuracy in dealing with the IQ controversy that one generally finds in the mass media is quite poor and largely at variance with expert opinion on these topics. If anyone wants full documentation on this point, I again refer them to Snyderman and Rothman's book *The IQ Controversy: The Media and Public Policy.*

Miele: Then are you ready to declare victory for Jensenism, at least as regards the scientific journals?

Jensen: I think so. Not in the sense that everyone or even a majority believe everything I have written on these subjects, but in the sense that they are now open for discussion on that basis.

Miele: Given your generally low evaluation of the media, let me turn the tables on you. Sit in my seat for a moment. You've been assigned to cover a new controversy in science or history and you know little about the specifics. How would you go about it? How would you prepare? Or determine who is "qualified" and who is "unbiased"?

Jensen: I'd like to see these really tough questions tried on a journalist or a professor of journalism! Not having worked on that side of the equation, I haven't given these matters as much thought as they deserve. But I have been interviewed by many journalists, in the print, radio, and TV media, and what I have noticed is that some do a much better job than others, and this usually has to do with their preparation and understanding of the subject under discussion. Theirs is really an exceedingly difficult task, because they're not in a position to become highly expert in every particular subject that they are assigned to write or interview about. I really admire the people who, in my own experience, have done this exceptionally well. The names that immediately come to mind are Joseph Alsop, Lee Edson, Morton Hunt, Dan Seligman, and Mike Wallace, who interviewed me on two occasions for the *60 Minutes* TV programs. I was rather amazed at how well prepared and knowledgeable they came for their interviews with me. They're all obviously brilliant fellows.

I don't know how these men prepared, but I can tell you how I think you might go about it. Talk to the editors of the specialist journals for the topic in question. Tell them the topic you're working on and ask for two things: a minimum basic reading list on the specific topic, and the names of the five or six most qualified persons you could talk with about the particular topic. If you have the time, look these people up in, say, *Psychological Abstracts*, the *Science Citation Index*, *Who's Who*, and the author index of textbooks on the subject of interest, to get some idea of their background and contributions to the field. The number of a textbook's page references to the cited works of a person is a strong clue as to the leading contributors to a given field. Talk with them about the topic of your assignment. The rest is up to your intelligence, understanding, and judgment.

Miele: How would you determine the scientific consensus, or does that really mean anything?

Jensen: The idea of a consensus is not very meaningful or important in science, especially at the frontiers of knowledge. At first, a consensus is nearly always opposed to any innovation. The technical competence of the work is a better guide. Behind the frontiers of a developing science, of course, a consensus of generally accepted opinion among workers in a given field may be quite meaningful. For example, there is now such a consensus among experts in psychometrics and behavioral genetics regarding the practical validity of IQ tests, the existence of a g factor, and its substantial heritability, to mention only a few points.

Miele: What does it mean to, as they say, "have an agenda"? Is someone with an agenda necessarily wrong as to the science involved? Doesn't everyone have some agenda?

Jensen: Having an agenda per se, of course, can have nothing to do with the truth in a scientific sense. A scientist's personal beliefs are of no importance when it comes to evaluating the scientific truth of that scientist's theories. Newton, for example, believed many things, such as alchemy, that today we would consider false and even bizarre, but that in no way invalidates his scientific discoveries, which have held up now for over three hundred years. When there is evidence, however, that a person has a philosophical, religious, or political agenda that, instead of scientific considerations, determines the kinds of evidence to be accepted or rejected, it becomes especially important to evaluate the person's claims in light of all the relevant empirical evidence, the methodology used in arriving at conclusions, and the logic and internal consistency of the arguments based thereon. I assume everyone has some kind of agenda.

Miele: Okay. Then what's Arthur Jensen's agenda?

Jensen: My own agenda is to bring psychology more fully into the larger domain of biology, and to apply the methods of differential psychology, psychometrics, and behavioral genetics to bear on some of the questions concerning the causes of individual and group differences that have arisen especially in the field of education. My aim in this is to produce good science, as best I can, not to change the world or push any social or political program.

Miele: Most important of all, what should make my BS-Detector hit red alert?

Jensen: Your "red alert" should go off whenever you see wishful thinking replace the reality principle or encounter any form of dogmatism, which is an anathema to science. On this, there's a memorable passage in Bertrand Russell's *Mysticism and Logic* that I especially like and that I recommend to scientists and science writers alike:

> The man of science, whatever his hopes may be, must lay them aside while he studies nature; and the philosopher, if he is to achieve truth, must do the same. Ethical considerations can only legitimately appear as determining our feelings towards the truth, and our manner of ordering our lives in view of the truth, but not as themselves dictating what the truth is to be.

Further Reading

The statements by Nixon can be found in: Ehrlichmann, J. (1982). *Witness to power.* New York: Simon and Schuster. Pp. 223. For the historical record of presidential statements on race, see: O'Reilly, K. (1995). *Nixon's piano: Presidents and racial politics from Washington to Clinton.* New York: Free Press.

Jerry Hirsch's article criticizing Jensen is: Hirsch, J. (1981). To defrock the charlatans. *Race Relations Abstracts*, 6.2, 1–66. For Barry Mehler's criticisms of the Pioneer Fund, see: Mehler, B. (1989–1990). Foundation for fascism: The new eugenics movement in the United States. *Patterns of Prejudice*, 23 (Winter), 17–26. Other critiques that appeared as part of "*The Bell Curve* Wars" include: Lane, C. (1994). The tainted sources of "the bell curve." *New York Review of Books* (1 December), 15; Lane, C. (1995). IQ, race and heredity. *Commentary*, 100 (August), 15–25; Miller, A. (1994). Professors of hate. *Rolling Stone* (20 October), 106–114; and Sedgwick, J. (1994). The mentality bunker. *Gentlemen's Quarterly* (November), 228–251.

For biographies of the Pioneer Fund's principal grantees and summaries of their research, written from a pro-Pioneer perspective, see Lynn, R. (2001). *The science of human diversity: A history of the Pioneer Fund*. New York: University Press of America. The book also contains a lengthy preface by the late Harry F. Weyher, long-time president of the Pioneer Fund, in which he responded to many of the charges made against the Fund in the articles cited above. He also published defenses of the Pioneer Fund in: Weyher, H. F. (1998a). The pioneer fund, the behavioral sciences, and the media's false stories. *Intelligence*, 26 (4), 319–336; and in: Weyher, H. F. (1998b). Contributions to the history of psychology, CXII: Intelligence, behavior genetics, and the Pioneer Fund. *Psychological Reports*, 82, 1347–1374.

The books recommended by Jensen for the general reader are: Jensen, A. R. (1981). *Straight talk about mental tests*. New York: Free Press; Seligman, D. (1992). *A question of intelligence: The IQ debate in America*. Secaucus, NJ: Birch Lane; and Eysenck, H. J. (1998). *Intelligence: A new look*. New Brunswick, NJ: Transaction. The opposing, anti-Jensenist point of view is well presented in: Gould, S. J. (1996). *The mismeasure of man*. (Revised and expanded edition). New York: Norton; and Graves, J. L. (2001). *The emperor's new clothes: Biological theories of race at the millennium*. New Brunswick, NJ: Rutgers University Press.

The evidence of media bias cited by Jensen is based on: Snyderman, M., and Rothman, S. (1987). Survey of expert opinion on intelligence and aptitude tests. *American Psychologist*, 42, 137–144; and on their 1988 follow-up book, Snyderman, M., and Rothman, S. (1988). *The IQ controversy: The media and public policy*. New Brunswick, NJ: Transaction.

The statement signed by 50 behavioral scientists, reproduced in Appendix B, originally appeared as Gottfredson, L. (1994), Mainstream science on intelligence, *Wall Street Journal* (December 13), A18. It was later republished as Gottfredson, L. (1997), Mainstream science on intelligence: An editorial with 52 signatories, history, and bibliography, *Intelligence*, 24 (1), 13–23.

For more information on these subjects, see the bibliography of Jensen's publications in Appendix A.

6

SCIENCE AND POLICY

What's to Be Done?

The final chapter deals with an area that Jensen has rarely entered—policy. When Jensenism became an issue, he avoided drawing policy implications. Only recently and tentatively has he done so. After all, the severest critics of Jensenism and other "race research" have always argued that it is a smoke screen to hide a reactionary political agenda. We debate whether there is some general rule, such as "science and politics don't mix," and whether questions about human beings should be treated differently from other scientific questions. Jensen argues that successful policy must be based on reality, not wishful thinking, and that's where science gets involved.

I question whether Jensenism didn't have a policy angle from the opening line of his famous *Harvard Educational Review* article: "Compensatory education has been tried and apparently it has failed." He explains that when the findings of the U.S. Commission on Civil Rights showed that compensatory education programs did not raise the IQ and scholastic achievement of the culturally disadvantaged, it contradicted what he and educators thoroughly believed at that time. He wondered why. Then another government-financed study, the famous 1966 Coleman Report, compared our nation's schools in terms of per-pupil expenditures, pupil/teacher ratios, and teacher qualifications. Taken all together, they failed to explain more than 10 percent of the variation in scholastic performance. Just spending more money per pupil, hiring new teachers, or providing them with better training would not eliminate the differences. They were the result of something in the pupils' family background factors, something the schools couldn't influence. Jensen began to think that he and others weren't asking the right questions and were looking in the wrong places for the answers.

We then turn to what that means for two of the major policies in this area—Equal Opportunity and Affirmative Action. Jensen says that he has always believed in equal opportunity for every individual, regardless of sex, race, religion, national origin, or any other classification, but that this doesn't ensure that everyone will achieve equal results. For Jensen, opportunities, like everything else, only make sense in terms of individual differences. The aim of public education should not be to produce equality (which it can't), but to provide a variety of opportunities to allow children to benefit in whatever way works best for them.

When Affirmative Action was introduced it was not a quota system. Its original purpose was to make special efforts to ensure that educational and employment opportunities were open to those groups that had historically been shut out, provided they met the usual qualifications, and to actively recruit them. Jensen states that he has supported this approach from the beginning. However, he says that when this failed to yield enough qualified minority members, Affirmative Action was turned into a reverse discrimination quota. He finds that to be unfair and simply wrong.

While that all sounds very morally uplifting, I ask Jensen whether a genetic role in the Black-White average-IQ difference means that de facto, if not de jure, segregation will be with us forever and that any attempts to produce truly integrated, quality education are doomed to failure. Jensen rejects my argument because he believes it contains two false premises. First, *quality* education is not "one size fits all" education. Instead, we now have computer technology to give every child an educational program specifically tailored to abilities, regardless of race, ethnicity, or social class. We wouldn't have to worry about whether there were enough members of any group in the honors classes, because in Jensen's system there wouldn't be honors classes. Every student would be honored by being given his or her best chance to succeed. Second, it has to be emphasized that the Black-

White difference in average IQ is only slightly greater than the average difference in IQ that occurs between full siblings reared together. As a society, we have no trouble dealing with that. The race difference is simply more visible.

We also discuss dysgenics, that is, the decline in the average IQ (which Jensen argues is taking place); eugenics (which Jensen favors, though on the basis of family choice rather than societal mandate); genetic engineering (a possibility, and an acceptable one, he believes—again, on an individual basis); population growth (in Jensen's view, the world's number-one problem, more than dysgenics) and its control (requiring some government role); immigration (which he also believes should be regulated); and brain drains and brain gains, and what they will mean as society becomes more and more dependent on an educated and—in Jensen's view—high-g population.

We conclude with Jensen's thoughts on how three tenets of Jensenism—the failure of compensatory education, the heritability of the g factor, and the genetic component in the Black-White difference in average IQ—have held up since his famous 1969 article in the *Harvard Educational Review*. More importantly, we discuss why it is not important to Jensen whether he turns out in the end to have been right or wrong, only that scientific research on these questions be allowed to advance.

Miele: So far we've talked a lot about the science and a little about the history and politics of the race-IQ debate. Now I want to talk about policy, which for the most part you've avoided. What is your overall view of the relationship between science and policy? Do you think there is a general rule we should follow, such as "Science and politics don't mix"?

Jensen: I have intentionally avoided policy questions in writing about mental abilities because I think of the scientific research as distinct from public policy. Policy concerns decisions about how the knowledge gained through research should be used in ways that would affect people's lives. The acquisition of factual knowledge should stand apart from policy. But to be effective, policy making must take into account our best factual knowledge about the alternatives under consideration.

In the world of practical affairs, any given policy decisions must also take into account a number of factors besides the relevant scientific data. Some of these other considerations may be in conflict. Policy decisions then emerge from weighing scientific knowledge along with all the other, and at times conflicting, factors outside the province of science—ideals and goals; economic feasibility; traditional social, cultural, and religious values; and the prevailing consensus of public opinion at a given time. Policy is often a matter of compromise.

Miele: But do you think policy questions that deal with human beings have to be treated differently?

Jensen: Successful policies, no matter how well intended, should not be based on purely wishful thinking or on speculative and untestable philosophy. They must recognize the reality principle, and that is where science plays an important role. I believe this is widely recognized. In the case of education, however, some of the government decisions have simply ignored any research findings that do not support the politically popular policies. Too many politicians take research results less seriously than purely political considerations. The popular media seldom help either, as they are also more politically than scientifically oriented.

Miele: What you've just said leads us back to the three points in your 1969 *Harvard Educational Review* article that gave rise to the word *Jensenism:* (1) the failure of compensatory education, (2) the evidence for a genetic basis to IQ, and (3) the likelihood of some genetic component in the Black-White IQ difference. The first element clearly involves an evaluation, even if a scientific one, of public policy. Back in 1969, most educators and psychologists considered compensatory education as a scientifically based method to eliminate the Black-White IQ difference.

So didn't Jensenism at least straddle the line between science and policy from the onset?

Jensen: I don't believe I straddled the line because policy itself can be a test of a theory. If a course of action is based on defective theory, it won't work. It was the failure of that policy, one in which I believed at the time, that was largely responsible for my becoming involved in the IQ controversy. The report of the U.S. Commission on Civil Rights on the failure of compensatory education programs to raise the IQ and scholastic achievement of the "culturally disadvantaged" came as a shock to me and to most other educators. It clearly contradicted the expectations of the psychological and educational theories that prevailed in the 1950s and 1960s.

This was immediately followed by the famous Coleman Report, commissioned by Congress in 1966. It looked at whether per-pupil expenditure, pupil/teacher ratio, teacher qualifications, special services, and the like really could explain regional, social class, and racial group differences in pupils' scholastic achievement. The report showed that all these school variables together accounted for only about 10 percent of the variation in scholastic performance. The rest was attributable to pupils' family background factors, something over which the schools have no influence.

The clear-cut finding rang the alarm that something was seriously wrong with the prevailing theory of individual and group differences in scholastic performance. Faced with this evidence, educational psychologists could either reassess their shaken theory, or try to explain away its failures with one excuse after another. For some people, a wish-fulfilling theory can become an unshakable article of faith, and so there are some psychologists and educators who still advocate the failed theories of the past.

Miele: Then let me turn to two of the most important policies— Equal Opportunity and Affirmative Action. What do those terms mean to you? What were your views on Equal Opportunity and

Jensen taking a break outside his home. (February 2002)

Affirmative Action back in 1969? How has thirty years of research changed your opinions, if at all?

Jensen: My thoughts about equal opportunity haven't changed at all. I have always believed in equal opportunity for every individual, regardless of sex, race, religion, national origin, or any other classification—provided that it is understood that ensuring equal opportunity for everyone doesn't ensure that everyone will benefit equally from the very same opportunity. To a large degree, we select our opportunities, and opportunities select those with the necessary mental maturity, special abilities, and proclivities to profit from them. The aim of public education should be to provide a sufficiently wide range and variety of different opportunities that all children can benefit in the ways that will be most apt to serve them in adulthood. Given these opportunities, each child's particular abilities and proclivities as demonstrated by frequent assessments of their performance should guide their course through school.

Miele: And Affirmative Action?

Jensen: When the original concept of Affirmative Action was just catching on in the 1960s it was not a quota system. That only came later. I approved two main facets of its original intent, and I still do: (1) We should make special efforts to ensure that historically underrepresented minorities are fully aware that educational opportunities in colleges and universities, in job training programs, and in employment opportunities are open to all, provided they meet the usual qualifications; and (2) colleges and universities, job training programs, and employers should actively seek out and recruit minority persons who could qualify by the usual standards, including the use of academic talent searches at the high school level, special inducements, and scholarships to encourage academically promising minority students to go on to college.

Miele: And what about the "quota" system you mentioned?

Jensen: That only came about when the measures I described didn't yield as high a percentage of qualified minority students or of qualified job applicants as was hoped for. Then the program turned into one of relaxing the selection standards for certain minorities in order to meet Affirmative Action guidelines—in effect, a quota or reverse discrimination system. Since there is usually only a limited number of admissions possible for a given institution, some substantial number of better-qualified White and Asian applicants would be denied admission in favor of applicants who were designated as members of underrepresented minorities, mostly Blacks and Hispanics. Such discrimination based on race is patently unfair and an anathema to those who were brought up in an era that taught that racial discrimination is simply wrong. And it is now apparent that there are certain tangible disadvantages to the supposed beneficiaries themselves resulting from this form of reverse discrimination. First, in the eyes of many, it depreciates the merit of those minority members who could have competed successfully without any special dispensation. It can also lower the self-esteem of those individuals who come to realize that they were selected because of their race, not their ability. And biased selection procedures have a cascading effect at later points in the career where less Affirmative Action is implemented. Those who weren't qualified for entrance will experience only failure and frustration as they try to climb up the ever more demanding rungs of the vocational or educational ladder.

Miele: But without such programs, doesn't the 15-point Black-White difference in average IQ mean that segregated schooling, de facto if not de jure, will be with us forever and that any attempts to produce truly integrated, quality education are doomed to failure?

Jensen: No, I don't agree. Nor do I agree that there is any advantage in de jure, or legally enforced, "racial balance." Parents should be able to send their children to the school of their choice. I favor any measures that would maximize free choice. It won't lead to either complete segregation or complete racial balance. I have repeatedly emphasized, particularly in talks before educational organizations and in a recent publication, that quality education does not mean the very *same* program of instruction for every child, but equal opportunity for all children to receive a *specific* program tailored to their *individual differences* in general ability and in special aptitudes. I especially stress the words *individual differences* to emphasize that these differences cut across all racial, ethnic, and social class groups. In a recent publication, I have described the kind of revolution in educational methods with the technology now available that I believe would best be able to provide the optimal educational experiences for virtually all children in the school-age population.

Miele: But doesn't a purely meritocratic educational policy like the one you suggest mean that there would be only token Blacks in advanced or honors classes in grade school and high school, and at the most selective universities?

Jensen: In the system I have proposed there wouldn't be honors classes in grade school or high school. With individualized, computer-assisted instruction, and small group interactions with teachers, there would still be a wide range of individual differences, but every pupil wouldn't be moving in lockstep on one and the same academic track.

We can't eliminate individual differences, but we can adapt instruction optimally to take account of individual differences. When it comes to admission to colleges and universities, the selection criteria will be based largely on students' achievements in academic subjects, of course, because that's what college is about. And colleges will differ greatly, as they do now, in their selectivity on academic criteria and on the relative weights given to other selection criteria. If there are racial, ethnic, social class, or any other kind of group differences in the proportions of the groups that meet these selection criteria, so be it, as long as every applicant, regardless of group membership or background, has been evaluated objectively on his or her own individual achievements.

Miele: Okay, suppose you were appointed not Secretary of Education, but Education Czar. You have complete dictatorial power over America's entire educational system from preschool to postdoctoral programs.

What would you do and how much would it be based on the three tenets of Jensenism—the failure of compensatory education, the heritability of the *g* factor, and the existence of some genetic component in the Black-White IQ difference?

Jensen: I find the very idea of a federally appointed "Education Czar" unappealing, undemocratic, and contrary to what I believe. Free enterprise in public education, with variety and competition among methods of schooling, is more likely to result in successful programs than a centrally dominated educational system. In the article I previously referred to, I described the kinds of innovations in schooling that I think would best take account of the very wide range of individual differences in learning abilities in our school population—a wide range exists within every racial or ethnic group. It's a program I would suggest even in countries or communities that are homogeneous racially or socially.

The key point I want to make is that full siblings within the same family, on average, differ in IQ by about as much (around 12 IQ points) as the average difference between Blacks and Whites of the same social class. (Equating the two groups for social class reduces the overall 15-point Black-White average IQ difference by about three points). Most people are surprised by this, but it's a fact. At least half of the population variation in IQ is *within* families.

The reason group differences are the focus of so much attention is because certain group characteristics are highly visible. So the highly publicized social and political problems of education are commonly seen as involving group differences. But the real problems of education exist at the level of individual differences, and these would exist even if there were no racial or other group differences. Let's not forget that the group differences are just aggregated individual differences and should be taken account of in the same way. Nothing I have discovered about the science of mental ability contradicts anything I believe ethically about the primacy of the individual over the group.

Miele: Do you think there's any real-world evidence of dysgenics, a genetic "dumbing-down" of the American population?

Jensen: The matrix of possible causes is way too complex and too poorly understood to serve as a reliable basis for inferring anything about the quality of the nation's gene pool or average level of *g* at any point in time. You'd have to look at the trend, from decade to decade, in the birthrates in different segments of the population that differ in IQ or any other trait that may be of interest to you.

The proper analysis is to examine the number of live births per woman (including those with no children, and regardless of their marital status) at approximately the end of the child-bearing years, say, age 45. Such data are available from the U.S. Census. We know that the number of years of education completed by adult women correlates about 0.60 with their IQs. The Census data show higher birthrates at the lower levels of education than at the higher levels, for both Blacks and Whites. But there is a greater disparity in birthrates between poorly educated and well-educated Blacks than is true for Whites. If this trend continues over a number of generations, the Black and White populations will be pulled increasingly further apart in average IQ. And the same thing will happen for any other traits that are correlated with educational level and IQ.

Miele: But I've heard very competent geneticists and demographers dismiss these claims of dysgenic doom because they don't take into account the people at the very low end of the IQ distribution who don't reproduce.

Jensen: That percentage is actually very small compared to the statistics I've just given. The data in the study most frequently cited to make that point were gathered in a small, middle-to-upper-middle-class, predominantly White city—Kalamazoo, Michigan. So they are not representative of the U.S. population of today.

Miele: The armed forces are one segment of American society for which we have extensive information. There were problems, and even race riots, during the Vietnam War years. But the military have probably been the most successful sector of American society in getting over racial segregation. Does that mean that achieving full integration requires autocratic measures?

Jensen: I agree the armed forces have been successful, not because they are autocratic, but because they are meritocratic. The armed forces are not an Affirmative Action employer. The military select their personnel on the same criteria, regardless of race. And Congress has mandated that those below the tenth percentile (that is, with an IQ of about 80) are not eligible for military service. The military evenhandedly use a test of mental ability, the Armed Services Vocation Aptitude Battery (ASVAB), to assign enlisted personnel to the many different training programs that require different levels of aptitude for acquiring specialized knowledge and skills. And the ASVAB is a very good measure of g, which it must be in order to successfully predict success or failure in the various training programs.

Miele: The United States substantially reduced welfare programs, effectively eliminating the political right to public assistance. Political liberals tell us this is not only inhumane but will have disastrous results should the economy take a serious downturn. But political conservatives tell us the marketplace will take care of all this if government just gets out of the way. Given the importance you attach to g, what do you see as the result of eliminating or severely reducing welfare?

Jensen: My guess is that it will be impossible to eliminate welfare, or at least it is incompatible with having a humane society in which people are not allowed to fall below some minimum decent standard of living. In a humane society, the limitations on the growth of the segment of a nation's population that will be in need of welfare will depend on measures taken to greatly diminish the birthrate in that segment of the population. The correlation between parents and their offspring in g and other important traits, whatever the cause, makes it *statistically predictable* which parents will contribute the largest proportion of the welfare dependents of the next generation—those at the lower 10 or 15 percent of the distribution of g in the general population. I emphasize that this is a statistical estimate, and applies to any particular pair of parents only with some quite large probable error. But in psychology we can statistically speak of a person's being "at risk" for, say, educational failure, delinquency, or welfare dependency just as in medical practice one can identify those who are statistically "at risk" for obesity, diabetes, heart disease, or cancer.

Miele: Then do you consider some form of eugenics to be feasible and ethically acceptable?

Jensen: Yes, but more ethical than feasible in the present climate of public opinion. Negative eugenics is already available on a personal, individual basis, in the form of genetic counseling of married couples who wish to minimize the risk of having a child with a high liability of some genetic disease. Few people object to that.

Singapore is the only country I know of that has instituted measures intended to promote positive eugenics, essentially by giving tax credits to parents who are college graduates for every child they have, and awarding college scholarships to all of their offspring who can qualify for admission. These and other such measures should, I think, be taken in other countries as well, provided they do not conflict with the need for zero population growth or even a birthrate that would reduce the present size of the world's population. Reducing population seems more urgent to me than eugenics per se. But unless people in the upper half of the bell curve for g have at least as many offspring as those of the lower half, there will inevitably result a dysgenic trend in the overall ability level and the educability of the population as a whole.

Adam Smith was correct, I believe, when he wrote in *The Wealth of Nations* that a country's most important natural resource is the level of educated ability of its population. This depends in large measure on the overall level of g as well as on the quality of the educational system and the cultural environment, which in turn reflect the society's level of g. The distribution of g in a society and the environmental, cultural, and educational conditions that affect the outward manifestations of g are not independent forces. Generally, environmental conditions are created by people, not imposed on them, and g is one of the crucial factors determining that creation.

Miele: Then what about the question of population in general?

Jensen: The growth of populations worldwide, especially in the Third World, is by far the most serious problem we have to face. Population growth certainly cannot continue indefinitely. It's even questionable whether the present world population of six billion already exceeds the earth's carrying capacity. One wonders if population growth will continue to the point that the human misery it causes is so massive and so profound as to be utterly unconscionable and intolerable. It has already reached that point in certain parts of the world. As far as I know, China is the only country that has officially recognized this problem and actually has taken measures to do something about it, with its policy of one child per family. They know that only enforcement of such measures, however draconian, that restrict population growth will save them. The totalitarian conditions that are apparently needed to accomplish this goal seem tolerable if one considers the eventual consequences of ignoring the problem. It seems the lesser of two evils, considering the consequences of overpopulation. Overpopulation pressure in a nation not only reduces the quality of life and creates personal misery for millions, but it is also a threat to neighboring countries and even to other countries worldwide. It may engender the political conditions that could lead to global war.

Miele: But whether the economy is in a boom or a decline, there is a demand for high-tech professionals and for agricultural and domestic workers. Doesn't that mean the United States needs more immigrants, not fewer?

Jensen: No First World country can expect to have an open border with a Third World country without serious risk to its own economy and quality of life. As for employment demands, it seems unreasonable that unskilled or semi-skilled workers from other countries should be brought in if they take jobs that could be filled from a country's own citizens. Low-skill work could probably be performed by many people who would otherwise need to rely on welfare. As to the kinds of highly skilled workers—engineers, scientists, physicians, and the like—who are usually in short supply in a highly technological society, the world actually resembles a free market to a large extent, with high ability generally following the laws of supply and demand, within nations and across national borders.

This economic demand for higher levels of professional and technical skills naturally makes for brain drains in some countries and brain gains in others. I read not long ago, for example, that India has the largest brain drain of any large country, while a few other countries, including the United States, are beneficiaries of a corresponding brain gain. At about the same time I read a report from the Educational Testing Service saying that the minority group getting the highest SAT scores in recent years are the children of immigrants from India. The supply of highly educated, technical talent in India exceeded the demands of their industry and economy, but has helped to fill the otherwise unmet demand for engineers and computer scientists in the United States. The same thing is seen in many other First World countries. This seems to be inevitable in the modern world.

Miele: As genetic screening and gene replacement techniques, even cloning, become economically more affordable, do you see better-off couples signing up for that sort of thing, even taking out loans if necessary? And if the United States and other major nations ban these procedures, won't a black market spring up in Cuba (which actually has been a leader in some aspects of biotech) or on some small offshore nation, or via cyberspace, as is the case with certain "designer drugs"?

Jensen: I can't predict the future, but it is likely that public opinion and government policies in various countries will differ in their attitudes toward eugenics and, if their population growth rate is no longer threatening, some countries may decide to do as Singapore has done, or something similar. If and when that happens, it will highlight Adam Smith's words that I just mentioned. National populations will begin to differ more than they do now, not only in behavioral qualities but in many aspects of health as well. I'm talking about large-scale effects over a period of several generations, not about cloning, or individuals' personal positive eugenics. Those things may happen, but they would be a drop in the bucket, and a highly suspect one at that. They wouldn't make a significant difference, except perhaps in the number of questionable characters who took advantage of some people's overweening ambition for their offspring.

Sir Francis Galton's original idea of eugenics, which he defined in his autobiography as "the scientific study of the biological and social factors which improve or impair the inborn qualities of human beings and of future generations," didn't include the kinds of biotechnology that may one day be possible, nor did it rule them out.

Miele: Then are we looking at a multi-tiered "brave new world" that is meritocratic at the high end and in the middle, but the low end can only hope that some form of welfare is provided?

Jensen: Every complex society in history has been multi-tiered. Ours is no different in that respect. As a society becomes more technological and information-intensive, however, the g factor comes increasingly into play in determining where people and groups come out in the hierarchy of prestige and rewards. In general, societies have valued and rewarded most those individuals who can do things that very few others can do and have rewarded least those who can only do things that many other people could do at least as well. With the increasing complexity of the functions needed for a society to maintain a competitive position in the modern world, the g factor and its manifestations in the workplace become more salient and more highly valued. Hence those in the lower quarter of the distribution of g in the population are at an increasingly greater risk for lacking the knowledge and skills that are most in demand in our modern society, and may even lack the requisite educability for acquiring them. To the extent that certain socially identifiable groups within the population differ on average in this respect, this problem has political overtones.

Miele: What advice, then, can you give to all those in the United States and around the world who are in that group? What can you say to those who because of genes, environment, or accident feel they are being left behind by the "brave new world" so many others are building and enjoying?

Jensen: I think the progress of civilization benefits everyone. No one is really being "left out" of whatever benefits come from science and invention, except for some pockets of deplorable destitution in parts of the Third World. In every society there has always been a wide range of individual differences in material advantages, wealth, abilities, talents, looks, and sheer luck. An individual has little control over some of these things.

My philosophy has been simply to try and do one's best with what one has to work with, and that in itself can bring satisfaction, knowing that you have applied your best effort to something, to have met responsibilities, and to have discharged your duties and dealt with others honorably. This becomes its own reward.

That, in fact, is the basic teaching of the *Bhagavad Gita*, which I have long enjoyed reading in many different translations, though I am not a Hindu or even a religious person. In one of the Mahatma Gandhi museums in India I recall seeing a letter on display that he had written to someone in which he said, "What you are doing may not be important, but it is very important that you do it." That attitude can often help one not feel discouraged, but instead carry on with what one believes has to be done. Having ideals, perhaps more than anything else, makes life seem worthwhile.

Miele: Looking back at the three tenets of Jensenism—the failure of compensatory education, the heritability of the g factor, and the genetic factor in the Black-White difference in average IQ—are you more or less confident of each of them than you were in 1969 when you published your famous article in the *Harvard Educational Review*?

Jensen: As to the failure of compensatory education, I think the evidence accumulated since 1969 shows that purely psychological and educational manipulations have relatively little if any enduring effect on individuals' level of *g*. Regarding the heritability of *g*, it has proven to be the most highly heritable component of human mental abilities. The most difficult question to resolve scientifically—and the one that causes the most controversy, of course—is the role of genes in the Black-White IQ difference. Many different lines of evidence are consistent with the Default Hypothesis that both genes and environment play a part in the overall mean Black-White difference in *g*, just as they do for individual differences within both populations. Predictions from the Default Hypothesis have been tested and they have held up. The purely environmental or "culture-only" theory, on the other hand, has had to fall back on series of ad hoc hypotheses. They lack any underlying theoretical basis and are often inconsistent with each other, since each one was invented to explain some single phenomenon.

If there's anything on which my judgment has changed significantly since 1969, it is the scientific value of typical IQ tests. Psychological tests are limited by the fact that they do not provide absolute scales, that is, those that have a true zero point and equal intervals throughout their range. As is well known in the physical sciences, the mathematical, and not just statistical, analysis of data is much greater with measurements based on absolute, or ratio-property, scales. These are virtually absent in psychological measurement. There's no doubt, however, that IQ tests and many other conventional psychological tests have real practical value. They are unquestionably valid predictors of certain kinds of performance in education and employment, and can be most useful in educational selection, and in hiring and promotion decisions.

As I've worked on my book-in-progress on mental chronometry (the real-time measurement of cognitive processes while they are going on), it has become ever clearer to me that the standard tests used in psychology only allow us to see "through a glass darkly." I now believe the precise response-time measures of cognitive processes will put psychology and the study of human differences on a much more scientific basis, comparable to that of the physical sciences. The study of human mental abilities is now going directly into the brain, and for this to progress apace we will need to measure behavior in physical units, namely time measured in milliseconds. Time is a natural scale of measurement for many mental processes. I view this line of research, which has great potential for brain research in relation to the questions of differential psychology, as the extension of what can be called the Galton paradigm. It is yet another case where Sir Francis Galton (1822–1911) was on the right track to begin with. The field of scientific psychology erred in straying from it for so long.

Miele: Finally, is there anything else you'd like to say, modify, or correct?

Jensen: All I will say in conclusion is that it won't matter to me in the long run if what I have said in these interviews eventually turns out to be proven either true or false, right or wrong. It is only what I think at present, based on my own research and all my reading, study, and thinking about the subjects you have questioned me about. I have tried to express my answers clearly and forthrightly. Whether I'm right or wrong in any particular instance isn't the really important thing. What is important is that scientific research on these matters should be encouraged and allowed to advance unfettered.

Finally, let me say that though I have been interviewed about my work a great many times in the last thirty years, by figures such as Joseph Alsop, Dan Rather, Phil Donahue, and Mike Wallace, to name a few, I haven't met another interviewer who came as well prepared and as sharply informed on all the topics of our discussion as you have been. I'm rather amazed. I appreciate it, and I thank you very much.

Miele: Then thank you for giving so generously of your time, for going on record in such depth and breadth, and for those extremely kind words.

Further Reading

Jensen describes in detail his views on Affirmative Action, and on how the educational system should be changed to better meet individual differences, in: Jensen, A. R. (1997a). Spearman's *g* and the problem of educational equality. *Oxford Review of Education, 17* (2), 169–187; and in: Jensen, A. R. (1997b). The *g* factor in the design of education. In Sternberg, R. J., and Williams, W. M. (Eds.), *Intelligence, instruction, and assessment.* Hillsdale, NJ: Erlbaum. (The latter book also contains essays by other, equally distinguished contributors, many of whom express views very different from Jensen's.)

The most recent biography of the founder of differential psychology, eugenics, mental chronometry, and the London School of psychology (of which Jensen is the foremost living exponent) is: Gillham, N. W. (2001). *A life of Sir Francis Galton.* New York: Oxford University Press. (Galton also pioneered the use of twins in scientific studies aimed at assessing the relative effects of nature and nurture.)

For more information on these subjects, see the bibliography of Jensen's publications in Appendix A.

APPENDIX A

BIBLIOGRAPHY OF
ARTHUR R. JENSEN

1955

1. Symonds, P. M., and Jensen, A. R. (1955). A review of six textbooks in educational psychology. *Journal of Educational Psychology, 46,* 56–64.

1956

2. Jensen, A. R. (1956). Aggression in fantasy and overt behavior. Unpublished doctoral dissertation, Columbia University, New York.

1957

3. Jensen, A. R. (1957). Aggression in fantasy and overt behavior. *Psychological Monographs, 71,* No. 445, Whole No. 16.
4. Jensen, A. R. (1957). Authoritarian attitudes and personality maladjustment. *Journal of Abnormal and Social Psychology, 54,* 303–311.
5. Pope, B., and Jensen, A. R. (1957). The Rorschach as an index of pathological thinking. *Journal of Projective Techniques, 21,* 59–62.

1958

6. Jensen, A. R. (1958). Personality. *Annual Review of Psychology, 9,* 295–322.
7. Jensen, A. R. (1958). The Maudsley Personality Inventory. *Acta Psychologica, 14,* 312–325. Reprinted in: Savage, R. D. (Ed.), *Readings in Clinical Psychology.* Pergamon Press, 1958.
8. Symonds, P. M., and Jensen, A. R. (1958). The predictive significance of fantasy. *American Journal of Orthopsychiatry, 28,* 73–84.

1959

9. Jensen, A. R. (1959). The reliability of projective techniques: Review of the literature. *Acta Psychologica, 16,* 3–31.

10. Jensen, A. R. (1959). *The reliability of projective techniques: Methodology.* Amsterdam: North-Holland Publishing Co. Pp. 32–67.

11. Jensen, A. R. (1959). A statistical note on racial differences in the Progressive Matrices. *Journal of Consulting Psychology, 23,* 272.

12. Jensen, A. R. (1959). Review of the Thematic Apperception Test. In O. K. Buros (Ed.), *Fifth mental measurements yearbook.* Highland Park, NJ: Gryphon Press. Pp. 310–313.

13. Jensen, A. R. (1959). Review of the Family Relations Test. In O. K. Buros (Ed.), *Fifth mental measurements yearbook.* Highland Park, NJ: Gryphon Press. Pp. 227–228.

14. Jensen, A. R. (1959). Review of *Perceptual processes and mental illness,* by H. J. Eysenck, G. W. Granger, and J. D. Brengelmann. *Journal of Nervous and Mental Diseases, 128,* 469–471.

1960

15. Jensen, A. R. (1960). Holistic personality. Review of *Understanding personalities,* by R. Leeper and P. Madison. *Contemporary Psychology, 5,* 353–355.

16. Jensen, A. R. (1960). Some criticisms of automated teaching. *California Journal of Instructional Improvement, 3,* 32–35.

17. Jensen, A. R. (1960). Teaching machines and individual differences. *Automated Teaching Bulletin, 1,* 12–16. Reprinted in: Smith, W. I., and Moore, J. W. (Eds.), *Programmed learning.* New York: Van Nostrand, 1962. Pp. 218–226.

1961

18. Jensen, A. R. (1961). On the reformulation of inhibition in Hull's system. *Psychological Bulletin, 58,* 274–298.

19. Jensen, A. R. (1961). Learning abilities in Mexican-American and Anglo-American children. *California Journal of Educational Research, 12,* 147–159.

20. Symonds, P. M., and Jensen, A. R. (1961). *From adolescent to adult.* New York: Columbia University Press. Pp. viii + 413.

1962

21. Jensen, A. R. (1962). The von Restorff isolation effect with minimal response learning. *Journal of Experimental Psychology, 64,* 123–125.

22. Jensen, A. R. (1962). An empirical theory of the serial-position effect. *Journal of Psychology*, 53, 127–142.

23. Jensen, A. R. (1962). Temporal and spatial effects of serial position. *American Journal of Psychology*, 75, 390–400. Reprinted in: Slamecka, N. J. (Ed.), *Human learning and memory: Selected Readings*. New York: Oxford University Press, 1967. Pp. 117–124.

24. Jensen, A. R. (1962). Is the serial position curve invariant? *British Journal of Psychology*, 53, 159–166.

25. Jensen, A. R. (1962). Transfer between paired-associate and serial learning. *Journal of Verbal Learning and Verbal Behavior*, 1, 269–280.

26. Jensen, A. R. (1962). Spelling errors and the serial position effect. *Journal of Educational Psychology*, 53, 105–109. Reprinted in: Otto, W., and Koenke, K. (Eds.), *Readings on corrective and remedial teaching*. Boston: Houghton-Mifflin, 1969. Pp. 346–352.

27. Jensen, A. R. (1962). Extraversion, neuroticism, and serial learning. *Acta Psychologica*, 20, 69–77.

28. Jensen, A. R. (1962). The improvement of educational research. *Teachers College Record*, 64, 20–27. Reprinted in: *Education Digest*, 1963, 28, 18–22.

29. Jensen, A. R. (1962). Review of *Programmed learning: Evolving principles and industrial applications. Foundation for Research on Human Behavior*, edited by J. P. Lysaught. *Contemporary Psychology*, 7, 33.

30. Jensen, A. R. (1962). Reinforcement psychology and individual differences. *California Journal of Educational Research*, 13, 174–178.

31. Jensen, A. R., and Blank, S. S. (1962). Association with ordinal position in serial rote-learning. *Canadian Journal of Psychology*, 16, 60–63.

32. Jensen, A. R., Collins, C. C., and Vreeland, R. W. (1962). A multiple S-R apparatus for human learning. *American Journal of Psychology*, 75, 470–476.

1963

33. Jensen, A. R. (1963). Serial rote-learning: Incremental or all-or-none? *Quarterly Journal of Experimental Psychology*, 15, 27–35.

34. Jensen, A. R. (1963). Learning abilities in retarded, average, and gifted children. *Merrill-Palmer Quarterly*, 9, 123–140. Reprinted in: DeCecco, J. P. (Ed.), *Educational technology: Reading in programmed instruction*. New York: Holt, Rinehart, and Winston, Inc., 1964. Pp. 356–375.

35. Jensen, A. R. (1963). Learning in the preschool years. *Journal of Nursery Education*, 18, 133–139. Reprinted in: Hartup, W. W., and Smothergill, Nancy L. (Eds.),

The young child: Reviews of research. Washington, DC: National Association for the Education of Young Children, 1967. Pp. 125–135.

36. Jensen, A. R., and Roden, A. (1963). Memory span and the skewness of the serial-position curve. *British Journal of Psychology, 54,* 337–349

37. Jensen, A. R., and Rohwer, W. D., Jr. (1963). Verbal mediation in paired-associate and serial learning. *Journal of Verbal Learning and Verbal Behavior, 1,* 346–352.

38. Jensen, A. R., and Rohwer, W. D., Jr. (1963). The effect of verbal mediation on the learning and retention of paired-associates by retarded adults. *American Journal of Mental Deficiency, 68,* 80–84.

1964

39. Jensen, A. R. (1964). The Rorschach technique: A re-evaluation. *Acta Psychologica, 22,* 60–77.

40. Jensen, A. R. (1964). Learning, briefly. Review of *Learning: A survey of psychological interpretations,* by W. F. Hill. *Contemporary Psychology, 9,* 228–229.

1965

41. Jensen, A. R. (1965). An adjacency effect in free recall. *Quarterly Journal of Experimental Psychology, 17,* 315–322.

42. Jensen, A. R. (1965). Rote learning in retarded adults and normal children. *American Journal of Mental Deficiency, 69,* 828–834.

43. Jensen, A. R. (1965). *Individual Differences in Learning: Interference Factor.* Cooperative Research Project No. 1867, U.S. Office of Education. Pp. 1–160.

44. Jensen, A. R. (1965). Scoring the Stroop Test. *Acta Psychologica, 24,* 398–408.

45. Jensen, A. R. (1965). Review of the Maudsley Personality Inventory. In O. K. Buros (Ed.), *Sixth mental measurements yearbook.* Highland Park, NJ: Gryphon Press. Pp. 288–291.

46. Jensen, A. R. (1965). Review of the Rorschach Test. In O. K. Buros (Ed.), *Sixth mental measurements yearbook.* Highland Park, NJ: Gryphon Press. Pp. 501–509. Reprinted in: Bracht, G. H., Hopkins, K., and Stanley, J. C. (Eds.), *Perspectives in education and psychological measurement.* New York: Prentice-Hall, 1972. Pp. 292–311.

47. Jensen, A. R. (1965). Review of the Make a Picture Story Test. In O. K. Buros (Ed.), *Sixth mental measurements yearbook.* Highland Park, NJ: Gryphon Press. Pp. 468–470.

48. Jensen, A. R., and Rohwer, W. D., Jr. (1965). Syntactical mediation of serial and paired-associate learning as a function of age. *Child Development, 36,* 601–608.

49. Jensen, A. R., and Rohwer, W. D., Jr. (1965). What is learned in serial learning? *Journal of Verbal Learning and Verbal Behavior, 4,* 62–72. Reprinted in: Slamecka,

N.J. (Ed.), *Human learning and memory.* New York: Oxford University Press, 1967. Pp. 98–110.

50. Battig, W. F., Allen, M., and Jensen, A. R. (1965). Priority of free recall of newly learned items. *Journal of Verbal Learning and Verbal Behavior, 4,* 175–179.

1966

51. Jensen, A. R. (1966). The measurement of reactive inhibition in humans. *Journal of General Psychology, 75,* 85–93.

52. Jensen, A. R. (1966). Social class and perceptual learning. *Mental Hygiene, 50,* 226–239. Reprinted in: Rogers, Dorothy (Ed.), *Readings in child psychology.* New York: Brooks-Cole Publishing Co., 1969.

53. Jensen, A. R. (1966). Individual differences in concept learning. In H. Klausmeier and C. Harris (Eds.), *Analyses of concept learning.* New York: Merrill, 1966. Pp. 139–154. Reprinted in: Butcher, H. J., and Lomax, L., Readings in human intelligence. London: Methuen, 1971. Pp. 100–114.

54. Jensen, A. R. (1966). Cumulative deficit in compensatory education. *Journal of School Psychology, 4,* 37–47.

55. Jensen, A. R. (1966). Verbal mediation and educational potential. *Psychology in the Schools, 3,* 99–109. Reprinted in: Torrance, E. P., and White, W. F. (Eds.), *Issues and advances in educational psychology.* (2nd Ed.). Itasca, IL: F. E. Peacock, 1975. Pp. 175–188.

56. Jensen, A. R. (1966). Conceptions and misconceptions about verbal mediation. In M. P. Douglas (Ed.), *Claremont Reading Conference,* Thirtieth Yearbook, Claremont Graduate School. Pp. 134–141.

57. Jensen, A. R. (1966). Intensive, detailed, exhaustive. Review of *Paired-associates learning: The role of meaningfulness, similarity and familiarization,* by A. E. Goss and C. F. Nodine. *Contemporary Psychology, 11,* 379–380.

58. Jensen, A. R., and Rohwer, W. D., Jr. (1966). The Stroop Color-Word Test: A review. *Acta Psychologica, 25,* 3693.

1967

59. Jensen, A. R. (1967). Varieties of individual differences in learning. In R. M. Gagne (Ed.), *Learning and individual differences.* Columbus, OH: Merrill. Pp. 117–135. Reprinted in: Roweton, W. E. (Ed.), *Humanistic trends in educational psychology.* New York: Xerox Co., 1972.

60. Jensen, A. R. (1967). Estimation of the limits of heritability of traits by comparison of monozygotic and dizygotic twins. *Science, 156,* 539. Abstract.

61. Jensen, A. R. (1967). Estimation of the limits of heritability of traits by comparison of monozygotic and dizygotic twins. *Proceedings of the National Academy of Science, 58*, 149–156.

62. Jensen, A. R. (1967). The culturally disadvantaged: Psychological and educational aspects. *Educational Research, 10*, 4–20.

63. Jensen, A. R. (1967). How much can we boost IQ and scholastic achievement? *Proceedings of the California Advisory Council on Educational Research.*

1968

64. Jensen, A. R. (1968). Social class, race and genetics: Implications for education. *American Educational Research Journal, 5*, 1–42 Reprinted in: Gordon, I. J. (Ed.), *Readings in research in developmental psychology.* Glenview, IL: Scott, Foresman, and Co., 1971. Pp. 54–67.Clarizio, H. F., Craig, R. C., and Mehrens, W. H. (Eds.), *Contemporary issues in educational psychology.* New York: Allyn and Bacon, 1970.

65. Jensen, A. R. (1968). Patterns of mental ability and socioeconomic status. *Science, 160*, 439. Abstract.

66. Jensen, A. R. (1968). Patterns of mental ability and socioeconomic status. *Proceedings of the National Academy of Sciences, 60*, 1330–1337.

67. Jensen, A. R. (1968). Social class and verbal learning. In M. Deutsch, I. Katz, and A. R. Jensen (Eds.), *Social class, race, and psychological development.* New York: Holt, Rinehart, and Winston. Pp. 115–174. Reprinted in: DeCecco, J. P. (Ed.), *The psychology of language, thought, and instruction.* New York: Holt, Rinehart, and Winston, 1967. Pp. 103–117.

68. Jensen, A. R. (1968). The culturally disadvantaged and the heredity-environment uncertainty. In J. Hellmuth (Ed.), *Disadvantaged child.* Vol. 2. Seattle, WA: Special Child Publications. Pp. 29–76.

69. Jensen, A. R. (1968). Another look at culture-fair testing. In *Western Regional Conference on Testing Problems Proceedings for 1968*, Measurement for Educational Planning. Berkeley, California: Educational Testing Service, Western Office. Pp. 50–104. Reprinted in: Hellmuth, J. (Ed.), *Disadvantaged child. Vol. 3, Compensatory education: A national debate.* New York: Brunner/Mazel, 1970. Pp. 53–101.

70. Jensen, A. R. (1968). Influences of biological, psychological, and social deprivations upon learning and performance. In *Perspectives on human deprivation.* Washington, DC: US. Department of Health, Education, and Welfare. Pp. 125–137.

71. Jensen, A. R. (1968). Discussion of Ernst Z. Rothkoph's two scientific approaches to the management of instructions. In R. M. Gagne and W. J. Gephart (Eds.), *Learning research and school subjects.* Itasca, IL: F. E. Peacock. Pp. 134–141.

72. Jensen, A. R. (1968). The biology of maladjustment. Review of *Studies of troublesome children,* by D. H. Stott. *Contemporary Psychology, 13,* 204–206.

73. Jensen, A. R., and Rohwer, W. D., Jr. (1968). Mental retardation, mental age, and learning rate. *Journal of Educational Psychology, 59,* 402–403.

74. Deutsch, M., Katz, I., and Jensen, A. R. (Eds.). (1968). *Social class, race, and psychological development.* New York: Holt, Rinehart, and Winston. Pp. v + 423.

75. Lee, S. S., and Jensen, A. R. (1968). Effect of awareness on 3-stage mediated association. *Journal of Verbal Learning and Verbal Behavior, 7,* 1005–1009.

1969

76. Jensen, A. R. (1969). How much can we boost IQ and scholastic achievement? *Harvard Educational Review, 39,* 1–123. Reprinted in: Environment, heredity, and intelligence. *Harvard Educational Review,* Reprint Series No. 2, 1969. Pp. 1–123. *Congressional Record,* May 28, 1969, Vol. 115, No. 88. Pp. H4270–4298. Bracht, G. H., Hopkins, K., and Stanley, J. C. (Eds.), *Perspectives in educational and psychological measurement.* New York: Prentice-Hall, 1972. Pp. 191–213. Barnette, W. L., Jr. (Ed.), *Readings in psychological tests and measurements.* (3rd ed.). Baltimore: Williams and Wilkins, 1976. Pp. 370–380.

77. Jensen, A. R. (1969). Reducing the heredity-environment uncertainty. *Harvard Educational Review, 39,* 449–483. Reprinted in: Environment, heredity, and intelligence. *Harvard Educational Review,* Reprint Series No. 2, 1969. Pp. 209–243.

78. Jensen, A. R. (1969). Intelligence, learning ability, and socioeconomic status. *Journal of Special Education, 3,* 23–35. Reprinted in: *Mental Health Digest,* 1969, *1,* 9–12.

79. Jensen, A. R. (1969). *Understanding readiness: An occasional paper.* Urbana, IL: ERIC Clearinghouse on Early Childhood Education, National Laboratory on Early Childhood Education. Pp. 1–17.

80. Jensen, A. R. (1969). Jensen's theory of intelligence: A reply. *Journal of Educational Psychology, 60,* 427–431.

81. Jensen, A. R. (1969). The promotion of dogmatism. *Journal of Social Issues, 25,* 212–217, 219–222.

82. Jensen, A. R. (1969). Criticism or propaganda? *American Psychologist, 24,* 1040–1041.

83. Jensen, A. R. (1969). An embattled hypothesis [interview]. *Center Magazine, 2,* 77–80.

84. Jensen, A. R. (1969). Education ills: Diagnosis and cure? Review of *Who can be educated?,* by M. Schwebel. *Contemporary Psychology, 14,* 362–364.

85. Jensen, A. R. (1969). Review of *Pygmalion in the classroom,* by R. Rosenthal and Lenore Jacobson. *American Scientist, 57,* 44A–45A.

86. Jensen, A. R. (1969). Race and intelligence: The differences are real. *Psychology Today, 3,* 4–6. Reprinted in: Sexton, Patricia C. (Ed.), *Problems and policy in education.* New York: Allyn and Bacon, 1970.

Jacoby, R., and Glauberman, N. (Eds.) *The Bell Curve debate: History, documents, opinions.* New York: Random House, 1995.

87. Rohwer, W. D., Jr., and Jensen, A. R. (1969). A reply to Glass. *Journal of Educational Psychology, 60,* 417–418.

1970

88. Jensen, A. R. (1970). A theory of primary and secondary familial mental retardation. In N. R. Ellis (Ed.), *International reviews, of research in mental retardation.* Vol. 4. New York: Academic Press. Pp. 33–105.

89. Jensen, A. R. (1970). Hierarchical theories of mental ability. In B. Dockrell (Ed.), *On intelligence.* Toronto: Ontario Institute for Studies in Education. Pp. 119–190.

90. Jensen, A. R. (1970). IQ's of identical twins reared apart. *Behavior Genetics, 1,* 133–148. Reprinted in: Eysenck, H. J. (Ed.), *The measurement of intelligence.* Lancaster, UK: Medical and Technical Publishing Co., 1973. Pp. 273–288.

91. Jensen, A. R. (1970). Race and the genetics of intelligence: A reply to Lewontin. *Bulletin of the Atomic Scientists, 26,* 17–23. Reprinted in: Baer, D. (Ed.), *Heredity and society: Readings in social genetics.* New York: Macmillan, 1973. Pp. 300–311. Block, N. J., and Dworkin, G. (Eds.), *The IQ controversy.* New York: Pantheon, 1976. Pp. 93–106.

92. Jensen, A. R. (1970). Can we and should we study race differences? In J. Hellmuth (Ed.), *Disadvantaged child,* Vol. 3, *Compensatory education: A national debate.* New York: Brunner/Mazel. Pp. 124–157. Reprinted in: Grigham, J. C., and Weissbach, T. A. (Eds.), *Racial attitudes in America: Analysis and findings of social psychology.* New York: Harper and Row, 1971. Pp. 401–434. *Journal of the American Anthropological Association,* 1971, Anthropological Studies. No. 8. Wrightsman, L. S., and Brigham, J. C. (Eds.), *Contemporary issues in social psychology.* (2nd ed.). Monterey, CA: Brooks/Cole, 1973. Pp. 218–227.

93. Jensen, A. R. (1970). Learning ability, intelligence, and educability. In V. Ilen (Ed.), *Psychological factors in poverty.* Chicago: Markham. Pp. 106–132.

94. Jensen, A. R. (1970). The heritability of intelligence. *Science & Engineering, 33,* 40–43. Reprinted in: *Saturday Evening Post,* Summer, 1972. Rubinstein, J., and Slife, B. D. (Eds.), *Taking Sides: Clashing views on controversial psychological issues.* Guilford, CT: Dushkin Publishing Group, 1980. Pp. 232–238. Zimbardo, P., and Maslach, C. (Eds.), *Psychology for our times: Readings.* Glenview, IL: Scott, Foresman, 1973. Pp. 129–134.

95. Jensen, A. R. (1970). Statement of Dr. Arthur R. Jensen to the General Subcommittee on Education of the Committee on Education and Labor, House of Representatives, 92nd Congress, second session. *Hearings on Emergency School Aid Act of 1970.* (H.R. 17846). Washington DC: U.S. Government Printing Office. Pp. 333–342.

96. Jensen, A. R. (1970). Review of *Behavioral genetics: Methods and research,* edited by M. Manosevitz, G. Lindzey, and D. D. Thiessen. *Social Biology, 17,* 151–152.

97. Jensen, A. R. (1970). Parent and teacher attitudes toward integration and busing. *Research Resume,* No. 43, California Advisory Council on Educational Research, May 1970.

98. Jensen, A. R. (1970). Selection of minority students in higher education. *Toledo Law Review,* Spring–Summer, Nos. 2 and 3, 304–457.

99. Jensen, A. R., and Rohwer, W. D., Jr. (1970). *An experimental analysis of learning abilities in culturally disadvantaged children.* Final Report. Office of Economic Opportunity, Contract No. OEO 2404, 1970. Pp. 1–181.

1971

100. Jensen, A. R. (1971). Individual differences in visual and auditory memory. *Journal of Educational Psychology, 62,* 123–131.

101. Jensen, A. R. (1971). Controversies in intelligence: Heredity and environment. In D. W. Allen and E. Seifman (Eds.), *The teacher's handbook.* Glenview, IL: Scott, Foresman and Co. Pp. 642–654.

102. Jensen, A. R. (1971). The role of verbal mediation in mental development. *Journal of Genetic Psychology, 118,* 39–70.

103. Jensen, A. R. (1971). Heredity, environment, and intelligence. In L. C. Deighton (Ed.), *Encyclopedia of education,* Vol. 4. New York: Macmillan. Pp. 368–380.

104. Jensen, A. R. (1971). The race x sex x ability interaction. In R. Cancro (Ed.), *Contributions to intelligence.* New York: Grune and Stratton, 1971. Pp. 107–161.

105. Jensen, A. R. (1971). A note on why genetic correlations are not squared. *Psychological Bulletin, 75,* 223–224.
106. Jensen, A. R. (1971). Hebb's confusion about heritability. *American Psychologist, 26,* 394–395.
107. Jensen, A. R. (1971). Twin differences and race differences in IQ: A reply to Burgess and Jahoda. *Bulletin of the British Psychological Society, 24,* 195–198.
108. Jensen, A. R. (1971). Erblicher I.Q. oder Pädagogischer Optimismus vor einem anderen Gericht. *Neue Sammlung, 11,* 71–76.
109. Jensen, A. R. (1971). Do schools cheat minority children? *Educational Research, 14,* 3–28.
110. Jensen, A. R. (1971). The phylogeny and ontogeny of intelligence. *Perspectives in Biology and Medicine, 15,* 37–43.
111. Jensen, A. R. (1971). Heredity and environment: A controversy over IQ and scholastic achievement. In H. C. Lindgren and Fredrica Lindgren (Eds.), *Current readings in educational psychology.* (2nd ed.). New York: Wiley. Pp. 323–327.

1972
112. Jensen, A. R. (1972). *Genetics and education.* London: Methuen (New York: Harper and Row). Pp. *vii* + 379.
113. Jensen, A. R. (1972). A two-factor theory of familial mental retardation. In J. deGrouchy, F. J. G. Ebling, and I. W. Henderson (Eds.), *Human genetics.* Proceedings of the 4th International Congress of Human Genetics, Paris, September 1971. Amsterdam: Excerpta Medica, 1972. Pp. 263–271.
114. Jensen, A. R. (1972). Review of Analysis of Learning Potential. In O. K. Buros (Ed.), *Seventh mental measurements yearbook.* Highland Park, NJ: Gryphon Press. Vol. I. Pp. 622–625.
115. Jensen, A. R. (1972). The case for IQ tests: Reply to McClelland. *The Humanist, 32,* 14.
116. Jensen, A. R. (1972). The causes of twin differences in IQ: A reply to Gage. *Phi Delta Kappan, 53,* 420–421.
117. Jensen, A. R. (1972). Genetics and education: A second look. *New Scientist, 56,* 96–98.
118. Jensen, A. R. (1972). Scholastic achievement and intelligence (Statement to the U. S. Senate Select Committee on Equal Educational Opportunity). In *Environment, Intelligence, and Scholastic Achievement* (A compilation of testimony to the Select Committee on Equal Educational Opportunity, United States Senate, 92nd Congress, 2nd Session, June 1972). Washington, DC: U.S.

Government Printing Office. Pp. 55–68. Reprinted in: *Saturday Evening Post*, 1972, *244* (2), 150–152.

119. Jensen, A. R. (1972). Interpretation of heritability. *American Psychologist, 27*, 973–975.

120. Jensen, A. R. (1972). I.Q. and Race: Ethical issues. *The Humanist, 32*, 5–6.

121. Jensen, A. R. (1972). Heritability and teachability. In J. E. Bruno (Ed.), *Emerging issues in education*. Lexington, MA: D. C. Heath. Pp. 57–88.

122. Jensen, A. R. (1972). Comment on De Fries's paper. In Lee Ehrman, G. S. Omenn, and E. Caspari (Eds.), *Genetics, environment, and behavior*. New York: Academic Press, 1972. Pp. 23–25.

123. Jensen, A. R. (1972). Discussion of Tobach's paper. In Lee Ehrman, G. S. Omenn, and E. Caspari (Eds.), *Genetics, environment, and behavior*. New York: Academic Press, 1972. Pp. 240–246.

124. Jensen, A. R. (1972). Educabilité, transmission héréditaire et différences entre populations. (Educability, heritability, and population differences.) *Revue de Psychologie Appliqué, 22*, 21–34.

125. Jensen, A. R. (1972). Review of *Race, culture and intelligence*, edited by K. Richardson, D. Spears, and M. Richards. *New Society, 491*, 408–410.

126. Jensen, A. R. (1972). Sir Cyril Burt [Obituary]. *Psychometrika, 37*, 115–117.

127. Jensen, A. R. (1972). Jensen on Hirsch on "jensenism." *Educational Researcher, 1*, 15–16.

128. Jensen, A. R. (1972). Assessment of racial desegregation in the Berkeley Schools. In D. Adelson (Ed.), *Man as the measure: The crossroads*. (Community Psychology Series, No. 1. American Psychological Association, Div. 27.) New York: Behavioral Publications, Inc. Pp. 116–133.

129. Jensen, A. R. (1972). Educability, heritability, and population differences. *Proceedings of the 17th International Congress of Applied Psychology*. Brussels, Belgium: Editest.

130. Jensen, A. R. (1972). Letter-to-the-Editor on genetic IQ differences among social classes. *Perspectives in Biology and Medicine, 116*, 154–156.

131. Jensen, A. R. (1972). Review of WLW Culture Fair Inventory. In O. K. Buros (Ed.), *Seventh mental measurements yearbook*. Highland Park, NJ: Gryphon Press, Vol. 1. Pp. 720–721.

132. Jensen, A. R. (1972). The IQ controversy: A reply to Layzer. *Cognition, 4*, 427–452.

133. Jensen, A. R. (1972). Empirical basis of the periodic table of human cultures. In E. Haskell (Ed.), *Full circle: The moral force of unified science*. New York: Gordon and Breach, 1972. Pp. 156–164.

1973

134. Jensen, A. R. (1973). A case for dysgenics. *The Journal: Forum for Contemporary History*, 2 (4), 1–6.

135. Jensen, A. R. (1973). Some facts about the IQ. *The Journal: Forum for Contemporary History*, 2 (7), 68.

136. Jensen, A. R. (1973). Expanding the thesis: The IQ controversy. Review of *IQ in the meritocracy*, by R. J. Herrnstein. *Book World, Chicago Tribune*, June 24, 1973.

137. Jensen, A. R. (1973). On "Jensenism": A reply to critics. In B. Johnson (Ed.), *Education yearbook, 1973–74.* New York: Macmillan Educational Corporation. Pp. 276–298.

138. Jensen, A. R. (1973). Race, intelligence and genetics: The differences are real. *Psychology Today*, 7, 80–86. Reprinted in: Durland, W. R., and Bruening, W. H. (Eds.). *Ethical issues.* Palo Alto, CA: Mayfield, 1975. Pp. 403–414. Whitehead, Joan M. (Ed.). *Personality and learning 1.* London: Hodder and Stoughton, 1975. Pp. 345–351. Schell, R. E. (Ed.). *Readings in developmental psychology today.* (2nd ed.). New York: Random House, 1977. Pp. 230–234. Brigham, J. C., and Wrightsman, L. S. (Eds.). *Contemporary issues in social psychology.* (3rd ed.). Monterey, CA: Brooks/Cole, 1977.

139. Jensen, A. R. (1973). Critics of the IQ. Review of *The fallacy of IQ*, edited by C. Senna. *Georgia Review*, 27, 439–445.

140. Jensen, A. R. (1973). Personality and scholastic achievement in three ethnic groups. *British Journal of Educational Psychology*, 43, 115–125.

141. Jensen, A. R. (1973). Let's understand Skodak and Skeels, finally. *Educational Psychologist*, 10, 30–35.

142. Jensen, A. R. (1973). Skinner and human differences. In H. Wheeler (Ed.), *Beyond the punitive society.* San Francisco: W. H. Freeman. Pp. 117–198.

143. Jensen, A. R. (1973). *Educability and group differences.* London: Methuen (New York: Harper and Row). Pp. xiii + 407.

144. Jensen, A. R. (1973). *Educational differences.* London: Methuen. (New York: Barnes and Noble). Pp. xiii + 462.

145. Jensen, A. R. (1973). Bildungsfähigkeit, Erblichkeit und Bevölkerungsunterschiede. *Neue Anthropologie*, 1, 37–43.

146. Jensen, A. R. (1973). Level I and Level II abilities in three ethnic groups. *American Educational Research Journal*, 4, 263–276.

147. Jensen, A. R. (1973). Wie sehr können wir Intelligenz Quotient und schulische Leistung steigern? In H. Skowronek (Ed.), *Umwelt Lind Begabung.* Stuttgart, W. Germany: Klett/Cotta. (Paperback edition published by Ullstein Taschenbuch Verlag, 1982.)

148. Jensen, A. R., and Frederiksen, J. (1973). Free recall of categorized and uncategorized lists: A test of the Jensen hypothesis. *Journal of Educational Psychology, 65,* 304–312.

1974

149. Jensen, A. R. (1974). What is the question? What is the evidence? [Autobiography.] In T. S. Krawiec (Ed.), *The psychologists.* Vol. 2. New York: Oxford University Press. Pp. 203–244.

150. Jensen, A. R. (1974). Kinship correlations reported by Sir Cyril Burt. *Behavior Genetics, 4* (1), 1–28.

151. Jensen, A. R. (1974). Review of *Abilities: Their structure, growth, and action,* by R. B. Cattell. *American Journal of Psychology, 87,* 290–296.

152. Jensen, A. R. (1974). Review of *Genetic diversity and human equality,* by Th. Dobzhansky. *Perspectives in Biology and Medicine, 17,* 430–434.

153. Jensen, A. R. (1974). How biased are culture-loaded tests? *Genetic Psychology Monographs, 90,* 185–244.

154. Jensen, A. R. (1974). Effects of race of examiner on the mental test scores of white and black pupils. *Journal of Educational Measurement, 11,* 1–14.

155. Jensen, A. R. (1974). Ethnicity and scholastic achievement. *Psychological Reports, 34,* 659–668.

156. Jensen, A. R. (1974). Cumulative deficit: A testable hypothesis? *Developmental Psychology, 10,* 996–1019.

157. Jensen, A. R. (1974). Interaction of Level I and Level II abilities with race and socioeconomic status. *Journal of Educational Psychology, 66,* 99–111. Reprinted in: Wittrock, M. C. (Ed.), *Learning and instruction.* Berkeley, CA: McCutchan, 1977. Pp. 270–290.

158. Jensen, A. R. (1974). Equality for minorities. In H. J. Walberg (Ed.), *Evaluating educational performance.* Berkeley, CA: McCutchan. Pp. 175–222.

159. Jensen, A. R. (1974). The strange case of Dr. Jensen and Mr. Hyde? *American Psychologist, 29,* 467–468.

160. Jensen, A. R. (1974). Educability and group differences. *Nature, 250,* 713–714.

161. Jensen, A. R. (1974). Race and intelligence: The case for genetics. *Times Educational Supplement,* London, September 20, 1974, No. 3095, 20–21.

1975

162. Jensen, A. R. (1975). The price of inequality. *Oxford Review of Education, 1* (1), 13–25.

163. Jensen, A. R. (1975). Les fondements scientifiques des inégalités ethniques. *Le Monde Diplomatique,* June 1975, No. 255, 19.

164. Jensen, A. R. (1975). A theoretical note on sex linkage and race differences in spatial ability. *Behavior Genetics, 5,* 151–164.

165. Jensen, A. R. (1975). The meaning of heritability in the behavioral sciences. *Educational Psychologist, 11,* 171–183.

166. Jensen, A. R. (1975). Panorama of modern behavioral genetics. Review of *Introduction to behavioral genetics,* by G. E. McCleam and J. C. DeFries. *Contemporary Psychology, 20,* 926–928.

167. Jensen, A. R. (1975). Race and mental ability. In J. F. Ebling (Ed.), *Racial variation in man.* London: Institute of Biology/Blackwell. Pp. 71–108.

168. Jensen, A. R. (1975). Es gibt Unterschiede zwischen Schwarzen und Weissen? *Psychologie Heute,* Jan. 1975, 63–75.

169. Jensen, A. R. (1975). Interview: Rasse und Begabung. *Nation Europa,* September 1975, 19–28.

170. Jensen, A. R., and Figueroa, R. A. (1975). Forward and backward digit span interaction with race and IQ: Predictions from Jensen's theory. *Journal of Educational Psychology, 67,* 882–893.

1976

171. Jensen, A. R. (1976). Race differences, strategy training, and improper inference. *Journal of Educational Psychology, 68,* 130–131.

172. Jensen, A. R. (1976). Equality and diversity in education. In Ashline, N. F., Pezullo, T. R.., and Norris, C. I. (Eds.), *Education, inequality, and national policy.* Lexington, MA: Lexington Books, 1976. Pp. 125–136.

173. Jensen, A. R. (1976). Addendum to human diversity discussion. In B. D. Davis and Patricia Flaherty (Eds.), *Human diversity: Its causes and social significance.* Cambridge, MA: Ballinger, 1976. Pp. 223–228.

174. Jensen, A. R. (1976). Twins' IQ's. A reply to Schwartz and Schwartz. *Behavior Genetics, 6,* 369–371.

175. Jensen, A. R. (1976). Eine Zweifactorentheorie des familiären Schwachsinns. *Neue Anthropologie, 4,* 5360.

176. Jensen, A. R. (1976). Test bias and construct validity. *Phi Delta Kappan, 58,* 34–346.

177. Jensen, A. R. (1976). Heritability of IQ [Letter-to-the-Editor]. *Science, 194,* 6–14.

178. Jensen, A. R. (1976). The problem of genotype-environment correlation in the estimation of heritability from monozygotic and dizygotic twins. *Acta Geneticae Medicae et Gemellologiae, 25*, 86–99.

1977

179. Jensen, A. R. (1977). An examination of culture bias in the Wonderlic Personnel Test. *Intelligence, 1,* 5164.
180. Jensen, A. R. (1977). Cumulative deficit in IQ of blacks in the rural South. *Developmental Psychology, 13,* 1841–1891.
Reprinted in: Willerman, L., and Turner, R. G. (Eds.), *Readings about individual and group differences.* San Francisco: W. H. Freeman, 1979. Pp. 83–91.
181. Jensen, A. R. (1977). Race and mental ability. In A. H. Halsey (Ed.), *Heredity and environment.* London: Methuen. Pp. 215–262.
182. Jensen, A. R. (1977). An unfounded conclusion in M. W. Smith's analysis of culture bias in the Stanford-Binet intelligence scale. *Genetic Psychology Monographs, 130,* 113–115.
183. Jensen, A. R. (1977). Did Sir Cyril Burt fake his research on heritability of intelligence? *Phi Delta Kappan, 58,* 471–492. Reprinted in: *Education Digest,* March 1977, 42, 43–45.
184. Jensen, A. R. (1977). Die falschen Anscullidigungen gegen Sir Cyril Burt. *Neue Anthropologie, 5,* 15–16.

1978

185. Jensen, A. R. (1978). Genetic and behavioral effects of nonrandom mating. In R. T. Osborne, C. E. Noble, and N. Weyl (Eds.), *Human variation.* New York: Academic Press. Pp. 51–105.
186. Jensen, A. R. (1978). Sex linkage and race differences in spatial ability: A reply. *Behavioral Genetics, 8,* 213–217.
187. Jensen, A. R. (1978). Sir Cyril Burt in perspective. *American Psychologist, 33,* 499–503.
188. Jensen, A. R. (1978). The current status of the IQ controversy. *Australian Psychologist, 13,* 7–28.
189. Jensen, A. R. (1978). The nature of intelligence and its relation to learning. In S. Murray-Smith (Ed.), *Melbourne studies in education.* Melbourne University Press. Pp. 107–133. Reprinted in: *Journal of Research and Development in Education, 12,* 79–95.
190. Jensen, A. R. (1978). Racism refuted [Correspondence]. *Nature, 274,* 738.

191. Jensen, A. R. (1978). Zum Stand des Streits um die Intelligenz. *Neue Anthropologie, 6,* 29–40.

192. Jensen, A. R. (1978). IQ controversy. *Baltimore Sun,* Nov. 24, 1978, A12.

193. Jensen, A. R. (1978). Citation Classics (How much can we boost IQ and scholastic achievement?). *Current Contents,* No. 41 (October 9), 16.

1979

194. Jensen, A. R. (1979). *g:* Outmoded theory or unconquered frontier? *Creative Science and Technology, 2,* 16–29.

195. Jensen, A. R. (1979). Review of *Inheritance of creative intelligence,* by J. L. Karlsson. *Journal of Nervous and Mental Diseases, 167,* 711–713.

196. Jensen, A. R., and Marisi, D. Q. (1979). A note on the heritability of memory span. *Behavior Genetics, 9,* 379–387.

197. Jensen, A. R., and Munro, E. (1979). Reaction time, movement time, and intelligence. *Intelligence, 3,* 121–126.

198. Jensen, A. R., and Osborne, R. T. (1979). Forward and backward digit span interaction with race and IQ: A longitudinal developmental comparison. *Indian Journal of Psychology, 54,* 75–87.

1980

199. Jensen, A. R. (1980). *Bias in mental testing.* New York: The Free Press (London: Methuen). Pp. *xiii* + 786.

200. Jensen, A. R. (1980). Uses of sibling data in educational and psychological research. *American Educational Research Journal, 17,* 153–170.

201. Jensen, A. R. (1980). Chronometric analysis of intelligence. *Journal of Social and Biological Structures, 3,* 103–122.

202. Jensen, A. R. (1980). Précis of *Bias in Mental Testing. Behavioral and Brain Sciences, 3,* 325–333.

203. Jensen, A. R. (1980). Correcting the bias against mental testing: A preponderance of peer agreement. *Behavioral and Brain Sciences, 3,* 359–371.

204. Jensen, A. R. (1980). A critical took at test bias: Fallacies and manifestations. *New Horizons, 21,* 44–64.

205. Jensen, A. R., and Inouye, A. R. (1980). Level I and Level II abilities in Asian, White, and Black children. *Intelligence, 4,* 41–49.

1981

206. Jensen, A. R. (1981). *Straight talk about mental tests.* New York: Free Press. Pp. *xiv* + 269.

207. Jensen, A. R. (1981). Raising the IQ: The Ramey and Haskins Study. *Intelligence, 5,* 29–40.

208. Jensen, A. R. (1981). Obstacles, problems, and pitfalls in differential psychology. In S. Scarr, *Race, social class, and individual differences in IQ.* Hillsdale, NJ: Erlbaum. Pp. 483–514.

209. Jensen, A. R. (1981). Reaction time and intelligence. In M. Friedman, J. P. Das, and N. O'Connor (Eds.), *Intelligence and learning.* New York: Plenum. Pp. 39–50.

210. Jensen, A. R. (1981). Impressions of India. *Update* (Graduate School of Education, University of California, Berkeley), Winter.

211. Jensen, A. R. (1981). Citation Classic (The Stroop color-word test: A review). *Current Contents, 13,* 20.

212. Jensen, A. R. (1981). An interview with Arthur Jensen. *Communique* (National Association of School Psychologists), *10,* 3–5.

213. Jensen, A. R. (1981). Taboo, constraint, and responsibility in educational research. *New Horizons, 22,* 11–20.

214. Jensen, A. R. (1981). A nontechnical guide to the IQ controversy. *New Horizons, 22,* 1–26.

215. Jensen, A. R., Schafer, E. W. P., and Crinella, F. (1981). Reaction time, evoked brain potentials, and psychometric *g* in the severely retarded. *Intelligence, 5,* 179–197.

1982

216. Jensen, A. R. (1982). Intelligence. In S. B. Parker (Ed.), *Encyclopedia of science and technology.* (5th ed.). New York: McGraw-Hill.

217. Jensen, A. R. (1982). Bias in mental testing: A final word. *Behavioral and Brain Sciences, 5,* 339–340.

218. Jensen, A. R. (1982). The chronometry of intelligence. In R. J. Sternberg (Ed.), *Advances in the psychology of human intelligence, Vol. 1.* Hillsdale, NJ: Erlbaum. Pp. 255–310.

219. Jensen, A. R. (1982). Reaction time and psychometric *g*. In H. J. Eysenck (Ed.), *A model for intelligence.* New York: Springer. Pp. 93–132.

220. Jensen, A. R. (1982). Changing conceptions of intelligence. *Education and Training of the Mentally Retarded, 17,* 3–5.

221. Jensen, A. R. (1982). The debunking of scientific fossils and straw persons. Essay-review of *The mismeasure of man,* by S. J. Gould. *Contemporary Education Review, 1,* 121–135.

222. Jensen, A. R. (1982). Level I/Level II: Factors or categories? *Journal of Educational Psychology, 74,* 868–873.

223. Jensen, A. R. (1982). The race concept: Physical variation and correlated social-
     ly significant behavioral variation. *Current Anthropology, 23,* 649–650.
224. Jensen, A. R., and Reynolds, C. R. (1982). Race, social class, and ability pat-
     terns on the WISC-R. *Personality and Individual Differences, 3,* 423–438.

1983

225. Jensen, A. R. (1983). Sir Cyril Burt: A personal recollection. *Association of
     Educational Psychologists Journal, 6,* 13–20.
226. Jensen, A. R. (1983). Effects of inbreeding on mental-ability factors. *Personality
     and Individual Differences, 4,* 71–87.
227. Jensen, A. R. (1983). The nonmanipulable and effectively manipulable variables
     in education. *Education and Society,* 51–62. Reprinted in: *New Horizons,* 1983, *24,*
     31–50.
228. Jensen, A. R. (1983). Review of *The testing of Negro intelligence* (Vol. II), edited by
     R. T. Osborne and F. C. J. McGurk. *Personality and Individual Differences, 4,*
     234–235.
229. Jensen, A. R. (1983). Review of *The inheritance of personality and ability,* by R. B.
     Cattell. *Personality and Individual Differences, 4,* 365–368.
230. Jensen, A. R. (1983). The definition of intelligence and factor score indeter-
     minacy. *Behavioral and Brain Sciences, 6,* 313–315.
231. Jensen, A. R. (1983). Again, how much can we boost IQ? Review of *How and
     how much can intelligence be increased?,* edited by D. K. Detterman and R. J.
     Sternberg. *Contemporary Psychology, 28,* 756–758.
232. Jensen, A. R. (1983). Critical flicker frequency and intelligence. *Intelligence, 7,*
     217–225.
233. Jensen, A. R. (1983). Taboo, constraint, and responsibility in educational
     research. *Journal of Social, Political and Economic Studies, 8,* 301–311.
234. Jensen, A. R. (1983). Beyond Groth's sociological criticism of psychometrics.
     Wisconsin Sociologist, 20, 102–105.
235. Jensen, A. R., and Reynolds, C. R. (1983). Sex differences on the WISC-R.
     Personality and Individual Differences, 4, 223–226.
236. Reynolds, C. R., and Jensen, A. R. (1983). WISC-R subscale patterns of abil-
     ities of blacks and whites matched on full scale IQ. *Journal of Educational
     Psychology, 75,* 207–214.
237. Sen, A., Jensen, A. R., Sen, A. K., and Arora, I. Correlation between reaction
     time and intelligence in psychometrically similar groups in America and India.
     Applied Research in Mental Retardation, 4, 139–152.

1984

238. Jensen, A. R. (1984). Francis Galton (1822–1911). In R. J. Corsini (Ed.), *Encyclopedia of psychology* (Vol. 2, p. 43). New York: Wiley.

239. Jensen, A. R. (1984). Karl Pearson (1857–1936). In R. J. Corsini (Ed.), *Encyclopedia of psychology* (Vol. 2, pp. 490–491). New York: Wiley.

240. Jensen, A. R. (1984). Charles Edward Spearman (1863–1945). In R. J. Corsini (Ed.), *Encyclopedia of psychology* (Vol. 3, pp. 353–354). New York: Wiley.

241. Jensen, A. R. (1984). Louis Leon Thurstone (1887–1955). In R. J. Corsini (Ed.), *Encyclopedia of psychology* (Vol. 3, pp. 426–427). New York: Wiley.

242. Jensen, A. R. (1984). Law of filial regression. In R. J. Corsini (Ed.), *Encyclopedia of psychology* (Vol. 2, pp. 280–281). New York: Wiley.

243. Jensen, A. R. (1984). Cultural bias in tests. In R. J. Corsini (Ed.), *Encyclopedia of psychology* (Vol. 1, pp. 331–332). New York: Wiley.

244. Jensen, A. R. (1984). Inbreeding in human factors. In R. J. Corsini (Ed.), *Encyclopedia of psychology* (Vol. 2, pp. 191–192). New York: Wiley.

245. Jensen, A. R. (1984). General intelligence factor. In R. J. Corsini (Ed.), *Encyclopedia of psychology* (Vol. 2, p. 48). New York: Wiley.

246. Jensen, A. R. (1984). Heritability. In R. J. Corsini (Ed.), *Encyclopedia of psychology* (Vol. 2, p. 108). New York: Wiley.

247. Jensen, A. R. (1984). Test bias: Concepts and criticisms. In C. R. Reynolds and R. T. Brown (Eds.), *Perspectives on bias in mental testing.* New York: Plenum. Pp. 507–586.

248. Jensen, A. R. (1984). Political ideologies and educational research. *Phi Delta Kappan, 65,* 460–462.

249. Jensen, A. R. (1984). The limited plasticity of human intelligence. *New Horizons, 25,* 18–22.

250. Jensen, A. R. (1984). Mental speed and levels of analysis. *Behavioral and Brain Sciences, 7,* 295–296.

251. Jensen, A. R. (1984). Test validity: *g* versus the specificity doctrine. *Journal of Social and Biological Structures, 7,* 93–118.

252. Jensen, A. R. (1984). Jensen oversimplified: A reply to Sternberg. *Journal of Social and Biological Structures, 7,* 127–130.

253. Jensen, A. R. (1984). Review of *Intelligence and national achievement,* edited by R. B. Cattell. *Personality and Individual Differences, 5,* 491–492.

254. Jensen, A. R. (1984). Sociobiology and differential psychology: The arduous climb from plausibility to proof. In J. R. Royce and L. P. Mos (Eds.), *Annals of theoretical psychology* (Vol. 2). Pp. 49–58. New York: Plenum.

255. Jensen, A. R. (1984). The black-white difference on the K-ABC: Implications for future tests. *Journal of Special Education, 18*, 377–408.

256. Jensen, A. R. (1984). Objectivity and the genetics of IQ: A reply to Steven Selden. *Phi Delta Kappan, 66*, 284–286.

257. Agrawal, N., Sinha, S. N., and Jensen, A. R. (1984). Effects of inbreeding on Raven Matrices. *Behavior Genetics, 14*, 579–585.

258. Vernon, P. A., and Jensen, A. R. (1984). Individual and group differences in intelligence and speed of information processing. *Personality and Individual Differences, 5*, 411–423.

1985

259. Jensen, A. R. (1985). Compensatory education and the theory of intelligence. *Phi Delta Kappan, 66*, 554–558. Reprinted in: Slife, B. (Ed.), *Taking sides: Clashing views on controversial issues* (8th ed.). Guilford, CT: Dushkin.

260. Jensen, A. R. (1985). Armed Services Vocational Aptitude Battery. *Measurement and Evaluation in Counseling and Development, 18*, 32–37.

261. Jensen, A. R. (1985). Review of the Predictive Ability Test, Adult Edition. In J. V. Mitchell, Jr. (Ed.), *The ninth mental measurements yearbook* (Vol. 2). Lincoln: University of Nebraska Press. Pp. 1184–1185.

262. Jensen, A. R. (1985). Review of Minnesota Spatial Relations Test, Revised Edition. In J. V. Mitchell, Jr. (Ed.), *The ninth mental measurements yearbook* (Vol. 2). Lincoln: University of Nebraska Press. Pp. 1014–1015.

263. Jensen, A. R. (1985). Methodological and statistical techniques for the chronometric study of mental abilities. In C. R. Reynolds and V. L. Willson (Eds.), *Methodological and statistical advances in the study of individual differences*. New York: Plenum. Pp. 51–116.

264. Jensen, A. R. (1985). Race differences and Type II errors: A comment on Borkowski and Krause. *Intelligence, 9*, 33–39.

265. Jensen, A. R. (1985). The nature of the black-white difference on various psychometric tests: Spearman's hypothesis. *Behavioral and Brain Sciences, 8*, 193–219.

266. Jensen, A. R. (1985). The black-white difference in *g*: A phenomenon in search of a theory. *Behavioral and Brain Sciences, 8*, 246–263.

267. Jensen, A. R. (1985). Humphrey's attenuated test of Spearman's hypothesis. *Intelligence, 9*, 285–289.

268. Jensen, A. R. (1985). Immunoreactive theory and the genetics of mental ability. *Behavioral and Brain Sciences, 8*, 453.

269. Cohn S. J., Carlson, J. S., and Jensen, A. R. (1985). Speed of information processing in academically gifted youths. *Personality and Individual Differences, 6,* 621–629.

1986

270. Jensen, A. R. (1986). Intelligence: "Definition," measurement, and future research. In R. J. Sternberg and D. K. Detterman (Eds.), *What is intelligence? Contemporary viewpoints on its nature and definition.* Norwood, NJ: Ablex.
271. Jensen, A. R. (1986). The theory of intelligence. In S. Modgil and C. Modgil (Eds.), *Hans Eysenck: Searching for a scientific basis for human behavior.* London: Falmer Press.
272. Jensen, A. R. (1986). *g*: Artifact or reality? *Journal of Vocational Behavior, 29,* 301–331.
273. Jensen, A. R. (1986). Review of *Academic work and educational excellence: Raising student productivity,* edited by T. M. Tomlinson and H. J. Walberg. *Educational Evaluation and Policy Analysis, 8,* 447–451.
274. Jensen, A. R., and Vernon, P. A. (1986). Jensen's reaction time studies: A reply to Longstreth. *Intelligence, 10,* 153–179.

1987

275. Jensen, A. R. (1987). Citation Classic: (Educability and group differences). *Current Contents: Social & Behavioral Sciences, 19* (46).
276. Jensen, A. R. (1987). Citation Classic: (Bias in mental testing). *Current Contents: Social & Behavioral Sciences, 19* (46).
277. Jensen, A. R. (1987). Process differences and individual differences in some cognitive tasks. *Intelligence, 11,* 107–136.
278. Jensen, A. R. (1987). Unconfounding genetic and nonshared environmental effects. *Behavioral and Brain Sciences, 10,* 26–27.
279. Jensen, A. R. (1987). The plasticity of "intelligence" at different levels of analysis. In J. Lochhead, J. Bishop, and D. Perkins (Eds.), *Thinking: Progress in research and teaching.* Philadelphia: Franklin Institute Press.
280. Jensen, A. R. (1987). Individual differences in mental ability. In J. A. Glover and R. R. Ronning (Eds.), *A history of educational psychology.* New York: Plenum.
281. Jensen, A. R. (1987). The *g* beyond factor analysis. In R. R. Ronning, J. A. Glover, J. C. Conoley, and J. C. Witt (Eds.), *The influence of cognitive psychology on testing.* Hillsdale, NJ: Erlbaum. Pp. 87–142.

282. Jensen, A. R. (1987). Differential psychology: Towards consensus. In M. Modgil and C. Modgil (Eds.), *Arthur Jensen: Consensus and controversy*. London: Falmer Press.

283. Jensen, A. R. (1987). *g* as a focus of concerted research effort [Editorial]. *Intelligence, 11*, 193–198.

284. Jensen, A. R. (1987). Intelligence as a fact of nature. *Zeitschrift für Pädagogische Psychologie, 1*, 157–169.

285. Jensen, A. R. (1987). Individual differences in the Hick paradigm. In P. A. Vernon (Ed.), *Speed of information processing and intelligence*. Norwood, NJ: Ablex.

286. Jensen, A. R. (1987). Mental chronometry in the study of learning disabilities. *Mental Retardation and Learning Disability Bulletin, 15*, 67–88.

287. Jensen, A. R. (1987). Further evidence for Spearman's hypothesis concerning black-white differences on psychometric tests. *The Behavioral and Brain Sciences, 10*, 512–519.

288. Jensen, A. R., and McGurk, F. C. J. (1987). Black-white bias in "cultural" and "noncultural" test items. *Personality and Individual Differences, 8*, 295–301.

289. Naglieri, J. A., and Jensen, A. R. (1987). Comparison of black-white differences on the WISC-R and the KABC: Spearman's hypothesis. *Intelligence, 11*, 21–43.

1988

290. Jensen, A. R. (1988). Mongoloid mental ability: Evolution or culture? *Mensa Research Bulletin, 24*, 23–25.

291. Jensen, A. R. (1988). Review of *Practical intelligence: Nature and origins of competence in the everyday world*, edited by R. J. Sternberg and R. K. Wagner. *Personality and Individual Differences, 9*, 199–200.

292. Jensen, A. R. (1988). Speed of information processing and population differences. In S. H. Irvine (Ed.), *The cultural context of human ability*. London: Cambridge University Press.

293. Jensen, A. R. (1988). Review of the Armed Services Vocational Aptitude Battery. In J. T. Kapes and M. M. Mastie (Eds.), *A counselor's guide to career assessment instruments*. Alexandria, VA: National Career Development Association. Pp. 59–62.

294. Jensen, A. R. (1988). Sex differences in arithmetic computation and reasoning in prepubertal boys and girls. *Behavioral and Brain Sciences, 11*, 198–199.

295. Jensen, A. R., and Faulstich, M. E. (1988). Psychometric *g* in black and white prisoners. *Personality and Individual Differences, 9*, 925–928.

296. Jensen, A. R., Larson, J., and Paul, S. M. (1988). Psychometric *g* and mental processing speed on a semantic verification test. *Personality and Individual Differences, 9*, 243–255.

297. Jensen, A. R., Saccuzzo, D. P., and Larson, G. E. (1988). Equating the Standard and Advanced Forms of the Raven Progressive Matrices. *Educational and Psychological Measurement, 48,* 1091–1095.
298. Cohn, S. J., Cohn, C. M. G., and Jensen, A. R. (1988). Myopia and intelligence: A pleiotropic relationship? *Human Genetics, 80,* 53–58.
299. Kranzler, J. H., Whang, P. A., and Jensen, A. R. (1988). Jensen's use of the Hick paradigm: Visual attention and order effects. *Intelligence, 12,* 371–391.

1989
300. Jensen, A. R. (1989). The relationship between learning and intelligence. *Learning and Individual Differences, 1,* 37–62.
301. Jensen, A. R. (1989). Philip Ewart Vernon (1905–1987) [Obituary]. *Psychologist, 44,* 844.
302. Jensen, A. R. (1989). "Revised" Updated. Review of *Intelligence: Its structure, growth and action,* by R. B. Cattell. *Contemporary Psychology, 34,* 140–141.
303. Jensen, A. R. (1989). Raising IQ without increasing *g?* A review of *The Milwaukee Project: Preventing mental retardation in children at risk. Developmental Review, 9,* 234–258.
304. Jensen, A. R. (1989). "Total perceived value" as the basis of assortative mating in humans. *Behavioral and Brain Sciences, 12,* 531.
305. Jensen, A. R. (1989). New findings on the intellectually gifted. *New Horizons, 30,* 73–80.
306. Jensen, A. R., Cohn, S. J., and Cohn, C. M. G. (1989). Speed of information processing in academically gifted youths and their siblings. *Personality and Individual Differences, 10,* 29–34.
307. Buckhalt, J., and Jensen, A. R. (1989). The *British Ability Scales* Speed of Information Processing subtest: What does it measure? *British Journal of Educational Psychology, 59,* 100–107.
308. Kranzler, J. H., and Jensen, A. R. (1989). Inspection time and intelligence: A meta-analysis. *Intelligence, 13,* 329–347.
309. Reed, T. E., and Jensen, A. R. (1989). Short latency visual evoked potentials (VEPs), visual tract speed, and intelligence. Significant correlations. Abstract. *Behavior Genetics, 19,* 772–773.

1990
310. Jensen, A. R. (1990). Speed of information processing in a calculating prodigy. *Intelligence, 14,* 259–274.

311. Jensen, A. R. (1990). Straight history. Review of *Schools as sorters: Lewis M. Terman, applied psychology, and the intelligence testing movement, 1890–1930*, by P. D. Chapman. *Contemporary Psychology, 35,* 1147–1148.

312. Jensen, A. R., and Reed, T. E. (1990). Simple reaction time as a suppressor variable in the chronometric study of intelligence. *Intelligence, 14,* 375–388.

1991

313. Jensen, A. R. (1991). Spearman's *g* and the problem of educational equality. *Oxford Review of Education, 17* (2), 169–187.

314. Jensen, A. R. (1991). General mental ability: From psychometrics to biology. *Psychodiagnostique, 16,* 134–144.

315. Jensen, A. R. (1991). Speed of cognitive processes: A chronometric anchor for psychometric tests of *g*. *Psychological Test Bulletin, 4,* 59–70.

316. Jensen, A. R. (1991). IQ and Science: The mysterious Burt affair. *The Public Interest, 105,* 93–106.

317. Jensen, A. R. (1991). Review of *U. S. race relations in the 1980s and 1990s: Challenges and alternatives,* edited by G. E. Thomas. *Personality and Individual Differences, 12,* 321–322.

318. Jensen, A. R. (1991). Spirmanov *g* factor: Veze izmedu psihometrije i biologije. *Psihologija, 24,* 167–193.

319. Kranzler, J. H., and Jensen, A. R. (1991). The nature of psychometric *g*: Unitary process or a number of independent processes? *Intelligence, 15,* 397–422.

320. Kranzler, J. H., and Jensen, A. R. (1991). Unitary *g*: Unquestioned postulate or empirical fact? *Intelligence, 15,* 437–448.

321. Reed, T. E., and Jensen, A. R. (1991). Arm nerve conduction velocity (NCV), brain NCV, reaction time, and intelligence. *Intelligence, 15,* 33–47.

1992

322. Jensen, A. R. (1992). Understanding *g* in terms of information processing. *Educational Psychology Review, 4,* 271–308.

323. Jensen, A. R. (1992). Spearman's hypothesis: Methodology and evidence. *Multivariate Behavioral Research, 27,* 225–233.

324. Jensen, A. R. (1992). More on Psychometric *g* and "Spearman's hypothesis." *Multivariate Behavioral Research, 27,* 257–260.

325. Jensen, A. R. (1992). Scientific fraud or false accusations? The case of Cyril Burt. In D. J. Miller and M. Hersen (Eds.), *Research findings in the behavioral and biomedical sciences.* New York: Wiley and Sons, Inc.

326. Jensen, A. R. (1992). The importance of intraindividual variability in reaction time. *Personality and Individual Differences, 13,* 869–882.

327. Jensen, A. R. (1992). Preface. In R. Pearson (Ed.), *Shockley on race, eugenics, and dysgenics.* Washington, DC: Scott-Townsend. Pp. 1–13.

328. Jensen, A. R. (1992). Mental ability: Critical thresholds and social policy. *Journal of Social, Political and Economic Studies, 17,* 1–11.

329. Jensen, A. R. (1992). The Cyril Burt scandal, research taboos, and the media. *The General Psychologist, 28,* 16–21.

330. Jensen, A. R. (1992). The relation between information processing time and right/wrong responses. *American Journal on Mental Retardation, 97,* 290–292.

331. Jensen, A. R. (1992). Vehicles of *g. Psychological Science, 3,* 275–278.

332. Jensen, A. R., and Reed, T. E. (1992). The correlation between reaction time and the ponderal index. *Perceptual and Motor Skills, 75,* 843–846.

333. Jensen, A. R., and Wilson, M. (1992). Henry Felix Kaiser (1927–1992). *In Memoriam,* pp. 88–91. Berkeley: University of California.

334. Reed, T. E., and Jensen, A. R. (1992). Conduction velocity in a brain nerve pathway of normal adults correlates with intelligence level. *Intelligence, 16,* 259–278.

1993

335. Jensen, A. R. (1993). Psychometric *g* and achievement. In B. R. Gifford (Ed.), *Policy perspectives on educational testing.* Norwell, MA: Kluwer Academic Publishers. Pp. 117–227.

336. Jensen, A. R. (1993). Test validity: *g* versus "tacit knowledge." *Current Directions in Psychological Science, 2,* 9–10.

337. Jensen, A. R. (1993). Why is reaction time correlated with psychometric *g?* *Current Directions in Psychological Science, 2,* 53–56.

338. Jensen, A. R. (1993). Spearman's hypothesis tested with chronometric information processing tasks. *Intelligence, 17,* 47–77.

339. Jensen, A. R. (1993). Spearman's *g:* Links between psychometrics and biology. *Annals of the New York Academy of Sciences, 702,* 103–131.

340. Jensen, A. R., and Sinha, S. N. (1993). Physical correlates of human intelligence. In P. A. Vernon (Ed.), *Biological approaches to the study of human intelligence.* Norwood, NJ: Ablex. Pp. 139–242.

341. Jensen, A. R., and Whang, P. A. (1993). Reaction times and intelligence: A comparison of Chinese-American and Anglo-American children. *Journal of Biosocial Science, 25,* 397–410.

342. Kranzler, J. H., and Jensen, A. R. (1993). Psychometric *g* is still not unitary after eliminating supposed "impurities": Further comment on Carroll. *Intelligence, 17,* 11–14.

343. Reed, T. E., and Jensen, A. R. (1993). Choice reaction time and visual pathway nerve conduction velocity both correlate with intelligence but appear not to correlate with each other: Implications for information processing. *Intelligence, 17,* 191–203.

344. Reed, T. E., and Jensen, A. R. (1993). Cranial capacity: New Caucasian data and comments on Rushton's claimed Mongoloid-Caucasoid brain-size differences. *Intelligence, 17,* 423–431.

345. Reed, T. E., and Jensen, A. R. (1993). A somatosensory latency between the thalamus and cortex also correlates with level of intelligence. *Intelligence, 17,* 443–450.

1994

346. Jensen, A. R. (1994). Afterword: Deafness and the nature of mental abilities. In J. P. Braden, *Deafness, deprivation, and IQ.* New York: Plenum. Pp. 203–208.

347. Jensen, A. R. (1994). Phlogiston, animal magnetism, and intelligence. In D. K. Detterman (Ed.), *Current topics in human intelligence, Vol. 4: Theories of intelligence.* Norwood, NJ: Ablex. Pp. 257–284.

348. Jensen, A. R. (1994). Review of *Intelligence* (2nd ed.), by N. Brody. *American Journal on Mental Retardation, 98,* 663–667.

349. Jensen, A. R. (1994). Reaction time. In R. J. Corsini (Ed.), *Encyclopedia of Psychology,* 2nd. ed. Vol. 3. New York: Wiley. Pp. 282–285.

350. Jensen, A. R. (1994). Humphreys's "behavioral repertoire" an epiphenomenon of *g*. *Psychological Inquiry, 5,* 208–210.

351. Jensen, A. R. (1994). Francis Galton. In R. J. Sternberg (Ed.), *Encyclopedia of Intelligence.* Vol. 1. New York: Macmillan. Pp. 457–463.

352. Jensen, A. R. (1994). Charles Edward Spearman. In R. J. Sternberg (Ed.), *Encyclopedia of Intelligence.* Vol. 2. New York: Macmillan. Pp. 1007–1014.

353. Jensen, A. R. (1994). Hans Jurgen Eysenck. In R. J. Sternberg (Ed.), *Encyclopedia of Intelligence.* Vol. 1. New York: Macmillan. Pp. 416–418.

354. Jensen, A. R. (1994). Race and IQ scores. In R. J. Sternberg (Ed.), *Encyclopedia of Intelligence.* Vol. 2. New York: Macmillan. Pp. 899–907.

355. Jensen, A. R. (1994). Psychometric *g* related to differences in head size. *Personality and Individual Differences, 17,* 597–606.

356. Jensen, A. R. (1994). Paroxysms of denial. *National Review, 46* (Dec. 5), 48–50. Reprinted in: Jacoby, R., and Glauberman, N. (Eds.), *The Bell Curve debate: History, documents, opinion.* New York: Random House, 1995.

357. Jensen, A. R., and Johnson, F. W. (1994). Race and sex differences in head size and IQ. *Intelligence, 18,* 309–333.

358. Jensen, A. R., and Ruddell, R. B. (1994). Guy Thomas Buswell. *In Memoriam.* Berkeley: University of California. Pp. 46–49.

359. Jensen, A. R., and Weng, J.-J. (1994). What is a good *g*? *Intelligence, 18,* 231–258.

360. Jensen, A. R., and Whang, P. A. (1994). Speed of accessing arithmetic facts in long-term memory: A comparison of Chinese-American and Anglo-American children. *Contemporary Educational Psychology, 19,* 1–12.

361. Jensen, A. R., and Wilson, M. (1994). Henry Felix Kaiser (1927–1992) [Obituary]. *American Psychologist, 49,* 1085.

362. Kranzler, J. H., Whang, P. A., and Jensen, A. R. (1994). Task complexity and the speed and efficiency of elemental information processing: Another look at the nature of intellectual giftedness. *Contemporary Educational Psychology, 19,* 447–459.

363. Shaughnessy, M. F. (1994). An interview with Arthur R. Jensen. *The School Field, 4,* 129–154.

1995

364. Jensen, A. R. (1995). Psychological research on race differences [Comment]. *American Psychologist, 50,* 41–42.

365. Jensen, A. R. (1995). Wanted: A unified theory of individual and group differences. [Abstract]. *Behavior Genetics, 25,* 272.

366. Jensen, A. R. (1995). IQ and science: The mysterious Burt affair. In N. J. Mackintosh (Ed.), *Cyril Burt: Fraud or framed?* Oxford: Oxford University Press.

1996

367. Jensen, A. R. (1996). Secular trends in IQ: Additional hypotheses. In D. K. Detterman (Ed.), *Current topics in human intelligence, Vol. 4: The environment.* Norwood, NJ: Ablex. Pp. 147–150.

368. Jensen, A. R. (1996). Inspection Time and *g* [Letter]. *Nature, 381,* 729.

369. Jensen, A. R. (1996). The locus of biological *g.* In I. Mervielde (Ed.), *Abstracts of the 8th European Conference on Personality,* University of Ghent, Belgium, July 11, 1996, p. 54.

370. Jensen, A. R. (1996). Giftedness and genius: Crucial differences. In C. P. Benbow and D. Lubinski (Eds.), *Intellectual talent: Psychometric and social issues,* Baltimore: Johns Hopkins University Press. Pp. 393–411.

371. Jensen, A. R. (1996). Review of *Genetics and experience,* by R. Plomin. *Journal of Social and Evolutionary Systems, 19,* 307–311. Reprinted in: *European Sociobiological Newsletter,* May 1997, No. 44, 24–28.

1997

372. Jensen, A. R. (1997). The puzzle of nongenetic variance. In R. J. Sternberg and E. L. Grigorenko (Eds.), *Intelligence, heredity, and environment.* Cambridge: Cambridge University Press. Pp. 42–88.

373. Jensen, A. R. (1997). The neurophysiology of *g.* In C. Cooper and V. Varma (Eds.), *Processes in individual differences.* London: Routledge. Pp. 108–125.

374. Jensen, A. R. (1997). Psychometric *g* and the race question. In J. Kingma and W. Tomic (Eds.), *Reflections on the concept of intelligence.* Greenwich, CT: JAI Press. Pp. 1–23.

375. Jensen, A. R. (1997). Introduction (to section on intelligence). In H. Nyborg (Ed.), *The scientific study of human nature: Tribute to Hans J. Eysenck at eighty.* New York: Elsevier. Pp. 215–220).

376. Jensen, A. R. (1997). The psychometrics of intelligence. In H. Nyborg (Ed.), *The scientific study of human nature: Tribute to Hans J. Eysenck at eighty.* New York: Elsevier. Pp. 221–239.

377. Jensen, A. R. (1997). Eysenck as teacher and mentor. In H. Nyborg (Ed.), *The scientific study of human nature: Tribute to Hans J. Eysenck at eighty.* New York: Elsevier. Pp. 543–559.

378. Jensen, A. R. (1997). Intelligence. In S. P. Parker F (Ed.), *Encyclopedia of science and technology.* 8th edition. New York: McGraw-Hill. Pp. 288–289.

1998

379. Jensen, A. R. (1998). *The g factor.* Westport, CT: Praeger.

380. Jensen, A. R. (1998). Spearman's law of diminishing returns. In A. Sen and A. K. Sen (Eds.), *Challenges of contemporary realities: A psychological perspective.* New Delhi: New Age International, Ltd.

381. Jensen, A. R. (1998). The *g* factor in the design of education. In R. J. Sternberg and W. M.. Williams (Eds.), *Intelligence, instruction, and assessment.* Hillsdale, NJ: Erlbaum. Pp. 111–131

382. Jensen, A. R. (1998). The suppressed relationship between IQ and the reaction time slope parameter of the Hick function. *Intelligence, 26,* 43–52.

383. Jensen, A. R. (1998). Jensen on "Jensenism." *Intelligence, 26*, 181–208.

384. Jensen, A. R. (1998). Adoption data and two *g*-related hypotheses. *Intelligence, 25*, 1–6.

1999

385. Jensen, A. R. (1999). Review of *Psychological testing of American minorities*, by R. J. Samuda. *Personality and Individual Differences, 26*, 1143–1145.

386. Jensen, A. R. (1999). Review of *Intelligence: A new look*, by H. J. Eysenck. *Galton Institute Newsletter, 32*, 6–8.

387. Caryl, P. G., Deary, I. J., Jensen, A. R., Neubauer, A. C., and Vickers, D. (1999). Information processing approaches to intelligence: Progress and prospects. In I. Mervielde, I. Deary, F. de Fruyt, and F. Ostendorf (Eds.), *Personality psychology in Europe: Volume 7*. Tilburg University Press. Pp. 181–219.

2000

388. Jensen, A. R. (2000). Hans Eysenck's final thoughts on intelligence. Special review of *Intelligence: A New Look*, by H. J. Eysenck. *Personality and Individual Differences, 28*, 191–194.

389. Jensen, A. R. (2000). Review of *Eminent Creativity, Everyday Creativity, and Health*, edited by M. A. Runco and R. Richards. *Personality and Individual Differences, 28*, 198–199.

390. Jensen, A. R. (2000). Elementary cognitive tasks and psychometric *g*. In A. Harris (Ed.), *Encyclopedia of Psychology*. New York: APA/Oxford University Press. Pp. 156–157.

391. Jensen, A. R. (2000). Twins. In A. Harris (Ed.), *Encyclopedia of Psychology*. New York: APA/Oxford University Press. Pp. 132–135.

392. Jensen, A. R. (2000). Charles E. Spearman: Founder of the London School. *Galton Institute Newsletter, 36*, 2–4.

393. Jensen, A. R. (2000). Testing: The dilemma of group differences. *Psychology, Public Policy, and Law, 6*, 121–127.

394. Jensen, A. R. (2000). Hans Eysenck: Apostle of the London School. In G. A. Kimble and M. Wertheimer (Eds.), *Portraits of Pioneers in Psychology*. Vol. 4. Washington, DC: American Psychological Association; and Mahwah, NJ: Erlbaum. Pp. 338–357.

395. Jensen, A. R. (2000). Charles Spearman. Discoverer of *g*. In G. A. Kimble and M. Wertheimer (Eds.), *Portraits of Pioneers in Psychology*. Vol. 4. Washington, DC: American Psychological Association; and Mahwah, NJ: Erlbaum. Pp. 92–111.

396. Jensen, A. R. (2000). Was wir über den *g*-Faktor wissen (und nichtwissen). In K. Schweizer (Ed.). *Intelligenze und kognition: Die kognitiv-biologische Perspektive der Intelligenz.* Landau: Verlag für Empirische Pädagogik. Pp. 13–36.

397. Jensen, A. R. (2000). The *g* factor: Psychometrics and biology. Novartis Foundation Symposium No. 233. *The nature of intelligence.* Chichester, England: Wiley. Pp. 37–57.

398. Jensen, A. R. (2000). Some recent overlooked research on the scientific basis of *The Bell Curve.* Commentary on Reifman on Bell-Curve. *Psycoloquy, 11* (106).

399. Jensen, A. R. (2000). "The *g* Factor" is about variance in human abilities, not a cognitive theory of mental structure. Reply to Anderson. *Psycoloquy, 11* (041).

400. Jensen, A. R. (2000). A nihilistic philosophy of science for a scientific psychology? Reply to Barrett. *Psycoloquy, 11* (088).

401. Jensen, A. R. (2000). Name-calling is a disappointing substitute for real criticism. Reply to Brace. *Psycoloquy, 11* (009).

402. Jensen, A. R. (2000). Artificial intelligence and *g* theory concern different phenomena. Reply to Bringsjord. *Psycoloquy, 11* (086).

403. Jensen, A. R. (2000). The heritability of *g* proves both its biological relevance and its transcendence over specific cognitive abilities. Reply to Bub. *Psycoloquy, 11* (085).

404. Jensen, A. R. (2000). Processing speed, inspection time, and nerve conduction velocity. Reply to Burns. *Psycoloquy, 11* (019).

405. Jensen, A. R. (2000). The ubiquity of mental speed and the centrality of working memory. Reply to Conway et al. *Psycoloquy, 11* (038).

406. Jensen, A. R. (2000). Is there a self-awareness of one's own *g* level? Reply to Demetriou. *Psycoloquy, 11* (040).

407. Jensen, A. R. (2000). Mixing up eugenics and Galton's legacy to research on intelligence. Reply to Fancher. *Psycoloquy, 11* (017).

408. Jensen, A. R. (2000). Psychometric scepticism. Reply to Harrington. *Psycoloquy, 11* (039).

409. Jensen, A. R. (2000). The locus of the modifiability of *g* is mostly biological. Reply to Hunt. *Psycoloquy, 11* (012).

410. Jensen, A. R. (2000). A "simplest cases" approach to exploring the neural basis of *g.* Reply to Ingber. *Psycoloquy, 11* (023).

411. Jensen, A. R. (2000). A fuzzy boundary of racial classification attenuates IQ difference. Reply to Jorion. *Psycoloquy, 11* (022).

412. Jensen, A. R. (2000). A potpourri of *g*-related topics. Reply to Kovacs and Pleh. *Psycoloquy, 11* (087).

413. Jensen, A. R. (2000). IQ tests, psychometric and chronometric g, and achievement. Reply to Kush. *Psycoloquy, 11* (014).

414. Jensen, A. R. (2000). Race differences, g, and the "default hypothesis." Reply to Locurto. *Psycoloquy, 11* (004).

415. Jensen, A. R. (2000). Cognitive components as chronometric probes to brain processes. Reply to Mackintosh. *Psycoloquy, 11* (011).

416. Jensen, A. R. (2000). Behavioral and biological phenomena equally "real" and related. Reply to Partridge. *Psycoloquy, 11* (018).

417. Jensen, A. R. (2000). "Biological determinism" as an ideological buzz-word. Reply to Raymond. *Psycoloquy, 11* (021).

418. Jensen, A. R. (2000). Nothing "mystifying" about psychometric g. Reply to Richardson. *Psycoloquy, 11* (042).

419. Jensen, A. R. (2000). Correlated vectors, g, and the "Jensen effect." Reply to Rushton. *Psycoloquy, 10* (082).

420. Jensen, A. R. (2000). Evoked potentials, testosterone, and g. Reply to Tan. *Psycoloquy, 10* (085).

421. Jensen, A. R. (2000). Evoked brain potentials and g. Reply to Verleger. *Psycoloquy, 10* (084).

422. Nyborg, H., and Jensen, A. R. (2000). Testosterone levels as modifiers of psychometric g. *Personality and Individual Differences, 28*, 601–607.

423. Nyborg, H. and Jensen, A. R. (2000). Black-white differences on various psychometric tests: Spearman's hypothesis tested on American armed services veterans. *Personality and Individual Differences, 28*, 593–599.

2001

424. Jensen, A. R. (2001). Spearman's hypothesis. In S. Messick and J. Collis (Eds.), *Intelligence and personality: Bridging the gap in theory and measurement.* Mahwah, NJ: Erlbaum. Pp. 3–25

425. Jensen, A. R. (2001). Misleading caricatures of Jensen's statistics: A reply to Kaplan. *Chance, 14,* 22–26.

426. Nyborg, H., and Jensen, A. R. (2001). Occupation and income related to psychometric g. *Intelligence, 29,* 45–55.

2002

427. Jensen, A. R. (2002). Galton's legacy to research on intelligence (The 1999 Galton Lecture). *Journal of Biosocial Science, 34,* 145–172.

428. Jensen, A. R. (2002). General cognitive ability (g factor) assessment. In R. Femandos-Ballesteros (Ed.), *Encyclopedia of Psychological Assessment.* London: Sage.

429. Jensen, A. R. (2002). Review of *Intelligence testing and minority students: Foundations, performance factors, and assessment issues,* by R. R. Valencia and L. A. Suzuki. *Intelligence, 30,* 216–217.

430. Jensen, A. R. (2002). Psychometric *g*: Definition and substantiation. In R. J. Sternberg and E. L. Grigorenko (Eds.), *The general factor of intelligence: How general is it?* Mahwah, NJ: Erlbaum. Pp. 39–54.

In Press

431. Jensen, A. R. (in press). Regularities in Spearman's Law of Diminishing Returns. *Intelligence.*

432. Jensen, A. R. (in press). Do age-group differences on mental tests imitate racial differences? *Intelligence.*

433. Jensen, A. R. (in press). Vocabulary and general intelligence: Commentary on Bloom's *How children learn the meanings of words (2000). Behavioral and Brain Sciences.*

434. Jensen, A. R. (in press). The mental chronometry of giftedness. In D. Boothe and J. C. Stanley (Eds.), *Giftedness and cultural diversity.*

435. Rushton, J. P., and Jensen, A. R. (in press). African-White IQ differences from Zimbabwe on the Wechsler Intelligence Scale for Children—Revised. *Personality and Individual Differences.*

APPENDIX B

MAINSTREAM SCIENCE ON INTELLIGENCE[1]

The Meaning and Measurement of Intelligence

1. Intelligence is a very general mental capability that, among other things, involves the ability to reason, plan, solve problems, think abstractly, comprehend complex ideas, learn quickly and learn from experience. It is not merely book learning, a narrow academic skill, or test-taking smarts. Rather, it reflects a broader and deeper capability for comprehending our surroundings— "catching on," "making sense" of things, or "figuring out" what to do.

2. Intelligence, so defined, can be measured, and intelligence tests measure it well. They are among the most accurate (in technical terms, reliable and valid) of all psychological tests and assessments. They do not measure creativity, character, personality, or other important differences among individuals, nor are they intended to.

3. While there are different types of intelligence tests, they all measure the same intelligence. Some use words or numbers and require specific cultural knowledge (like vocabulary). Others do

---

[1]Reprinted with permission of *The Wall Street Journal,* copyright 1994, Dow Jones & Company, Inc. All rights reserved.

not, and instead use shapes or designs and require knowledge of only simple, universal concepts (many/few, open/closed, up/down).

4. The spread of people along the IQ continuum, from low to high, can be represented well by the bell curve (in statistical jargon, the "normal curve"). Most people cluster around the average (IQ 100). Few are either very bright or very dull: About 3% of Americans score above IQ 130 (often considered the threshold for "giftedness"), with about the same percentage below IQ 70 (IQ 70–75 often being considered the threshold for mental retardation).

5. Intelligence tests are not culturally biased against American blacks or other native-born, English-speaking peoples in the US. Rather, IQ scores predict equally accurately for all such Americans, regardless of race and social class. Individuals who do not understand English well can be given either a nonverbal test or one in their native language.

6. The brain processes underlying intelligence are still little understood. Current research looks, for example, at speed of neural transmission, glucose (energy) uptake, and electrical activity of the brain.

Group Differences

7. Members of all racial-ethnic groups can be found at every IQ level. The bell curves of different groups overlap considerably; but groups often differ in where their members tend to cluster along the IQ line. The bell curves for some groups (Jews and East Asians) are centered somewhat higher than for whites in general. Other groups (blacks and Hispanics) are centered somewhat lower than non-Hispanic whites.

8. The bell curve for whites is centered roughly around IQ 100; the bell curve for American blacks roughly around 85; and those for different subgroups of Hispanics roughly midway between those for whites and blacks. The evidence is less defin-

itive for exactly where above IQ 100 the bell curves for Jews and Asians are centered.

Practical Importance

9. IQ is strongly related, probably more so than any other single measurable human trait, to many important educational, occupational, economic, and social outcomes. Its relation to the welfare and performance of individuals is very strong in some arenas in life (education, military training), moderate but robust in others (social competence), and modest but consistent in others (law-abidingness). Whatever IQ tests measure, it is of great practical and social importance.

10. A high IQ is an advantage in life because virtually all activities require some reasoning and decision-making. Conversely, a low IQ is often a disadvantage, especially in disorganized environments. Of course, a high IQ no more guarantees success than a low IQ guarantees failure in life. There are many exceptions, but the odds for success in our society greatly favor individuals with higher IQs.

11. The practical advantages of having a higher IQ increase as life settings become more complex (novel, ambiguous, changing, unpredictable, or multifaceted). For example, a high IQ is generally necessary to perform well in highly complex or fluid jobs (the professions, management); it is a considerable advantage in moderately complex jobs (crafts, clerical and police work); but it provides less advantage in settings that require only routine decision making or simple problem solving (unskilled work).

12. Differences in intelligence certainly are not the only factor affecting performance in education, training, and highly complex jobs (no one claims they are), but intelligence is often the most important. When individuals have already been selected for high (or low) intelligence and so do not differ as much in IQ, as in graduate school (or special education), other influences on performance loom larger in comparison.

13. Certain personality traits, special talents, aptitudes, physical capabilities, experience, and the like are important (sometimes essential) for successful performance in many jobs, but they have narrower (or unknown) applicability or "transferability" across tasks and settings compared with general intelligence. Some scholars choose to refer to these other human traits as other "Intelligences."

Source and Stability of Within-Group Differences

14. Individuals differ in intelligence due to differences in both their environments and genetic heritage. Heritability estimates range from 0.4 to 0.8 (on a scale from 0 to 1), most thereby indicating that genetics plays a bigger role than does environment in creating IQ differences among individuals. (Heritability is the squared correlation of phenotype with genotype.) If all environments were to become equal for everyone, heritability would rise to 100% because all remaining differences in IQ would necessarily be genetic in origin.

15. Members of the same family also tend to differ substantially in intelligence (by an average of about 12 IQ points) for both genetic and environmental reasons. They differ genetically because biological brothers and sisters share exactly half their genes with each parent and, on the average, only half with each other. They also differ in IQ because they experience different environments within the same family.

16. That IQ may be highly heritable does not mean that it is not affected by the environment. Individuals are not born with fixed, unchangeable levels of intelligence (no one claims they are). IQs do gradually stabilize during childhood, however, and generally change little thereafter.

17. Although the environment is important in creating IQ differences, we do not know yet how to manipulate it to raise low IQs permanently. Whether recent attempts show promise is still a matter of considerable scientific debate.

18. Genetically caused differences are not necessarily irremedi-

able (consider diabetes, poor vision, and phenylketonuria), nor are environmentally caused ones necessarily remediable (consider injuries, poisons, severe neglect, and some diseases). Both may be preventable to some extent.

Source and Stability of Between-Group Differences

19. There is no persuasive evidence that the IQ bell curves for different racial-ethnic groups are converging. Surveys in some years show that gaps in academic achievement have narrowed a bit for some races, ages, school subjects and skill levels, but this picture seems too mixed to reflect a general shift in IQ levels themselves.

20. Racial-ethnic differences in IQ bell curves are essentially the same when youngsters leave high school as when they enter first grade. However, because bright youngsters learn faster than slow learners, these same IQ differences lead to growing disparities in amount learned as youngsters progress from grades one to 12. As large national surveys continue to show, black 17-year-olds perform, on the average, more like white 13-year-olds in reading, math, and science, with Hispanics in between.

21. The reasons that blacks differ among themselves in intelligence appears to be basically the same as those for why whites (or Asians or Hispanics) differ among themselves. Both environment and genetic heredity are involved.

22. There is no definitive answer to why IQ bell curves differ across racial-ethnic groups. The reasons for these IQ differences between groups may be markedly different from the reasons why individuals differ among themselves within any particular group (whites or blacks or Asians). In fact, it is wrong to assume, as many do, that the reason why some individuals in a population have high IQs but others have low IQs must be the same reason why some populations contain more such high (or low) IQ individuals than others. Most experts believe that environment is important in pushing the bell curves apart, but that

genetics could be involved too.

23. Racial-ethnic differences are somewhat smaller but still substantial for individuals from the same socioeconomic backgrounds. To illustrate, black students from prosperous families tend to score higher in IQ than blacks from poor families, but they score no higher, on average, than whites from poor families.

24. Almost all Americans who identify themselves as black have white ancestors—the white admixture is about 20%, on average—and many self-designated whites, Hispanics, and others likewise have mixed ancestry. Because research on intelligence relies on self-classification into distinct racial categories, as does most other social-science research, its findings likewise relate to some unclear mixture of social and biological distinctions among groups (no one claims otherwise).

Implications for Social Policy

25. The research findings neither dictate nor preclude any particular social policy, because they can never determine our goals. They can, however, help us estimate the likely success and side effects of pursuing those goals via different means.

The following professors—all experts in intelligence and allied fields—have signed this statement:

Richard D. Arvey, *University of Minnesota*
Thomas J. Bouchard, Jr., *University of Minnesota*
John B. Carroll, *University of North Carolina at Chapel Hill*
Raymond B. Cattell, *University of Hawaii*
David B. Cohen, *University of Texas at Austin*
Rene V. Dawis, *University of Minnesota*
Douglas K. Detterman, *Case Western Reserve University*
Marvin Dunnette, *University of Minnesota*
Hans Eysenck, *University of London*
Jack Feldman, *Georgia Institute of Technology*

Edwin A. Fleishman, *George Mason University*
Grover C. Gilmore, *Case Western Reserve University*
Robert A. Gordon, *Johns Hopkins University*
Linda S. Gottfredson, *University of Delaware*
Robert L. Greene, *Case Western Reserve University*
Richard J. Haier, *University of California at Irvine*
Garrett Hardin, *University of California at Santa Barbara*
Robert Hogan, *University of Tulsa*
Joseph M. Horn, *University of Texas at Austin*
Lloyd G. Humphreys, *University of Illinois at Urbana-Champaign*
John E. Hunter, *Michigan State University*
Seymour W. Itzkoff, *Smith College*
Douglas N. Jackson, *University of Western Ontario*
James J. Jenkins, *University of South Florida*
Arthur R. Jensen, *University of California at Berkeley*
Alan S. Kaufman, *University of Alabama*
Nadeen L. Kaufman, *California School of Professional Psychology at San Diego*
Timothy Z. Keith, *Alfred University*
Nadine Lambert, *University of California at Berkeley*
John C. Loehlin, *University of Texas at Austin*
David Lubinski, *Iowa State University*
David T. Lykken, *University of Minnesota*
Richard Lynn, *University of Ulster at Coleraine*
Paul E. Meehl, *University of Georgia*
R. Travis Osborne, *University of Georgia*
Robert Perloff, *University of Pittsburgh*
Robert Plomin, *Institute of Psychiatry, London*
Cecil R. Reynolds, *Texas A & M University*
David C. Rowe, *University of Arizona*
J. Philippe Rushton, *University of Western Ontario*
Vincent Sarich, *University of California at Berkeley*
Sandra Scarr, *University of Virginia*
Frank L. Schmidt, *University of Iowa*
Lyle F Schoenfeldt, *Texas A & M University*

James C. Scharf, *George Washington University*

Herman Spitz, *former Director of Research at the E. R. Johnstone Training and Research Center, Bordentown, N.J.*

Julian C. Stanley, *Johns Hopkins University*

Del Thiessen, *University of Texas at Austin*

Lee A. Thompson, *Case Western Reserve University*

Robert M. Thorndike, *Western Washington University*

Philip Anthony Vernon, *University of Western Ontario*

Lee Willerman, *University of Texas at Austin*

INDEX

234

INDEX